SAGE was founded in 1965 by Sara Miller McCune to support the dissemination of usable knowledge by publishing innovative and high-quality research and teaching content. Today, we publish more than 750 journals, including those of more than 300 learned societies, more than 800 new books per year, and a growing range of library products including archives, data, case studies, reports, conference highlights, and video. SAGE remains majority-owned by our founder, and after Sara's lifetime will become owned by a charitable trust that secures our continued independence.

Los Angeles | London | Washington DC | New Delhi | Singapore | Boston

ADVANCE PRAISE

Our children are our future. Our economic vitality depends on the capabilities of tomorrow's workforce. Our values depend on the responsibility and integrity of our young people, who will become the parents and community leaders of the future.

Yet we now know millions of young people who are not receiving nearly enough of the resources they need to become successful adults. A significant proportion of young people do not believe that they will achieve their goals and aspirations.

There is another equally troubling consequence: Because we as a nation are failing to prepare them for the future, many young people are beginning to lose hope. More than 40% of our young people say that they doubt they can ever achieve their goals and 70% wish they would have more opportunities to help themselves fulfil their dreams.

Instead of focusing on statistics that suggest the symptoms of a larger problem, Mr Gangadhar Joshi via *Campus to Corporate* sheds new light on transforming knowledge into skills and thus addressing employability.

Today the CUSP between educated student and a company hiring for skills is arguably the most important area that needs attention, focus and study. With his experience in both domestic and global corporations and heading up an MBA school, Mr Joshi is probably the only person who has the unique integrated skill to discuss employability and its execution from corporate to campus. Mr Joshi has done an incredible job of proposing the same via his *Campus to Corporate* detailed study which comes with recommendations and suggestions. It will be an invaluable handbook for colleges and corporations.

I wish him luck in his endeavour to translate his experience and ideas into a time-tested path for students and employers, both.

Jiten Sandu
Chief Operating Officer, TalentMAT

Wholesome and inclusive development has been conclusively 'voted' as the key aspiration as well as the mandate in India 2014. Some of the key economic drivers of this 'Jan Abhiyan' (bordering on to Jan Andolan) are Skilling India and Make in India. For the first time we are witnessing a concerted and determined effort for all the wheels of the nation to work with complete focus and synergy. Rightly the political leadership recognises that all stakeholders have to contribute meaningfully and energetically in providing the traction that the nation needs and deserves.

In this context, while it is important to improve individual platforms (like academia, industry, civic bodies, …), perhaps the bigger impact will come by strengthening the 'bridges' which connect these platforms. We witness huge 'transmission and distribution' losses/leakages for want of compatibility and understanding between various stakeholders in our system. In my 40 years of intense engagement with both industry and academia, I have witnessed serious talks about alliances in every forum, but unfortunately the two still operate in fair isolation. Everyone is a looser and certainly here lies a great opportunity to bring some convergence.

This calls for an insightful understanding of the two environments (corporate and academia), healthy respect for the strengths and compulsions of each other, and a tacit acknowledgement that we are in 'win-win' setting and not in a 'zero-sum' game.

Professor Joshi, through his eventful and rich professional journey, captures the understanding of the corporate world and the academia in a very friendly manner. He has been on both sides of the table (he has in fact tried to make it a round table, so that there are no sides). He has delivered in various key sectors and geographies in his innings with industry, and has helped build and lead a very vibrant academic institution. And he brings out key themes very effectively. Learnability and employability instead of teaching and employment as key pillars are very valid and timely propositions in today's fast-changing industrial and social world. He prompts industry to engage with academia with an open mind (not just a vendor for talent), and urges academia to get real-life perspective through the learnings from industry. The biggest learning is, however, for the youth who have to look at their tenure in academia as opportunity for wholesome development of their persona, and not marking time in a 'degree awarding' factory.

Campus to Corporate is not about a placement event, but about the evolution and culmination of a whole journey.

Would commend whole heartedly.

Pradeep Bhargava
Director, Cummins India Ltd

Campus
to Corporate

Campus
to Corporate

Your Roadmap to Employability

Gangadhar Joshi

*Former Director, Symbiosis Institute of Operations
Management (SIOM)*
and
Principal Consultant, Gangadhar Joshi & Associates

www.sagepublications.com
Los Angeles • London • New Delhi • Singapore • Washington DC • Boston

First published in 2015 by

SAGE Publications India Pvt Ltd
B1/I-1 Mohan Cooperative Industrial Area
Mathura Road, New Delhi 110 044, India
www.sagepub.in

SAGE Publications Inc
2455 Teller Road
Thousand Oaks, California 91320, USA

SAGE Publications Ltd
1 Oliver's Yard, 55 City Road
London EC1Y 1SP, United Kingdom

SAGE Publications Asia-Pacific Pte Ltd
3 Church Street
#10-04 Samsung Hub
Singapore 049483

Published by Vivek Mehra for SAGE Publications India Pvt Ltd, typeset in 10/12 pts Times New Roman by RECTO Graphics, Delhi, and printed at Saurabh Printers Pvt Ltd, New Delhi.

Library of Congress Cataloging-in-Publication Data

Joshi, Gangadhar.
  Campus to corporate : your roadmap to employability / Gangadhar Joshi, Symbiosis Institute of Operations Management (SIOM) and Principal Consultant, Gangadhar Joshi and Associates, Nashik.
  pages cm
  Includes index.
  1. College graduates—Employment—India. 2. College graduates—Vocational guidance—India. 3. Career development—India. I. Title.
  HD6278.I5J67   650.1—dc23   2015   2015018179

ISBN: 978-93-515-0279-1 (PB)

The SAGE Team: Amit Kumar, Indrani Dutta, Vandana Gupta, Rajib Chatterjee and Rajinder Kaur

CONTENTS

FOREWORD

There has been an increased awareness of human capital as one of the driving forces of economic development in recent years. The Government of India also has realised the importance of investing in education and training as a way of improving the existing stock of skills. By 2030, though amongst the youngest nations in the world, India will be the primary source of meeting the human resource of the entire world. With nearly 140 million in the college-going age group, one in every four graduates in the world will be a product of the Indian higher education system. There is a need, therefore, for the Indian higher education systems to be more focused on employability rather than on the employment of its graduating students. 'To be employed is to be at risk, to be *employable* is to be secure,' says Peter Hawkins (1999) in *The Art of Building Windmills*.

'Creating globally compatible human resource with broad-based knowledge, multi-disciplinary skills and positive attitude' was the vision of Professor Gangadhar Joshi, the Former Director of the Symbiosis Institute of Operations Management (SIOM), Pune, Mahrashtra, one of the premier institutes of the Symbiosis family and the writer of *Campus to Corporate*. As a Director, he focused on developing competencies rather than delivering degree certificates, and his book *Campus to Corporate* aptly presents his same focus.

I am particularly impressed with the title of this book, *Campus to Corporate*, which in itself signifies a transition from one world to another for the graduating students. It is a transition from convenience to inconvenience, known to unknown and friend circle to professional colleagues and superiors. It is a testing ground for real capabilities and competencies of the graduated entering the corporate world. It is a world where education ends and real learning begins. I would describe *Campus to Corporate* as a bridge for the gap that exists between the two worlds of education and work.

I have read many articles and literature dealing with various aspects of career and employability skills in isolation. I find *Campus to Corporate* a unique publication which provides a comprehensive coverage of the employability aspects in a structured manner. The book is focused on global employability. It provides an integrated understanding of the employability issues and a practical approach focused on acquiring skills to achieve sustainable employability. The book provides progressing skills acquisition programme starting from individual skills, then organisational skills, and finally the technological skills. The section on certifications and professional associations is unique in the sense that it takes care of most sectors such as operations, finance, and information technology (IT). While doing this, it also highlights the interrelationships of various skills and attributes in individual, group, and organisational settings.

I am sure this book will be of great help to the graduating students as well as the institutions to enhance their employability performance. It could also be a refresher to refer periodically as one grows in his/her career. Those who wish to get into entrepreneurship instead of employment can also derive tremendous value from the contents of this book.

Professor Gangadhar Joshi is a vastly experienced professional in the field of management consulting, education and training, and he will have a lot to share in future with the world of education in making it more meaningful and value adding. He has just made a beginning with *Campus to Corporate*.

I congratulate him for *Campus to Corporate* and wish all the success for his efforts and future endeavours.

Padma Bhushan Dr S.B. Mujumdar
Founder, Symbiosis, and Chancellor, Symbiosis International University

PREFACE

2014 has been a year of significance for India. A new government, its focus of governance, and its emphasis on skills development are all the key features which would lead India in the times to come. Our Ex-President Hon'ble Abdul Kalam highlighted in his Vision 2020 document India's demographic advantage of becoming a source of global cadre of skilled youth with specific knowledge of special skills for fulfilling the human resource requirements of various countries. Hon'ble Prime Minister Shri Narendra Modi, during his recent visit to the US, once again, reiterated this demographic advantage of India over the developed nations. His vision of transforming this young population into globally compatible and superior quality human resource is very clear. The purpose of higher education is no more just turning out graduates for employers who could be plugged in from day one. The need is to create employability amongst the graduates rather than just promising placements. It is more important to demonstrate 'what you can deliver' rather than 'what your qualifications are'. The institutes should be energising students to think and learn to develop new skills at work in preparation for life. It is my great pleasure that my book *Campus to Corporate* is coming out at the most appropriate time, when employability-based skills development has become a prime focus of the new government. *Campus to Corporate* has the same purpose of enabling globally compatible employability with broad-based knowledge, multi-disciplinary skills and the right attitude.

When I completed my post-graduation in 1975 from National Institute of Industrial Engineering (NITIE), Mumbai, placement was not a big issue. I had six jobs to select from without having an opportunity to go through any formal employability-enhancement programme like 'Campu2Corporate'. There were no Internet sources where I could learn the tricks of placement processes. However, after joining a company, I quickly realised that my degree, even from a premier institution like NITIE, was just a passport and not a visa for me to sustain in the corporate world. I realised that I lacked many skills described in this book, and it took me a long time to really gain confidence of facing the job challenges. In my first job, when I was just three months old in the industry, I had to negotiate with a strong union. I learnt everything the hard way, took risks on the way and remained on a roller coaster of aspiration, inspiration, perspiration and desperation for about eight years in different employment situations.

My venturing into own management consulting practice in 1983 gave me the same pleasure and satisfaction as that of a new swimmer who jumps in the water without any support and floats. That was one way of getting industry ready—a very hard and painful way.

My life has been characterised by unpredictable circumstances and full of challenges involved in managing those circumstances. Different industries, different locations, different organisations and different disciplines actually made me a person who could adapt to any situation and make a contribution. Doing difficult things possible has been the feature of my professional background and the word 'impossible' never appeared in my professional dictionary. Getting into higher education and now writing this book, *Campus to Corporate*, were totally unthinkable events until as late as 2004 when I returned from Bangladesh after completing a consulting assignment.

My thinking on employability started in 2005 when I took over as the Founder Director of SIOM at Pune. I had the challenge to ensure 100% placement of the first batch of 60 students who joined SIOM investing money with expectations of making a good career. Having spent years in the corporate world, the academic world was alien to me. I was very clear on 'What to Deliver?' but not so much on

'How to deliver?' I was not sure about the processes which could make it happen. A new institute, a new Director and an environment of heavy competition from other institutions for placement gave me a challenging situation to manage. That is where my corporate consulting experience and entrepreneurship background came into play. I prepared a strategic plan, first to survive and then to grow in leaps and bounds to make SIOM successful, and within a span of three years, at least 25 top class companies in diverse sectors recognised SIOM as a reliable source of globally compatible and competent manpower. I must have interacted with 100 top companies in all sectors with a view to understand their expectations. Apart from marketing SIOM to the corporate world, these visits were aimed at seeking answers to questions as follows:

1. Why is it that some institutes have better placement performance than others?
2. What do the companies mean when they say, 'We only go to campuses of top class institutes?'
3. Which specific needs of the companies my students could meet after graduation?
4. How do I differentiate my students from those of other B-schools?
5. How do I keep my institute always in the eyes of the corporate world?

SIOM is prospering today with the foundation created during the initial three years of my leadership. The questions apply to all institutes of higher education delivering graduate and post-graduate programmes. Most of them need to do a lot more than what is being done today in this area of employability enhancement.

This book is actually a sharing of my understanding and learning about the issues of employability enhancement as a Director of SIOM. Going into specifics of my initiatives and strategies of managing SIOM could be a subject matter of another book. The biggest lesson is that it is important for the institutes to go beyond just the completion of the syllabi and convince companies that the students they are having on board are exactly what they are looking for in terms of knowledge, skills and attitude. The match between the companies' expectations and the students' competencies need not be 100% and it would never be. What matters is the evidence that the students coming out of campus have the potential to meet most of the corporate expectations. Employability is not the same as just getting a job after graduation; it implies something about the capacity of the graduates to function in a job and be able to move between jobs and thus remaining employable for the lifetime. It means that the institutes must have an understanding of the current and future competency requirements and should align their input processes accordingly.

Section 1 provides answers to some of the questions previously mentioned and highlights the need for an integrated approach to employability enhancement. This integrated approach has the foundation skills identification and development. It provides an insight into corporate expectations and the scenario of most institutions, resulting in the gap to be bridged by initiatives such the *Campus to Corporate*. This section also provides a broad roadmap for the institutions to pursue. Students and institutes have to work together as we did in SIOM.

Your institute must have or should be able to create a unique selling proposition (USP) for the students to be placed. Unfortunately, most institutions do not have one and have no desire, willingness and capability to create the one. What is it that your institute is known for? During my young days when B-schools were very limited, we used to consider Indian Institute of Management Ahmadabad (IIMA), known for 'Marketing', and IIM Kolkata for 'Human Resource Management'. The Centre of Excellence (COE) concept also helps institutes to create a USP. Our USP in SIOM is 'Techo-Business Managers' meaning 'Managers with technology background'. With this USP, our basic competition significantly reduced as only few institutions could claim a similar USP on an all-India basis. It also helped us to position ourselves effectively in the placement market and to create mutually beneficial industry–institute partnerships. Subsequently, it was just an issue of identifying the skills and competencies required and ensuring that the students had them before they left the institute. It is the USP which enabled the placement of my entire first batch of 60 students in quick time.

This book is an attempt to present an integrated approach and a workable plan for students to pursue and add value to their careers and for the institutes to enhance their employability image. It prescribes an easy to understand and practical approach for students to develop life and business skills that could be seamlessly woven into a well-rounded personality. This book is expected to meet that need for the students as well as the institutions in terms of the following:

- Students will have the ability to succeed not only through the placement process but also while pursuing their careers in the corporate world.
- Students practising skills covered in this book will be able to differentiate themselves from others in terms of knowledge, skills and attitude.
- Understanding the transition from 'Campus' to 'Corporate' will allow the students to adopt their personality and disposition to different situations.
- Higher employability and placement would result in an enhanced quality of incoming students.
- The institute as a whole stands to benefit in the long run through the enhancement of its image as a source for industry-ready human capital and a better industry–institute partnership.

The book has a logical approach to addressing employability skills issues. Having established the need in Section 1, Section 2, on personal effectiveness skills, shows the importance of keeping pace with the continually changing world of work. Employers seek graduates who are enterprising, resourceful and adaptable, and who, in addition to a degree, possess a range of skills and attributes, which can be used in a wide variety of settings in their careers. It is also necessary to look at your personal value and professional competencies. Having a set of skills and personal attributes makes a person more likely to get a desired placement and sustained success in career. The 7Cs (**C**haracter, **C**ompetence, **C**oncern, **C**reativity, **C**ommunication, **C**ommitment and **C**ourage) model for managerial excellence is my attempt to logically bring together all those skills, qualities and attributes which are important from the employability point of view. It is not just important to have these 7Cs at the time of entry into the corporate world, but they are also very necessary for your long-term success in all your professional endeavours.

Section 3 is dedicated to the skills required to be effective in the organisation. The personal effectiveness skills and the demonstrated potential of organisation skills during the placement process will give you entry in the organisation. However, your success in the organisation depends entirely on the proven practice of skills described in this section. These skills are more behaviour oriented and involve interpersonal issues with regard to relationships, communication and teamwork. The 50 new rules of work set the framework for your new work environment which you need to accept and be prepared for. You need to be proactive to each of the 50 rules of work with a positive attitude and mindset.

Recognising the fact that today's businesses are managed on technology, particularly the IT, Section 4 is dedicated to the basic and advanced IT and other skills which will enable the students to secure better employability. Today's employers expect that their employees become familiar with a wide variety of IT applications. Your first job may or may not require the extensive use of IT. It is still worthwhile to at least get introduced yourself to this form of technology. The Internet assists in accessing information which can help you increase your knowledge, learn new skills and even test yourself on different qualities and attributes of personality, leaderships and the like. New applications and techniques are evolving all the time and you need to learn something beyond the basics to demonstrate your technological awareness and potential. The basics of IT are generally part of the syllabus of the graduate or post-graduate course you are pursuing. If you are pursuing the IT-related graduation programme you are better off than the others.

Section 4 also deals with two other important areas, which could enhance your employability and career prospects. They are obtaining certifications and obtaining membership of professional associations, institutions and societies. A certification makes an individual more marketable. When a candidate comes to an employer with recognised and accepted professional certifications, it gives the employer more confidence to hire. Particularly for freshers, new to the employment market without a great deal of past experience, the combination of an academic degree and an industry-recognised certification puts him/her in a stronger position.

Most companies in the current employment market such as enterprise resource planning (ERP), supply chain, information technology, IT-enabled services, consulting, retail and financial services are multinational companies (MNCs) or have foreign affiliations. It is assumed that certified professionals have greater ability to understand new or complex technologies and are globally compatible. Therefore, getting certified in your area of expertise or major interest gives significant advantages to you over others. This section also provides an overview of various certifications in areas of finance, IT and operations which could enhance employability and career prospects.

Section 4 also deals with the importance of membership of professional societies, associations and institutions. Memberships of professional associations and societies give tremendous advantages to enhance your career prospects, knowledge gain and networking. Most specialisations and industries have a professional body, normally an association or institute or institution or society, which people with the relevant background, experience or qualifications can join. It not only provides networking opportunities, but it is also an avenue to demonstrate professional expertise and obtain recognitions through participating in seminars, conferences and symposiums.

Section 5 is dedicated to actual placement process which happens at the campus or anywhere else. Although all the four previous sections would significantly help a student's performance during the placement process, clear understanding of the process steps and their requirements at each step is important. There are many resources available on 'how to succeed through the placement' by way of books and on-line, inclusion of this section really completes the integration and comprehensiveness of its title *Campus to Corporate*. You practise everything that is said in the first four sections and finally get ready for this last phase of your being on campus. Don't you agree that this is the primary purpose of your coming on campus at the first place?

This section takes you through the whole placement process commencing from developing a perfect CV, aptitude test, group discussions and interviews. Your preparation and approach at each of the stages are described in sufficient details.

This entire book, *Campus to Corporate* is like a recipe book. It describes various ingredients of employability and the ways of managing them. There is no theory in this book. It is best available in your syllabi and contributes to your acquiring subject knowledge. This book is focussed on skills building and attitude development. Your library may have books dealing in more details with individual sections and chapters of this book. This book will just orient you to different skills and their value to your career and work life. It would certainly be worthwhile for you to read further on each of the chapters and sections as per your need and requirement.

Finally, campus placement is a strategic issue for the institute and not just a campaign or activity. Your placement officer and placement committee should be preparing a placement plan very early. Students should be clear about the career which they want to pursue. Never hope for good placement results by preparing just a month or two before the placement season. Ideal time to get into the *Campus to Corporate* mode is right from the beginning of the first semester if it is a two-year post-graduate programme or the fifth semester if it is a four-year degree course. Reading this book and putting these skills into practice is the key to success. This is a tested and proven approach to enhance employability.

My best wishes to the world of higher education for its efforts towards skills development and employability enhancement. I welcome critiques, comments and suggestions from the readers for me to enhance the value of this book in its future editions. I also take the opportunity to thank all those who have directly or indirectly helped me in developing this concept and the book. My special thanks to Amit Kumar and the entire SAGE team for taking a keen interest in the publication of this book and to Ms Indrani Dutta for patiently reviewing the text and helping me to be a better author on the way.

ABOUT THE AUTHOR

Gangadhar Joshi, the Former Director of Symbiosis Institute of Operations Management (SIOM) (2005–8), is currently the Principal Consultant of Gangadhar Joshi & Associates, a multidisciplinary management consulting, education and training firm based at Pune, India. He is a mechanical engineer (1971) with Masters in Industrial Engineering (1975). With an extensive private and public sector experience in India and overseas, he has been involved in advising governments and industries at the strategic level, developing/implementing change management programmes, institutional strengthening, business re-engineering, cost reduction, lean manufacturing, manpower planning, management development and performance management.

He has been closely involved in counselling and advising senior executives on developing and implementing their business strategy. Over the years, he has developed and conducted workshops for top and senior managers in strategic planning, productivity management, total quality management, change management leadership, ISO 9000 Certification and executive performance management.

Joshi took over the leadership of the Symbiosis Institute of Operations Management (SIOM) in 2005, as its Founder Director, and within a short span of 3 years SIOM became known in the corporate world as reliable source of globally compatible managerial human resource which could meet its expectations. SIOM further prospered on this solid foundation in its mission of empowering operations excellence.

Putting Things in Perspective

1

Putting Things in Perspective

1. Introduction and Need for Transition
2. Corporate Expectations Scenario
3. Business Schools Scenario

Introduction and Need for Transition

When I completed my post-graduation from the National Institute for Industrial Engineering (NITIE) in 1975, I had six jobs to choose from. None of them, however, were through campus interviews. Campus placements were not very common in those days. Students graduating from reputed institutions in those days such as the Indian Institutes of Management (IIMs), the Jamnalal Bajaj Institute of Management Studies (JBIMS) had much better placement results as NITIE was still fairly new in the post-graduate management education space. Those reputed B-schools still excel in their placement results and enjoy priority status in the corporate world. Corporate world even pays some of the very prestigious schools for conducting campus placement drives.

The situation is drastically different for a large number of technical and business schools who meet tough competition to get their students placed in respectable jobs. The primary cause of this situation is the inadequacy of efforts of these colleges and institutions in ensuring industry readiness of their graduates and post-graduates. The focus of a large proportion of university-affiliated institutes is on ensuring compliance with the academic and administrative requirements of the university. Very little is being done to satisfy the real stakeholder and customer of the higher education sector, the corporate and the professional world. Premier institutions such as the IIMs, Indian Institutes of Technology (IITs) and a few other autonomous institutions have demonstrated better placement results. They understand the difference between employment and employability and develop their students accordingly by facilitating the whole lot of extraneous inputs to make them application oriented, industry-ready professionals with broad-based knowledge, multi-disciplinary skills and the right attitude.

Sam Pitroda, the chairman of Knowledge Commission, writes in his report on higher education (*National Knowledge Commission Report to the Nation 2006–2009*, March 2009, National Knowledge Commission, Govern ment of India):

1. We produce MBA certificate holders and not managers.
2. We test mental ability to remember and not the understanding and application capability.

Survey findings on Indian higher education reflect the authenticity of the earlier statements and somewhat alarmingly indicate the quality of higher education and training imparted to the youth of this country.

- **Tata Institute of Social Sciences (TISS) 2010**
  - 10% of fresh graduates are actually employable, while only 25% of MBA and engineering graduates are employable.

- **Merit Trac-MBA Universe Study (2011–12)**
  - Only 21% of MBAs are employable; the previous study of 2007 by Merit Trac placed employability index at 25%. (Reported in *Economic Times* of 7 August 2012.)

- **NASSCOM Survey (2011–12)**
  - Only 25% graduates in India are employable.
  - The NASSCOM report highlights that only about 17.45% of engineering graduates of the year 2011 were employable. Its survey of 2011 showcased that over 75% of IT graduates are not ready for jobs. (Published: Wednesday, 28 November 2012, in *Careers India*; Read more at: http://www.careerindia.com/news/2012/11/28/nasscom-only-25percent-graduate-in-india-are-employable-003361.html)
  - 'Our Engineers are not employable; they just don't have industry-ready talent. In other words, they lack the skills required for the jobs that are available to them,' says Sangeeta Gupta, Senior Vice President, NASSCOM.

The recent news about over 100+ B-schools planning closure is a reflection of the deteriorating value attached to the MBA programmes of these institutions. There is a need for a different approach to higher education programmes and ensuring employability in the light of the following:

- The fiercely competitive business environment in which the graduates/post-graduates are expected to deliver.
- Increasing complexity and competition in academic and business world.
- Constantly changing corporate needs and becoming more sector specific.
- Criticality of human competence in creating/sustaining business competitiveness.
- Rapidly increasing the number of institutions resulting in competition for placements.
- Growing pressure from the industry to make fresh inductees productive from day one to reduce the initial training costs.
- Increasing interdependence between the academia and the industry to satisfy the need for mutual sustenance and innovation in their respective areas.

While the institutions prepare students academically only through their syllabus, the real transformation of a student into an industry-ready manager/professional is not assured. The issue of employability of these graduates is not adequately addressed. The corporate world looks for entrants with broad-based knowledge, multi-disciplinary skills and positive attitude. The old tradition of hiring 'management trainees' and training them over a couple of years before they start delivering, has vanished. Employers do not want to invest in training of entry level graduates and expect that they start delivering immediately. It, therefore, becomes a specialised process of total development of students where life and business skills would be seamlessly woven to enable them to be successful in the corporate world. It is nicely said:

> There are three kinds of students who emerge from the institutions.
> ...Some make wonders happen..! Some see wonders happen...! Others wonder what happened!!

The primary objective of this book is to eliminate the third type of students from the institutes of higher education and achieve increments in the other two categories. It is necessary to imbibe professional and life skills in students. A transition is expected to happen from a raw graduate to a complete industry-ready employable person with professional and management skills. There are 12 clearly defined transition tracks as presented by Wipro CEO in his speech/presentation at FICCI Summit 2007 on Indian higher education (Table 1.1). These are progressive steps which will take its natural time to get inculcated in the students. While the responsibility of the institutes is to facilitate this transition in the most effective manner, the students' responsibility is to be honest with themselves and to instill these skills in their personality. Both the institutes and the students need to create a plan and execute it with full zest.

Table 1.1   Campus to Corporate Key Transitions

	Campus		Corporate
1	Individual based	To	Team based
	Value: Effective decision-making		
2	Self-planned	To	Project planned
	Value: Planning and resource optimisation		
3	Last minute preparation	To	Day-to-day work discipline
	Value: Disciplined and planned activities minimise risk.		
4	Answers available and known	To	Solution not known
	Value: Spirit of curiosity and reform, exploration		
5	Remember the answer	To	Arrive at an answer
	Value: Analysis and synthesis skills, problem solving skills, out of box thinking		
6	Marks-based Focus	To	Productivity Focused
	Value: Wider perspective of results/ outcomes. Looking beyond the counts and making impact		
7	Evaluated by someone else	To	Start with self-evaluation
	Value: Become your critic, buries ego, hold self-esteem		
8	Deadlines not all that tough	To	Very strict dead lines
	Value: Time and project management		
9	Canteen behaviour	To	Corporate manners and etiquettes
	Value: Discipline, responsibility and accountability		
10	Family and friends	To	Alone and corporate
	Value: Responsible behaviour, help yourself, courage		
11	Prescribed syllabus	To	Each day's activity is unique
	Value: Be fearless and always be ready for new challenges.		
12	Understanding theory	To	Activity-based learning
	Value: Applying theoretical knowledge to solve practical problems.		

Source: Speech/Presentation by Wipro CEO at FICCI Summit 2007 on Indian higher education.

The transitions need proper guidance and therefore students should seek advice from either the faculty or responsible educational/professional counsellors.

2 Corporate Expectations Scenario

Human resource heads from top companies such as ICICI Bank, Airtel, Big Bazaar and Network-18 got together during September 2009, at the MBAUniverse.com's Corporate Connect Series programme to share their thoughts on who and what they look for from campus placements. Some of their thoughts highlighted here should help the students and the institutions understand the corporate expectations from fresher graduates and post-graduates.

- Apart from the intelligence quotient (IQ), we look at the emotional quotient (EQ—an indicator of the candidate's value system), inter-personal skills and sensitivity. We look at their experiences and also their leadership potential.
- It is understood that if we are hiring from top colleges in India, we are dealing with the best minds. We choose those colleges which have a stringent filtering mechanism.
- Need to have a 'can-do' spirit for getting noticed. At campus, almost all the students are capable of the job on offer. But how do we choose among them is the question you need to really understand.
- Academics are certainly important and it has its own place, but competency becomes the differentiating factor while choosing a candidate.
- Employers check your education first. But more than that, your ethics, sense of responsibility and inherent capability are scrutinised. We look for the one who owns up. As long as you have the hunger to learn, you are in.
- Retail, for instance, is all about detail, confusion and chaos. We see if the candidate has the technical competencies and eagerness to learn. We try and see if he will fit into our own cultural DNA. We don't look at fresh college graduates for short term; we have longer plans for them. We look ahead for 15 years.
- There are two more things that we evaluate: the candidates' flexibility to timings and his/her choice for mobility. We never try to retain those who focus on salary. If there is any other reason, like any family or health concerns, we try and accommodate the employee whichever way possible. So keep yourself flexible and try to learn things, rather than thinking just about your salary.
- Different employers are collaborating with various colleges in India to provide on the job training and learning. ICICI Bank has also tied up with a few MBA colleges in India to help students gain practical knowledge with training.

When employers decide to hire graduates/post-graduates, they generally have two big questions:

- Which campuses are worth visiting and which ones should we visit?
- Whom should we select? Who does really fit the bill? And Why?

When the corporate company is on campus for placement, the question is what kind of students they would choose to hire. The earlier comments from various HR heads tell a lot about this aspect. Generally the placement teams look for specific traits and specific skills and attributes and decide on the candidates who could match their expectations. It is very important for the students to individually and collectively understand the earlier mentioned questions and be prepared with the appropriate responses to satisfy the corporate world on different accounts.

The US-based Graduate Management Admissions Council (GMAC) conducts periodic Corporate Recruiters Surveys (CRS) to determine the various trends of recruitment. The highlights of their 2011 CRS adequately answers the second of the questions mentioned earlier. The GMAC Corporate Recruiters Survey covered over 1,400 respondent corporate companies. Some of the findings of their 2011 survey (*Corporate Recruiters Survey 2011*, Graduate Management Admissions Council [GMAC], Virginia, USA) are presented here with permission from the GMAC (Tables 2.1 and 2.2).

Based on the earlier mentioned traits the students along with the institute management spend some time together, assess and establish where they stand as regards acceptability of the institute, of the MBA programme and also of the graduating students.

The issue of selection of the students only arise when the company first decides to visit their campus. Campus placement drive is a very expensive process for the corporate. Therefore, they are very choosy about visiting a particular campus. They prefer to visit campuses in metros and some bigger cities because they can cover more campuses in one visit. It is important for the institutions to understand the criteria used by the companies to visit campuses other than pure logistics conveniences. The corporate

Table 2.1   Primary Traits and Abilities Sought in MBA Candidates

	Percentage of Respondents
Professionalism	77
Initiative	77
Integrity	76
Motivation	76
Ability to deal effectively with pressure/unexpected obstacles	75
Achievement and/or goal orientation	74
Adaptability	68
Innovation and/or creativity	68
Collaboration	65
Efficiency	49
Listening ability	48
Discipline	45
Cross-cultural sensitivity	39
Persuasiveness	39
Diplomacy/tact	33
Capacity and willingness to follow a leader	30
Empathy	25
Delegation skills	21

Source: Corporate Recruiters Survey 2011 Report.

Table 2.2 Primary Skills, Knowledge and Experience Sought in MBA Candidates

	Percentage of Respondents
Communication skills	86
Strategic skills	67
Proven ability to perform	66
Core business knowledge	63
Ability to manage change	61
Technical and/or quantitative skills	59
Ability to manage decision-making processes	59
Ability to apply business discipline to any job or function	51
Ability to establish business structure, processes, procedures	45
Strong academic performance	45
Sufficient years of work experience	41
Ability to manage the task environment	40
Same or related industry in prior work experience	39
Negotiation skills	34
Similar occupation in prior work experience	31
Ability to manage subject-matter experts or technical experts	29
Ability to manage human capital	25
Similar job level in prior work experience	20
Specific language, country, and/or cultural expertise	17

Source: Corporate Recruiters Survey 2011 Report.

Table 2.3 Corporate Criteria for Choosing a Management Institute for Placement

• Reputation of business school	• School accreditation
• Past experience at the school	• Retention history of past hires
• Depth of the talent pool	• Students willing to relocate
• Quality of the curriculum	• Influence of alumni at the company
• Existing relationships at school	• Admissions standards at the school
• Quality of students, faculty/staff	• As a matter of prestige

Source: Corporate Recruiters Survey 2011 Report.

companies have specific criteria for visiting a particular campus. Some of the criteria which I had surveyed are given in Table 2.3.

The following presentation should help the institutions and student bodies to understand the criteria and prepare themselves to effectively demonstrate to the corporate world that their institute more than meets the criteria.

- **Reputation of the institute**
  The reputation of any educational institution gets built over the years. The corporate usually compete with each other to get the best students from such reputed institutes. When a particular

institute is yet to achieve such a level of reputation, it has to face stiff competition from other colleges to get placement for students. The first three years of any new college or B-school are critical for making the right impression with the corporate.

I have come across many companies which stick to the top 10 management institutes for all their placement needs. These companies take pride in associating only with these top institutes. Many of the second generation business owners are educated overseas in Ivy League schools. They obviously opt for students from institutes which have affiliation with such top ranked foreign institutions. The early success of the Institute of Business (IOB), promoted by Kellog and others from the US, is one such example.

- **Past experience with the institute**
Past experience of the corporate companies determines the chances of repeating their visits to the campuses. Capability and competence of the director/placement officer, number of students participating in the placement process, performance of students in earlier placement process (also known as 'Hit Rate') and the number of students actually joining after selection, are some of the influencing factors that motivate or de-motivate the corporate to re-visit a campus for placement.

- **Depth of the talent pool**
The talent pool at any institute comprises the director, faculty, staff and all groups and individuals associated with the institute. The accreditations, publications, participation by the director/faculty at various conferences/seminars, management development programmes (MDPs) and management consulting services by the institute provide good indication of the institutional talent level. The understanding of business and the corporate world further attracts the corporate world to visit the campus.

- **Quality of the curriculum**
Most institutes have same basic curriculum prescribed by the respective universities. The autonomous institutes too have similar basic curriculum but they offer a huge number of elective options for students. Some of them even offer many industry-oriented programmes and certifications like the American Production and Inventory Control Society (APICS) and Supply Chain Management (SCM). More details on such certifications are provided in Section IV. Some institutes align their syllabus and other inputs to a particular area or sector like operations, finance, retail, infrastructure, etc. This is a good way of presenting your institute as centre of excellence in that sector or domain.

- **Existing relationships at school**
Building sustainable industry–institute relationship is the key. If your institute has a relationship with the corporate chance is more that the corporate will look to your institute for campus placements. Such relationships could be developed through executive/MDPs, consulting services, guest speakers, visiting faculty, industry visits, visits by the director and placement staff/committee to companies and so on.

- **Quality of students, faculty/staff**
The quality of students is a result of many factors such as the quality of incoming students, education input processes, evaluation processes and extra-curricular inputs. Being employable and industry readiness are prime indicators of the quality of students leaving the institute. The quality of the faculty and the staff certainly is the primary driver to ensure students' employability and industry-readiness. Being eligible to become a faculty or director is one thing and being able to deliver value is different. There is abundance of 'eligible' faculty/staff; however tremendous shortage of 'qualified' management educators. The eligibility comes from meeting the minimum criteria set by the regulating bodies, but quality comes in with practical understanding and

experience of the business world. This makes most institutes adopt a coaching class approach to the placement process.

- **School accreditation**

  Although national and international accreditation enhances confidence of the corporate world in the quality of institutions, such accreditation, however, only creates evidence of the institute's potential to deliver and may not guarantee the actual delivery of competencies desired by the corporate world. From the corporate perspective, the only question is, 'Are the (students) of this particular institute worthy of hiring?'

- **Retention history of past hires**

  If students, hired in the past, leave the company within a short period, the corporate would refrain from visiting such institutes for campus placement. Companies do not like their employees joining and making it just a stepping stone for the next job. Such candidates are known as *job hoppers*. When they hire management graduates, they expect them to make a long-term career with the company. Students should keep this in mind before committing to any company.

- **Students willing to relocate**

  Students of institutions outside the metros, in B-class cities, generally are reluctant to accept job offers away from their place of residence or the nearest metro city. This reluctance limits their placement opportunities. This tendency also has negative influence on the corporates' willingness to visit a particular campus. In the modern world, the flexibility of job location is very important for career advancement and growth. The geographical boundaries should not be the barriers for accepting any employment.

- **Influence of alumni at the company**

  Alumni are the major industry–institution promotion link. Strong and active alumni of any institute enhance the corporate interaction and generate opportunities for acceptance of the institute and its students. New institutes have limitations of not having an alumni. Corporate background of the director and the faculty helps to bridge this gap to a great extent.

- **Admissions standards at the school**

  Corporates enquire about the admission standards and selection processes of incoming students. The centralised standard admissions process managed by the State Directorate of Technical Education (DTE) for all universities affiliated institutions makes it difficult for companies to make a choice of one over the other. Autonomous B-schools have more rigorous admission standards and admission processes. Companies like to see students with prior experience, zero backlogs and first class throughout.

Students need to be clear with their understanding as to why a particular company offers to come for campus placement. This would enable the institutes to prepare and approach the campus placement issue accordingly. For instance:

- Companies may visit your campus because MBAs from top schools are not affordable to them.
- Corporates visiting your campus during the early part of their recruitment schedule (September–October each year) come with a sincere desire to hire students from your institute.
- Corporates visiting your campus during the intermediate part of their recruitment schedule (November–January) come after exploring talent search at other institutes more reputed than yours.
- Corporates visiting your campus towards the last part of their recruitment schedule (February onwards) come with a view to get MBAs at lower compensation packages.

INDIA'S BEST EMPLOYERS

The Indian corporate sector employs a number of graduates and post-graduates from the institutes as fresh as well as lateral placements. But how many are lucky to find the best employers and the best workplaces? A great workplace ensures that employees have freedom to execute their ideas and enjoy the work.

While we are on the subject of corporate expectations, it would be worthwhile to review India's top ranked employers. Most of these companies are heavy recruiters of engineers and MBAs each year and most campuses strive hard to invite them for placement of students. Different organisations conduct surveys to identify great places to work not only in India but globally.

While surveying the companies, they use different criteria like career advancements, work-life balance, compensation and the like. The ranking given by different surveys to companies may differ. However, some of the companies do appear as common in most of the surveys, generally considered as great places to work.

The Annual BT-People Strong Survey for 2013, carried out in association with Naukri.com and published as cover story of *Business Today* of August 2014, shows the top 25 best employers in India (Table 2.4).

Table 2.4   Best 25 Companies to Work with (2013)

1st	Google India	Cool work culture and policy of pushing people to pursue their passion makes it the most attractive company for employees in India today.
2nd	Accenture	By listening to its employees, the company ensures that they stay engaged and happy.
3rd	Tata Consultancy Services (TCS)	Though known as a caring workplace, TCS slipped from no. 1 position in 2012. It has innovative HR initiatives such as 'Mpower,' aimed at resolving individual employee issues and 'Maitree,' which reaches out to employees' families.
4th	Infosys	It remains in the top-10 list, but has slipped from the no. 2 slot in 2012. The company encourages regular communication with the employees.
5th	Larsen and Toubro (L&T)	L&T moved up from the no. 10 position in 2012. It prefers to groom leaders within the organisation, believing that few outside can match the quality of its workforce in heavy engineering and construction.
6th	Bharat Heavy Electricals Limited (BHEL)	Few companies can match the employee benefits and training programmes BHEL provides.
7th	IBM	Closely associated with education initiatives, IBM encourages its people to have a sense of purpose and do things responsibly.
8th	Tata Motors	Tata Motors gives employees ample opportunities.
9th	Wipro	Wipro has fallen from no. 3 rank in 2012. It has undergone many changes. Employees now have greater clarity about their roles and more responsibilities.
10th	Hindustan Unilever Limited (HUL)	HUL is a name that spells trust. Employees are taken through various roles and given ample market exposure.

(Table 2.4 Contd)

(Table 2.4 Contd)

11th	Microsoft	The company has dropped from its no. 7 spot in 2012. It allows employees to work flexi-time and gives them enough freedom to set their agenda.
12th	Tata Steel	The company has set many benchmarks in employee benefits over the years and continues to be rated highly for its HR practices.
13th	ABB	The company hardly makes any noise about its HR practices, but those in the business know. It offers excellent opportunities.
14th	Bharti Airtel	Bharti Airtel is in sync with the need of bright young people for constant change.
15th	State Bank of India	It is not only customers who rely on the State Bank of India, employees too seek it out for career growth.
16th	ONGC	Few companies can match ONGC's infrastructure and range. It is a safe bet for a career, indeed a poaching ground for its competitors.
17th	Axis Bank	With its youthful workforce, Axis Bank combines the finest of the public and the private sectors.
18th	Mahindra & Mahindra (M&M)	The company believes in carefully choosing and nurturing its talent. It offers employees huge opportunities to innovate and even incubates some of their ideas.
19th	Indian Railways	With a staff of 1.4 million, whom it cossets with benefits, the Indian Railways is an employer like none other.
20th	ACC	The company has been ranked 20th in 2012 as well by *Business Today* 'Best Companies to Work For in India' survey.
21st	HDFC Bank	Consistent in its HR policies and quick to spot talent, the company encourages its employees by giving them challenging assignments.
22nd	HCL Technologies	The company gives people enough room to air their views and multiple platforms to execute their ideas.
23rd	Delhi Metro Rail Corporation	With its employee-centric policies, Delhi Metro has emerged as a sought after company in the job market.
24th	Abbott Laboratories	The company's people-friendly policies make it an attractive workplace.
25th	Vodafone	The company offers employees ample opportunities and aids their career growth.

Source: Corporate Recruiters Survey 2011 Report.

Most of the earlier mentioned companies have campus-to-connect programmes to promote industry–institute partnerships. It is a matter of pride for any institute who could place their students in one or more of the companies. It also places additional responsibility on the institutes to make it happen and sustain with the right positioning and right inputs given to its graduating students.

Business Schools Scenario

3

India has about 3,900 management institutes, collectively offering around 3.9 lakh seats. The number of engineering colleges is also of similar magnitude. Large number of new institutes mushroomed exponentially without consideration to the actual demand and the quality of education and training that needs to be imparted. Many of them were categorised as 'mediocre' while some as 'poor'. Very few institutes actually managed to climb the ladder to be amongst the top ones in the country. Generally, higher education institutes in India are being looked upon as machines that churn out students and get money.

Some institutes initially boasted of 'world-class' infrastructure. Soon it ceased to act as a differentiating factor and 'placements' became a unique selling proposition. Placements finally became a permanent feature, almost as important (or little more important!) as curriculum. Some institutions commenced boasting even of 'international placements'. Naturally, the focus of students shifted from academics to placements. 'Placements' became the sole purpose, aim and the right of the students joining higher education, particularly engineering and management education. The point now is whether the institutions accept this shift and adapt themselves to delivering employability based education.

With the number of institutes increasing drastically, problems such as limited focus on the completion of syllabus and lack of quality faculty plagued most of them. This, in turn, is reflected in the quality of graduates and post-graduates, and further widened the gap between corporate expectations and offerings by the institutes. The 'employability' of a graduate professional became questionable and still remains questionable. Some of corporate comments like 'MBA means mediocre but arrogant' or 'mediocre institutes producing mediocre graduates' are heard very often. It is also now a known fact that the job profiles being offered to majority of MBA graduates have been downgraded. The survey findings on Indian higher education reported earlier tell the whole story.

A close analysis of a few successful management institutes in terms of their overall ranking as 'Tier 1' institutes reveals that these institutes have built a very strong value proposition based on 'soft aspects' such as quality and service rather than on 'hard aspects'. Most of these institutes are known for their contemporary course content, pedagogy and delivery. Syllabus revisions, addition of case studies and adding new subjects are routine activities in such institutions. More importantly, faculty members have gained reputation for their contribution to the area of their competence, and the demand for a particular course, specialisation or subject is also related to the credibility of the faculty.

While we would all like to learn best practices from the good institutes, this book focuses on the large number of student population associated with Tier II and Tier III institutions. There is a need for a different approach to enhance the employability and enable students to succeed in the fiercely competitive and changing business environment. It is high time institutions start thinking about this and break free from inertia and complacency and evolve a roadmap.

My experience is, MBA institutions need to be managed as a corporate company doing business. Education is a business of value addition. It is a process of transformation from a raw graduate to an industry-ready professional. It has all the ingredients of an industrial enterprise, namely input, process and output. The supporting services of quality assurance, maintenance, human resource and financial management have a similar role to play even in institutions of higher education. Vertically also it has the same structure, hierarchy and roles to be played from trustees, director and downwards to faculty and staff.

My vision was to build a competency-building institution and not a mere academic institute. My definition of competency comprised of broad-based knowledge, multi-disciplinary skills and positive attitude. Academics provide the knowledge; however, for the corporate world multidisciplinary skills and positive attitude to work and organisation are paramount. Academics is measurable through marks and grades; however, skills and attitude are a promise from students and the institute during the placement process. It is a challenge for them to convince the corporate world of potential competencies students bring on board if selected.

Managing the management institutes could be a topic for my next book. The purpose here is to provide some tried, tested and proven tips in the form of '10 commandments' that might be useful in ensuring value addition to the MBA graduates and to their career prospects.

MY 10 COMMANDMENTS FOR EXCELLENCE IN MANAGING A B-SCHOOL

- Recognise and accept that higher education is a business of delivering value to stakeholders.
- Establish a clear vision and direction for the institute.
- Establish a clear definition of market for input (incoming students), output (outgoing students) and transformational processes and inputs.
- Treat students as product to be transformed from raw graduates to ready-to-use resources for the corporate.
- Go beyond AICTE, UGC or NAAC norms in resource planning and deployment, particularly faculty resources.
- Go beyond the university syllabi and create opportunities for experiential learning through the application of concepts in real life world.
- Focus on competency building rather than just giving MBA as a certificate.
- Establish, maintain and promote stakeholder (particularly students and corporate) interaction and involvement in the development and management of the B-school.
- Establish and promote an open and transparent work environment in the campus and carry the team with shared vision, goals and objectives.
- Continuously benchmark globally about curriculum and other student development initiatives, and create international alliances and networks.

Making the Placement Cell Effective

Institutes generally have a dedicated placement cell. It needs to be effective.

- Establish placement cell very early in the academic year comprising of
  - Head of placements (a faculty)
  - Student representatives from senior batch—60%
  - Student representatives from the junior batch—40%

- Director or head of the institute provides the overall direction and supervision.
- Budget the placement activity. The budget may be high during the initial years and could be tapered down as the institute becomes known in the corporate word.
- Facilitate the placement cell with infrastructure like communication systems, PCs/laptops, a corporate-like furnished conference room, etc.
- Prepare a database of prospective placement companies and include their requirements and expectations. This is a high level research activity. A well-prepared database of the prospective companies will enhance the effectiveness of the placement cell.
- Student members in the placement team should take ownership of prospective companies by sector or by region, etc.
- As the corporate thinks twice before visiting a campus for placements, you also must have your analysis of companies' suitability to your students before they come to campus.
- Entire batch of students should undertake placement drives both for summer and final placements.
- Director and the head of placements should have links with the key corporate all over the country to create and foster the corporate relationship. Their participation in various conferences and seminars also greatly helps networking and relationship building.
- An attractive placement brochure helps, but just mailing them is not adequate. The brochure should have a corporate response form to understand the corporate needs.
- Establish professional placement policies and procedures which should be transparent and corporate-friendly.
- Success of summer internship placements is a good indication of prospects for final placements.
- Identify all those skills, knowledge points, certifications and other inputs needed by the corporate those are not part of the MBA programme and ensure that those inputs are provided well before the placement season.

Industry–Institute Relationships

This is at the heart of employability improvement and, therefore, successful placement of students. There are a number of avenues through which students and B-schools collaborate with industry. Some of the commonly used avenues are:

- Guest lectures by industry representatives
- Feedback and suggestions in curriculum and content designing
- Executive education and management development programmes
- Consulting services by faculty on management and related business issues
- Joint seminars by institute and industry for both executives and students
- Institutes providing research support to industry and even acting as incubators to new business
- Inclusion of industry experts in governing councils and other board of studies
- Industry providing financial and infrastructure support to B-schools for their development
- Corporate funding academic and applied research

The rest of the book is intended to deal with bridging the real gap between

- Employable and not-employable
- What you receive at your institute and what the corporate needs
- What you are and what you should be in the corporate world

The skills and competencies expected by the corporate have been classified into three categories. A section deals with each of the categories below and the chapters within deal with the skill development issues.

1. Personality and personal effectiveness skills
2. Organisational skills
3. Technology-based skills including professional memberships and certifications

Let us now get ready to jump-start on the road map to be industry ready and employment worthy. Let us not focus on just getting a job but becoming employable. Getting a job is a risky proposition while gaining employability is a sustainable option.

 Suggested Activity

Establish a team of 8–10 members of your institute comprising of senior students, faculty, alumni and staff under the leadership of the director/principal of the institute.

Brainstorm and assess the current situation on various aspects of employability such as

- What is our institute known for?
- How do we differentiate our institute from similar other institutes?
- Our strengths, weaknesses, opportunities and threats (SWOT).
- In which sector our students could be absorbed the most?
- Do we have the understanding of the knowledge and skills required by the companies?
- What knowledge and skills we deliver to the students in relation to the above and what are the gaps?
- Which companies recruit our students? Which companies refused to come to our campus?
- What have been the role profiles and remuneration packages offered to our students?
- Do our students get placed at par with other institutes for same profiles?
- What is the current level of industry–institute partnership?

Establish specific goals and action plans to bridge the gaps if any with specific responsibilities and time frames.

Review the progress on the action plans once in 3 months.

Personal Effectiveness Enhancement

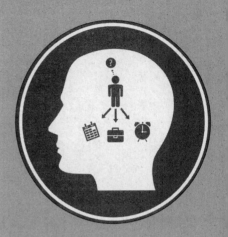

2

7Cs Model for Professional Excellence

4

The world of work is in a state of continual change. Your career today may involve moving between a number of different job functions and employers. Those jobs and employers are themselves likely to change and develop during the time you are employed with them. Employers, therefore, seek graduates who are enterprising, resourceful and adaptable to changes and who, in addition to formal degree, possess a range of skills and attributes, which can be used in a wide variety of settings during their careers. As engineering or MBA graduates seeking placement, it is necessary to have a look at the personal value and professional competencies coming on board. Having a set of skills, knowledge and personal attributes makes a person more likely to get a desired placement and sustained success in career.

The 7Cs model for professional excellence[1] is an attempt to logically bring together all those skills, qualities and attributes which are important from the employability point of view. It is not just important to have these 7Cs at the time of entry into the corporate world, they are also necessary for long-term success in all your professional endeavours (see Figure 4.1).

The 7Cs are mutually non-exclusive and complement each other. For example, if you have a high level of commitment, you are likely to have higher competence, or with good courage, your communication skill is likely to be better. The following brief description of 7Cs would help you understand them better and establish your own improvement plan.

Figure 4.1   7Cs of Professional Excellence

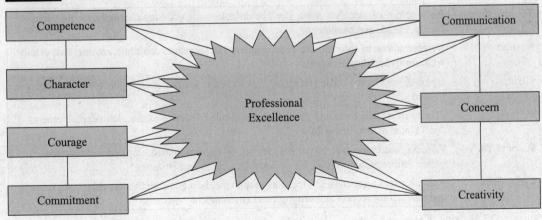

Source: Author.

[1] The idea of 7Cs has been adapted from: http://www.nsbe.org/trackback/77415a01-f74b-4763-bb99-6bee624cef33/The-7-C's"-of-Leadership.aspx?culture=en-US

CHARACTER

Your character is 'who and what you really are'. It is not just what you display for others to see, it is who you are, even when no one is watching. Abraham Lincoln said, 'Reputation is the shadow. Character is the tree.' Character comprises of your culture and conscience. Good character is thinking and doing the right thing because it is right to think and do what is right. The Rotary International, a 108 year old international service organisation, whose purpose is to bring together business and professional leaders in order to provide humanitarian services, encourages high ethical standards in all vocations and helps build international goodwill and world peace. Its 1.2 million members strive hard to create positive, lasting change in communities around the world. 'Service Above Self' is its motto and the four-way test which it prescribes is the standard of thinking and practicing. The four-way test says:

Of the things we think, say or do

1. Is it the TRUTH?
2. Is it FAIR to all concerned?
3. Will it build GOODWILL and better FRIENDSHIP?
4. Will it be BENEFICIAL to all concerned?

Your character is defined by some key attributes and could be assessed by the pattern of your thinking, behaviour and actions. These could best be remembered by the acronym TRC-FRC (Table 4.1).

A person may have money, position or power, but without 'good' character he/she will not be considered to be truly successful. The objective is to set a good example for everyone, demonstrate the citizenship value and make the world a better place to live for everybody.

Table 4.1 Key Determinants of Your Character

Trustworthiness	Be honest; don't deceive, cheat, steal; be reliable; build good reputation; be loyal to your family, friends and country
Respect	Respect others; be tolerant; use good manners and language; don't hurt anyone; deal calmly with insults and disagreements
Caring	Be kind; be compassionate and show you care; express gratitude; forgive others; help people in need
Fairness	Play by rules; take turns and share; be open-minded; listen to others; don't exploit others; don't blame others; treat all fairly
Responsibility	Plan; do your tasks; give 100%; keep trying; be self-disciplined; think of consequences before acting; be accountable for your words, actions and attitudes
Citizenship	Volunteer for community service; cooperate; vote; be a good neighbour; obey laws, rules and regulations; respect authority; protect environment

Source: The mentioned concept has been adapted from http://charactercounts.org/sixpillars.html of Josephson Institute, USA.

COMPETENCE

Competence is the ability of a person to perform a task successfully or efficiently. It is an indication of a person being physically, mentally, intellectually, emotionally, socially and culturally fit in any situation. Competence is a combination of knowledge, skills and attitude. Companies look for broad-based knowledge, multi-disciplinary skills and positive attitude when they hire graduates. Knowledge is available in classrooms, books and libraries, while skills and attitude building is a joint effort between you and your institution.

The recruiting team has a competency map in mind for the position for which you are being considered. Through questioning they try to assess the matching of what you have to offer with what is required for the job to be performed. You, therefore, need to carefully study and understand the competency profiles of the positions for which you seek to be considered. Building competencies to satisfy requirements and specifications of different job profiles and sectors increases the chances of the desired placement.

CONCERN

The word concern is sometimes linked to worry; however, both are quite different. Concern is an expression of recognising a problematic situation and showing seriousness to resolve the problem. A worried person sees a problem and a concerned person solves a problem. Expressing concern about a constraint and overcoming the same is a desired professional quality.

Concern also means to think about others' problems and shortcomings and help them to overcome those. They could be your family, neighbourhood, co-workers and community. It is important to realise that no one is perfect, and therefore people need your help in the same way as you may need theirs. You should be honest, loyal and consistent with the person you help.

There are many avenues available for community service. You can volunteer your services to charitable organisations such as the Rotary. Some students visited a remand home in Nashik and taught the children mathematics. Special programmes for slum children and senior citizens were also organised. It is always a great feeling to serve such disadvantaged and deprived class of society.

It is very true what Zig Ziglar, famous American author, said, 'You will get the things you want simply by helping enough other people get the things they want.' Or Charles Willey, a veteran international reporter said 'Make just one person happy each day and in forty years you will have made 14,600 people happy for a little time, at least.'

CREATIVITY

George Bernard Shaw said 'Some people see the things as they exist and ask the question WHY; I imagine things which don't exist and ask the question WHY NOT." That is creativity. Creativity is an ability to come up with new ideas and different ways of doing things. It involves challenging the status quo and thinking about a different situation to replace the same.

Creative thinking benefits all areas and activities of management. Thinking out of the box in solving problems, designing new systems to improve efficiency, developing new products, developing new software applications, all require a high level of creativity. Creativity turns up in every business situation where there is a possibility of doing things in a more profitable or more satisfying way. The subject of innovation and creativity is dealt with in more detail later in this section.

Famous baseball player Yogi Berra said 'If you keep doing things you have been doing, you will only get results you have been getting.' Think differently, act differently, be imaginative and you will be a different professional.

COMMUNICATION

The need for communication skills is ranked number 1 amongst the skill requirements by companies. It is important in virtually every career and sector that you may seek placement in. According to William Schaffer of Sun Microsystems, 'If there's one skill that's required for success in this industry, it's communication skill.' One study, published in Business Outlook, based on responses from over 1,000 employers from Fortune 1,000 companies revealed that employees send/receive an average of 1,798 messages each day via telephone, email, faxes, papers and face-to-face communications. Some experts have estimated that an average business executive spends 75–80% of his time communicating, that is, about 45 minutes of every hour. People with good communication skills have better prospects than those who are weak communicators.

A study published in the *Journal of Career Planning & Employment* asked almost 250 employers 'What skills are most important for college graduates?' Their overwhelming response was written and oral communication skills, followed by interpersonal skills, teamwork and analytical abilities. The importance of communicating effectively on the job is clear. However, realisation of the fact that communication skills often make the difference between being hired and being rejected in the first place is necessary. Therefore, having strong written and verbal business communication skills will make you more competitive, more promotable and more productive on the job. You must develop these skills now as a student, before you enter the job market. Being able to communicate well can boost your overall performance.

There is a separate chapter dedicated to this important subject of communication skills in a later section.

COMMITMENT

In corporate and professional life, commitment is *action*. No excuses. No debate. No lengthy analysis. No whining about how hard it is. No worrying about what others might think. No cowardly delays. Just go. Peter Drucker says 'Unless commitment is made, there are only promises and hopes … but no plans.' We all have experiences of how long the New Year resolutions last. To commit is to pledge yourself to a certain purpose or line of conduct or action. It also means practicing your beliefs consistently. There are, therefore, two fundamental conditions for commitment.

- The first is having a sound set of beliefs. It is said 'Stand for something or you'll fall for anything.' This links with the character.

- The second is faithful adherence to those beliefs with your behaviour and actions. Possibly the best description of commitment is 'persistence with a purpose'.

Being committed and staying committed is no easy task. Wavering commitment could be considered as no commitment at all. If you're really committed and genuine in that commitment, it will always stand the test of time. Current goals may have to be revamped or refined as the time goes on and your commitments will change. You may have to take some form of risk to make the changes necessary to fulfil your commitments. Keep your commitment in the forefront of your heart and mind and the things you always dreamed about will become a reality.

Commitment is most difficult and most readily proven during tough times. A ship's captain earns his reputation if he survives the storms. When your competition is tough, when money dries up or when the glamour of success wears off, this is when it is easiest to compromise your commitments. The real test comes when you can hold the line against the easy route of compromise.

COURAGE

Courage is not something that you display only in cases of emergencies or while performing some adventurous task. It is not something that can be borrowed from or lent to somebody when required through lessons. Courage is a way of life and comes from within. It is as much a habit as anything else, such as getting up, brushing your teeth in the morning or drinking coffee.

People tend to speak of courage only in terms of bravery. For instance, they speak of courage in battlefield. Soldiers and policemen are supposed to show courage. They tend to refer to courage in the face of devastations such as floods, earthquakes and others. However, courage is not merely related to your putting up with a bad situation. After all, in bad situations, there is not much one can do expect cope with whatever strength and forbearance one can muster.

The real test of courage is or should be in our normal daily lives. For example:

- The courage to speak truth at all times, because lies are the biggest and most obvious sort of cowardice that people hide behind.
- The courage to speak our mind and not stay silent. We are at times afraid that other people might not agree with us or there will be conflicting views and conflict is unpleasant. But not speaking your mind can lead to much worse unpleasantness.
- The courage to stand up for what we believe in. The courage to follow ethics, public laws, rules and regulations and make other people follow them too. The courage to resist those who take easy ways out, which leads to corruption and red tape.

Mark Twain has said, 'Courage is not the absence of fear. It is acting in spite of it.' A courageous person, then, is someone who feels fear, recognises fear and still goes on to do what he or she believes is right.

You should look at your life and lives of people around you and your family, friends and community. List the actions or decisions or behavioural patterns displayed by you or others during say the last 3 years. Try to link those actions and behavioural patterns into one of the Cs and evaluate its impact on the success of your career, life, business or organisation to which you belong and to your country and world. You may even carry out your own SWOT analysis to assess your situation on 7Cs and take appropriate actions to strengthen them. SWOT means strength, weakness, opportunities and threats.

Strengths and weakness are what you bring to a situation, and opportunities and threats are what the environment brings to you. SWOT analysis could be applied to any organisation or situation or even to your choice of career. If you choose to be an engineer, you apply the SWOT to yourself in relation to the demands of engineering as occupation. The SWOT analysis should generally result in a specific action plan to enhance strengths, eliminate weaknesses, exploit opportunities and hedge threats.

You need to put in sincere efforts to improve with or without the support from your institution. After all, it is your career which is at stake!! Mind you, your time in the institute is the best time for you to get better at each of the Cs. Once you get employed, you may not get the time and opportunity to work on your Cs.

Personality and Personality Development

5

We describe and comment on personalities of the people around us almost every day. Smart, pleasing, sweet, cute, attractive, strong, weak, shy and aggressive are few of the common adjectives used to describe personality. However, we mostly see the appearance of a person or persons in terms of external physical characteristics of height, weight, stature, complexion, etc., and consider them as the personality. It is true that physical appearance does matter; however, there are many other aspects that contribute to one's personality. Good appearance may impress someone initially but only personality can make a lasting impression. Annoyed with the service of a private sector bank, once I said to the manager, 'My old fashioned nationalised bank people are better because they do not wear a tie and do not claim to be efficient.' Good physical appearance can make you a publicity model but real good personality makes you a leader. The corporate world needs leaders and not just publicity models.

So, what is personality? A number of simple interactive personality tests are available on-line. You may use them to assess your personality type in terms of scores based on your responses to the questions. You do not get absolute answers about your personality; however, you will get some trends and behavioural patterns based on your responses to the questions asked. We used personality tests for our students at the beginning and towards the end of the programme to see the impact of our inputs. Generally, personalities are described in a vast number of different traits and their combinations. As an illustration, Wikipedia deals with the following five commonly used traits.

- Openness to experience
- Conscientiousness
- Extraversion
- Agreeableness
- Neuroticism

An easy way to remember this is with the acronym OCEAN.

- **Openness to experience**
  A high score on 'openness to experience' means appreciation for art, unusual ideas, curiosity and imagination. These people are more creative, open to new and different ideas. They are more likely to create stories, be better readers and have better writing skills.

  Low scorers on 'openness to experience' tend to be more closed-off and more analytical and resistant to change. They see imagination and art as waste of time. They are more concerned with grades and just work hard for the sake of hard work.
- **Conscientiousness**
  A high score on 'conscientiousness' means the tendency to show self-discipline, act dutifully and aim for achievement. Planned behaviour is preferred to spontaneous behaviour and responses.

These people achieve high levels of success through purposeful planning and persistence. They are regarded as responsible, reliable, compulsive perfectionists and workaholics. Their success is attributed to their focus on the work that needs to be done, timeliness and efficiency.

- **Extraversion**

A high score on 'extraversion' means the tendency to seek out the company and stimulation of others. The trait is marked by pronounced engagement with the external world. They tend to be enthusiastic, communicative, action-oriented people, who love excitement. In groups, they like to talk and draw attention to themselves.

Low scorers are introverts. They lack the exuberance, energy and activity level of extraverts. They tend to be quiet, low-key and not very involved in the social world. Introverts shouldn't be confused with depression or shyness; they simply lack the need for external stimulation that extraverts crave.

- **Agreeableness**

High scorers on 'agreeableness' are more compassionate and cooperative with others. This trait reflects individual differences for social harmony. They generally get along with others and have an optimistic view of human nature.

Low scorers are disagreeable individuals. They place self-interest at the top with no concern for others' well-being and are less likely to extend themselves to others. They tend to be sceptical of people's motives and human nature which can make them suspicious, unfriendly and uncooperative.

- **Neuroticism**

High scorers on 'neuroticism' experience negative emotions, such as anger, depression or anxiety. They are highly reactive in stressful situations. They are more likely to interpret ordinary situations as threatening or minor situations as too difficult or impossible. When presented with a difficult situation or a problem that they don't know how to solve, they just break down rather than being able to handle the situation. They also get angry easily and don't know what they are angry at.

Having high or low scores does not necessarily mean the person is good or bad; it is just an indication of the type of personality one may have. Based on the job profile you are targeting or that being considered by a company, some amendments to the earlier mentioned traits may be necessary. Just be aware of this fact and be ready to develop your personality traits accordingly. Personalities continue to develop throughout their lifetimes. Specific traits change at different rates and to different degrees.

Simply speaking, personality is the sum total of all physical, mental and emotional attitudes, values, interests and motivational factors. Your personality is shown by the way you behave or react to people, respond to things and circumstances. 'Students of your institute are the most humble MBAs, I have come across.' This was the description of my students by the Director of I2 Technologies in Bangalore. This is also an aspect of students' personality observed and appreciated by the employer.

Personality development is not just improving external appearance, public speaking or mannerisms. It is a struggle to march from lower mind to higher mind. It is a process of enhancing and grooming one's outer and inner self to bring about a positive change in your life. It is a tool that helps you realise your capabilities and your strengths making you a stronger, a happier and a cheerful person in addition to enabling improvements in behaviour, communication, interpersonal relationships, attitude towards life and ethics. An improvement in your personality can improve your chances for success in any undertaking.

Let us understand the development requirements towards a fine personality.

1. Be yourself
   - Think and feel good about yourself; high self-esteem but no ego or envy.
   - Don't compare yourself with anyone. If you do, you are insulting yourself.
   - Blindly following someone who is successful will never take you in right direction.
   - It is not who you are at the best of times that defines you as a person; it is who you are at the worst of times that shows your true nature.
2. Clarity of goals and purpose in life
   - Things will happen only if you want them to happen and you make them happen.
   - Goals can be achieved—systematic, determined, consistent efforts with self-control and by accepting setbacks without dejection.
   - Life laughs at you when you are unhappy.... Life smiles at you when you are happy.... Life salutes you when you make others happy!!
   - Uphold the ideal again and again even if failed a thousand times, never give up.
3. Initiative
   - Develop leadership qualities.
   - Make right decisions at right time.
   - Do beyond expectation; give more than what is expected, without expecting rewards in cash or kind. Rewards would come automatically.
   - Be adaptable to change; challenge your beliefs and fear.
4. Attitudes towards failures and mistakes
   - No one can go back and change a bad beginning; but anyone can start afresh and create a successful ending.
   - Accept your mistakes, learn from them. Most importantly, do not repeat mistakes.
   - Do not find fault with others for your mistakes; since others have to tolerate your faults, it is only fair that you tolerate theirs.
   - Every successful person has a painful story. Every painful story has a successful ending. Accept the pain and get ready for success.
5. Enthusiasm
   - Change 'Impossible' to 'I-M-Possible'.
   - Energy and excitement give you joy in work and life.
   - Enthusiasm leads to commitment and helps overcome tiredness, disappointments and failures.
   - 'Changing the face' can change nothing; but 'facing the change' can change everything.
6. Character
   - Inculcate honesty, integrity, sincerity, truthfulness and commitment in yourself.
   - Never feel insecure. It is the nature of life; to be uncomfortable with insecurity is to be uncomfortable with life. Use insecurity as a catalyst to develop self-reliance.
   - Faith, trust and confidence; unshakeable faith in yourself and the world will create a launching pad for success.
   - Compassion and love—the more you give away, the more of it comes back to you.
7. Self-discipline
   - An essential ingredient of success, and therefore a major strength.
   - It covers your thoughts, emotions, words, actions, habits and behaviours.
   - Balance your life at work and home. It is important to recognise each aspect of life and enjoy its journey; everyday of it, not waiting for a perfect day in future.

8. Positive attitude
   - Live your life to the fullest with a positive attitude.
   - 'Can do' instead of 'can't do' attitude.
   - 'I choose to do' instead of 'I have to do' or 'I need to do'.
   - Show an attitude of gratitude.
9. Hard work/Smart work
   - It is not the number of hours, but the output and results that are important.
   - Doing right things at the right time is paramount.
   - No one manufactures a lock without a key. Similarly God won't give problems without solutions.
10. Desiring and deriving pleasure and excitement
    - Respect and value people.
    - Develop multi-faceted hobbies and involvement avenues.
    - Spread love and happiness.
    - Communicate with clarity and conviction.
    - Give honest sincere acknowledgement.
11. Growing in one's knowledge and skills
    - Never develop a 'I know it all' attitude as the learning stops at that point.
    - Do not get hurt by criticism of others.
    - Books, meetings, personal visits and experiences increase ones knowledge and skills.
    - Continuously polish yourself.

Success is a Journey. Developing a winning personality is not a hit-and-miss affair or a matter of luck, but a conscious and focused effort.

Building Positive Mindset and Work Attitude

6

Aspiring for success in life requires a positive mindset and attitude. Good work attitude is crucial if you want to increase your chances of success at work. When people say that they are giving 100% they actually give far below 100%. There is a very simple and popular way of explaining the importance of attitude and its linkage with 'being 100%'.

If the alphabets A B C D E F G H I J K L M N O P Q R S T U V W X Y Z are represented as serial numbers 1 2 3 4 5 6 7 8 9 10 11 12 13 14 15 16 17 18 19 20 21 22 23 24 25 26, then ...

L-O-V-E	= 12+15+22+5	= 54%
L-U-C-K	= 12+21+3+11	= 47%
M-O-N-E-Y	= 13+15+14+5+25	= 72%
L-E-A-D-E-R-S-H-I-P	= 12+5+1+4+5+18+19+9+16	= 89%
S-K-I-L-L-S	= 18+11+9+12+12+18	= 64%
H-A-R-D-W-O-R-K	= 8+1+18+4+23+15+18+11	= 98%
K-N-O-W-L-E-D-G-E	= 11+14+15+23+12+5+4+7+5	= 96%

but....

A-T-T-I-T-U-D-E	= 1+20+20+9+20+21+4+5	= 100%

Dalai Lama says, 'It is very important to generate a good attitude, a good heart, as much as possible. From this, happiness in both the short term and the long term for both yourself and others will come.'

GETTING POSITIVE MINDSET AND ATTITUDE

It is true that employers look for people with the right skills and knowledge to complete a job. However, all else being equal, a majority of them would look for a positive attitude. You must practicse the following to demonstrate and apply a positive attitude.

- **Have a dream.** Dream is an essential motivator for something tangible to aim for. It shouldn't be just a daydream. It should be challenging and big enough to inspire you. It should stretch your ability beyond your comfort zone but within realistic bounds.

- **Develop hunger.** A simple desire won't get you anywhere beyond a wish list. You should develop hunger for something bad enough that you will do anything to satisfy it. If you have a cause you are passionate about and a dream that you can picture, hunger is the force that drives you.
- **Mind your own business.** Focus on your own performance. There is no point comparing yourself with others. Bill Gates said, 'If you compare yourself with others, you insult yourself.' The only one you have to compete with is yourself. Remember, there is always somebody out there who is better than you.
- **Never look back.** Driving vehicle by merely looking at the rear view mirror is absurd, isn't it? Periodically use the rear mirror to take stock of the past situation. Take the load of 'past' off your back. The past can never be brought back and can never be repeated. Your past mistakes should only serve as a lesson for the future.
- **Can do.** Say, 'It looks tough; let me see what I can do.' Instead of 'Oh no, this cannot be done.' Do not waste your precious time convincing others why certain things cannot be done. The right thing would be to figure out a way to complete the task at hand.
- **Never say die.** Nothing is impossible; it is I-M-POSSIBLE if you make it. You are bound to face some setbacks and failures with your projects. Do not quit and give up. Failure only happens when you give up. Richard Bach says, 'Sooner or later, those who win are those who think they can.' Hence, they say, a winner never quits.
- **Do not complain.** Complaining is giving opportunity for somebody else to succeed. It is an excuse for non-performance. Instead of complaining, discuss the issue with others including seniors. When you discuss, there is a next step in what you can do about the situation. Complaining is a bad habit and can be detrimental to your career success. Stop complaining and start thinking of solutions.
- **Excel in your work.** Remember there are no shortcuts to success. If there are, then there will be a lot more successful people in this world. You need to work hard as well. It means doing extra to make sure a job is done with pride. Make sure that it exceeds the basic qualities, requirement and expectations. It is your name and reputation that is at stake.
- **Be organised.** If you are organised, you become efficient and if you are efficient you become effective. This allows your superiors to consider giving you more important assignments. This is because they know you would make more efficient use of your productive time and be able to complete them on time.
- **Control your emotions.** Forgiveness is a gift to humankind. Getting angry results in lot of stress. Forgiveness has a more positive impact on those who make you angry and helps them to perform with more responsibility and accountability. Don't forget also to forgive yourself for everything you regret ever having done or not done.
- **Have gratitude for all of life.** Gratitude is another gift to humankind. Saying 'thank you' is a powerful way to create great relationships, but the real power of gratitude is internalising an immense thankfulness for your very existence. Just when you're about to blow your top for all the seeming misfortunes that befall you, remind yourself of all your blessings. This practice can be very sobering.
- **Be of service to others.** Being of service to others is one of the greatest paths to happiness. Remember, your greatest service to others is the kind of person you are, rather than the tasks you accomplish. Your greatest gift to others is happiness and the most powerful way to do that is 'Be happy and keep others happy.'
- **Dance lightly with life.** Life does not have to be taken very seriously. You will make mistakes and you will also feel regrets. Happiness comes from playing hopscotch on the river of life.

Be a hopper from joy to joy while laughing at the threats of calamity. Convert each constraint or obstacle or failure into an opportunity to make life better.

- **Know unity with spirit.** Be spiritual and not religious. Your life will be happier if you acknowledge that you are not alone; become open to that presence of almighty, and create rituals to celebrate your spirituality. You may feel your bond with spirit in songs of praise, in calls to prayer, in meditation, while doing yoga or while walking in the woods.

- **Be the master of your destiny.** Envision the future you want and then take action to create that future. Often, you will fail. Each failure is a new lesson to be learnt. Thomas Edison failed 1,000 times before he could develop a light bulb; but, he was a step nearer to success with each failure. Plan again and take action again. Remember, 'Positive thoughts beget positive results.' More positive you are and the more you believe in yourself, the more positive things will come your way.

GET RID OF THAT NEGATIVITY

Negativity is all around us and is not obvious at all times. You are most likely to have the presence of negativity if

- You were in very good mood at the beginning of your conversation with a friend and the end leads to your feeling down, empty or alone.
- You are more concerned with the drawbacks of doing something than actually doing it
- The thought of going into your office make you feel sick.

There are three sources from which negativity usually breeds: you yourself, your relationships and your environment. The following suggestions may be useful to reduce negativity in your life.

Negativity within yourself

- **Negativity feeds on fear and anxiety.** The fear and anxiety impair your ability to move forward. Focus on the things you want to do, push out fear and anxiety and experience the positive feelings and happiness you get from doing those things.
- **Meditate.** You can meditate through traditional ways such as yoga or deep breathing, or just by being 'alone'. The goal is to spend some time daily on clearing your mind, ridding it of negative thoughts and refocusing on those that are positive.
- **Work out and eat right.** If you look good on the outside, it'll be easier to feel good on the inside too.

Negativity in your relationships

- **Minimise toxic relationships.** Toxic relationship is one which makes you feel bad about yourself. Toxic people take pleasure in creating that feeling. Minimise the time you spend with them and work on cultivating healthier, happier relationships.
- **Set clear boundaries.** Set boundaries with negative people in your life. Let them know that although you love and care for them, their negativity isn't welcome. Explain to them that if they can't be positive or respectful, then you can't be around them.
- **Find positive people.** The more you surround yourself with positive high-energy people, the less room you have for those who are negative. A friend, relative or co-worker, who makes you feel

special, gives you more confidence, even makes you feel empowered, is the type of person who brings positivity into your life.

- **Accept challenges.** When people tell you that you can't do something, prove them wrong. Chances are, they themselves can't do it or are too afraid to try. If you show them it can be done, they might even be inspired by your success. You can be a living tip for positive thinking to them.

Negativity within your environment

- **Surround yourself only with things you love and make you feel good.** They could be framed family photos, favourite books, potted plants, adopting a pet and works of art or whatever else that is meaningful to you.
- **Love what you do and do what you love.** If the morale of the company is low, your work environment can have a tremendously negative impact on you and your outlook. Best option is to look for a new job with a company or another department in the same company, known for a healthy and positive culture.
- **Love where you live.** Your neighbourhood can have a big impact on your outlook. Whether something distasteful has happened in your community or you just don't get positive vibes from your neighbours, it may be the time to move.
- **Get involved.** Get involved in your local community. Get involved with non-profit organisations and do some community work. You will realise the sheer number of people who have bigger problems than you do. Be a big brother or sister. Getting involved in community service makes a positive impact on the world around you, ultimately making you feel positive about yourself and about life.

Recognise negative thoughts as they emerge and bury them before they take root. If you feel your mood darkening again, put a stop to these dangerous musings before you succumb to them. Rule your emotions; don't let your emotions rule you. Life often throws more obstacles in our path than we can handle. However, you can make the choice to be happy.

POSITIVE ENVIRONMENT AT WORKPLACE

Modern day workplaces are very stressful and demanding. Working under pressure is acceptable at times, because it increases productivity. However, too much pressure makes people think that the organisation is not the right place to work. Hence, creating a positive work environment is essential to keep up the spirit within the people working with you.

First and foremost you yourself should be happy with your work situation. If you are unhappy or frustrated, it is unlikely that you will be able to create a positive work environment at your workplace. You hear the flight attendant when you travel by air: 'Put your own oxygen mask on first.' You are of no use to others if you have not taken care of yourself first. Here are some tips for you to create an enjoyable and performing workplace. The following tips may be useful for you to practise in situations where you are supervising people or you are the owner of a business and have created an organisation for running that business.

- **Honour yourself.** It is your self-esteem which makes others have confidence in you as a leader. If you do not respect yourself, others will not. Make sure your self-esteem does not go to extremes and becomes ego.
- **Have a meaning and purpose.** Find a meaning and purpose in the job your staff are doing at the workplace. The office atmosphere should make them feel that their choice of organisation is right for showing their talents and improving their skills.
- **Promote team work.** *Together Each Achieves More* is the TEAM. One of the best ways of creating a positive working atmosphere is to group the individuals into teams. If employees work as a team, the distributed responsibilities increase their output.
- **Encourage employees.** Show appreciation for the performance of your employees and encourage them. Consider awarding prizes and certificates to the best performers. This will bring in a positive attitude towards work, as they know that they will be recognised and rewarded for their good performance.
- **Utilise their talents.** Utilise the special talent of your employees. Do it by dealing with them in a polite way, but with a degree of authority. Show appreciation for their talent and build relationships. That will make them feel that the workplace atmosphere is favourable and conducive for them to show their talents.
- **Make wise investments.** Right infrastructure at workplace creates and promotes positive work environment. Invest in things, such as furniture, computers, interiors and colour schemes, that provide a welcoming atmosphere. You may even consider providing music in office as music has been proved to increase productivity.
- **Communicate your expectations.** Your subordinates always would like to know what you expect from them. Clearer the expectations, more are their chances of meeting them. Set goals and performance standards for them to achieve. Specify the deadlines clearly, so that there is no room for any confusion in the mind of your employees.

Getting started is easy. It's the sustenance that's tricky. Make a habit of thinking positively till it becomes an indelible part of who you are. Keep it up. Remember Zig Ziglar who said, 'Your attitude, not your aptitude, will determine your altitude.'

7   Values and Ethics

Ethisphere, a US based Research Company dedicated to the creation, advancement and sharing of best practices in business ethics and corporate social responsibility, published a list of 110 companies from 100 countries and 36 industries for their ethical behaviour in 2011. Some of the ethical companies which appear in the list are Adidas, eBay, Microsoft and Colgate Palmolive. From India, only HDFC Bank found a place in the list.

Business ethics and corporate social responsibility are the subjects that aim at cleaning the systems, organisations and people who drift away from ethical practices. The world famous Enron in US and the most recent Satyam case in India are only few of the worst situations from the ethical and morality point of view. Scams and scandals have become rampant in recent times across business sectors including governments. The fundamental claim of any business cannot be ethical if it ignores unethical practices by itself, its employees, its suppliers or its marketing/purchasing channels. Good sign is that businesses increasingly find themselves facing pressure to improve their ethical practices from their customers, pressure groups and external stakeholders. They monitor the ethical practice of multinationals or industries and initiate combined direct and indirect actions and sanctions.

Ethics involves a discipline that examines good or bad practices within the context of a moral philosophy. It defines and recommends concepts of right and wrong behaviour. For us, ethics means living our life responsibly and to review whether our actions are right or wrong. Ethical behaviour is that which is morally accepted as 'good' and 'right' as opposed to 'bad' or 'wrong' in a particular setting. It is said, 'In love and war everything is fair.' That is supposed to be an exception and not a rule. Unfortunately, the world currently believes, 'Everything is fair until you are caught and proven guilty.' Most of the times, we live in an ethical illusion about ourselves with discrepancies between our beliefs, thoughts, behaviour and actions. It also includes our sense of reasoning for our wrong behaviour.

The class of 2009 graduates of Harvard Business School initiated an MBA oath with a mission to facilitate a widespread movement of MBAs aiming to lead in the interests of the greater good and committing to living out the principles articulated in the oath. The oath is a voluntary pledge for graduating and current MBAs to 'create value responsibly and ethically'. The objective is to create an MBA community with a high standard for ethical and professional behaviour. The group now has a broad coalition of MBA students and graduates representing over 250 schools from around the world including the World Economic Forum. You may find more information about it at www.mbaoath.com.

The MBA oath is expected to:

- Make a difference in the lives of MBAs who take the oath.
- Challenge other MBAs to work with a higher professional standard, whether they sign the oath or not.
- Transform the field of management into a true profession in which MBAs are respected for their integrity, professionalism and leadership.

I thought it may be useful to reproduce here the MBA oath verbatim (with permission from www. mbaoath.com) for possible adoption by young MBAs. Though, this oath is created by MBA fraternity for MBA fraternity, I see the value in its universal adaptation by all graduates who enter the employment world.

THE MBA OATH

As a business leader I recognise my role in society.

- My purpose is to lead people and manage resources to create value that no single individual can create alone.
- My decisions affect the well-being of individuals inside and outside my enterprise, today and tomorrow.

Therefore, I promise that:

- I will manage my enterprise with loyalty and care, and will not advance my personal interests at the expense of my enterprise or society.
- I will understand and uphold, in letter and spirit, the laws and contracts governing my conduct and that of my enterprise.
- I will refrain from corruption, unfair competition, or business practices harmful to society.
- I will protect the human rights and dignity of all people affected by my enterprise, and I will oppose discrimination and exploitation.
- I will protect the right of future generations to advance their standard of living and enjoy a healthy planet.
- I will report the performance and risks of my enterprise accurately and honestly.
- I will invest in developing myself and others, helping the management profession continue to advance and create sustainable and inclusive prosperity.

In exercising my professional duties according to these principles, I recognise that my behaviour must set an example of integrity, eliciting trust and esteem from those I serve. I will remain accountable to my peers and to society for my actions and for upholding these standards.

This oath I make freely, and upon my honour.

Ethics could be learnt and practised at any stage in life. Some business schools have included business ethics and social responsibility as a core and compulsory subject. These subjects are supposed to challenge students to look at issues from an ethical and moral perspective and move their thinking upward towards a clean world. The point is, do we accept and internalise the ethical and moral principles in our life as an individual, a group, an institution, a company or as a community of which we are a part.

This chapter aims to help individuals, who are entering the corporate world as future managers and leaders, to accept the ethical principles and practice them in real life situations. Following is a list of ethical principles which translate ethical values into active language, establishing standards or rules describing the kind of behaviour ethical professionals should and should not engage in. These principles describe the characteristics and values associated with ethical behaviour and ethical decision-making.

1. **Accountability:** Accountability is taking ownership. Ethical professionals acknowledge and accept personal accountability for the ethical quality of their decisions and omissions to themselves, their associates, clients, colleagues, their companies and their communities.

2. **Commitment to excellence:** Ethical professionals pursue excellence in performing their duties, and are well-informed and prepared. They constantly endeavour to increase their skill in all areas of responsibility.

3. **Concern for others:** Ethical professionals are caring, compassionate, benevolent and kind; they believe in, 'help those in need' and seek to accomplish their business goals in a manner that causes the least harm and the greatest positive good.

4. **Fairness:** Ethical professionals are fair and just in all dealings. They do not misuse their powers and do not use indecent means to gain or maintain any advantage. They also do not take undue advantage of other's mistakes or difficulties. They manifest a commitment to justice, equal treatment to all, and tolerance for and acceptance of diversity. They are open-minded and willing to admit their mistakes and where appropriate, change their positions and beliefs.

5. **Honesty:** Ethical professionals are honest and truthful in all their dealings and they do not deliberately mislead or deceive others by misrepresentations, over statements, partial truths, selective omissions or any other means.

6. **Integrity:** Ethical professionals show personal integrity and the courage of their convictions by doing what they think is right even when there is great pressure to do otherwise. They are principled, honourable and upright, and they fight for their beliefs. They will not sacrifice principle for expediency, or be hypocritical or unscrupulous.

7. **Law abiding:** Ethical professionals abide by laws, rules and regulations relating to their personal, professional and business activities.

8. **Leadership:** Ethical professionals are conscious of the responsibilities and opportunities of their place of leadership and seek to be positive ethical role models by their own conduct. They create and promote an environment in which principled reasoning and ethical decision-making are highly regarded and respected.

9. **Loyalty:** Ethical professionals are loyal to their clients, companies and colleagues. They avoid undue influences and conflicts of interest and make independent professional judgements. If they decide to accept other employment, they provide reasonable notice, respect the proprietary information of their former employer and refuse to engage in any activities that take undue advantage of their previous positions.

10. **Promise-keeping and trustworthiness:** Ethical professionals are worthy of trust. They are candid and forthcoming in supplying relevant information and correcting misapprehensions of facts. They make every effort to fulfil the spirit of their promises and commitments. They do not unreasonably try to rationalise non-compliance or create justifications for escaping their commitments.

11. **Reputation and morale:** Ethical professionals seek to protect and build good reputation for themselves, their profession and business. They enhance the morale of their associates, colleagues and employees by avoiding situations that might undermine respect and take whatever actions necessary to correct or prevent the creation of such situations by others.

12. **Respect for others:** Ethical professionals show respect for human dignity, autonomy, privacy, rights and interests of all those who have a stake in their decisions. They are courteous and treat all people with equal respect and dignity regardless of sex, race or national origin.

It is the people who bring ethical or unethical and moral or immoral values and practices to the organisation, society and community. It is worth noting that

- **Most people** behave ethically to avoid some punishment or to receive some reward.
- **Many** behave ethically to be good citizens and responsive to family, friends and seniors.
- **Very few** behave ethically to pursue some ideal of doing the right things.

Compliance is about doing what you are required to do by laws or rules. Ethics is about doing what you should do because it is right, just and fair. Compliance often represents an ethical minimum while ethics represents a standard that exceeds the legal minimum.

Legality is enforcement, ethics is obligatory and morality comes from within. My question to you is 'in which group you want to be in your profession and career?'

Many companies and professional associations have a practice of defining a code of conduct for its members. It communicates management's behavioural expectations from its employees. The code of conduct generally covers two aspects.

- Compliance-based, which defines the desired behavioural patterns and specifies the penal provisions in cases of defaults.
- Integrity-based, which positively supports ethical behaviour with value-based statements and announcements, and emphasises shared responsibility and accountability.

You may visit the websites of various professional associations and companies and can read the entire draft of the code of conduct which the members or employees have to sign and abide by.

I have followed the ethical principles for over 40 years of my professional career. If I could not help somebody, I have not done harm to anybody. It was not easy. I have lost many 'lucrative' opportunities and have suffered at the hands of some managements as well ... but ... even at the age of 66, I sleep peacefully for full 8 hours. Isn't it the prize for ethical behaviour?

Suggested Activity

Try this simple questionnaire, developed by the Pat Lucas Consulting Firm, on yourself and see where you place yourself on ethical platform.

		Always	Usually	Never
1.	Do/Will you maintain confidentiality of matters in employment?	☐	☐	☐
2.	Do/Will you say 'no' to inappropriate requests?	☐	☐	☐
3.	Do/Will you show respect for copyright laws?	☐	☐	☐
4.	Are/Will you be honest when sharing information with others?	☐	☐	☐
5.	Do/Will you balance organisational and personal needs?	☐	☐	☐

		Always	Usually	Never
6.	Are/Will you be able to manage your personal biases?	☐	☐	☐
7.	Do/Will you respect the diversity within your organisation?	☐	☐	☐
8.	Do/Will you utilise your authority properly?	☐	☐	☐
9.	Do/Will you challenge yourself to 'do the right thing'?	☐	☐	☐
10.	Does/Will favouritism ever enter into your decision-making?	☐	☐	☐
11.	Do/will you follow orders regardless if they appear unethical?	☐	☐	☐
12.	Are/Will you be able to avoid conflicts of interest?	☐	☐	☐

You may also able to assess the ethical status of the company which you have joined or likely to join using the following.

		Always	Usually	Never
1.	Does the organisation have a written ethics policy?	☐	☐	☐
2.	Does the company require its employees to sign a code of conduct statement?	☐	☐	☐
3.	Are ethical behaviours expected out of the leaders?	☐	☐	☐
4.	Are ethical behaviours rewarded?	☐	☐	☐
5.	Do the leaders in the organisation act ethically?	☐	☐	☐
6.	Are the leaders in the organisation honest?	☐	☐	☐
7.	Is the behaviour of the leaders consistent with the stated ethics and values of the organisation?	☐	☐	☐
8.	Do the leaders in the organisation employ favouritism?	☐	☐	☐
9.	Does the organisation offer training in business ethics?	☐	☐	☐
10.	Do the leaders in the organisation balance the needs of the business with ethical issues appropriately?	☐	☐	☐
11.	Does the organisation balance its short-term business goals with its long-term need for success?	☐	☐	☐
12.	Do the executives in the organisation lead by example?	☐	☐	☐

Innovation and Creativity

8

All businesses are facing the challenges of survival and growth in this market due to globalisation, increasing competition, diversity among consumers and access to new forms of technology. It is a survival of the fittest syndrome. Realising this, since 2001, world celebrates 15–21 April every year as World Creativity and Innovation Week (WCIW). Incidentally, WCIW starts on 15 April, which is the birthday of the great Leonardo da Vinci. Since its inception, businesses, communities and schools in over 40 countries use the week to enliven the creative spirit by inspiring people to spark their brains to use new ideas, imagination and make new decisions that make a positive difference at home, at work and at school. *Unlimited creative potential in all of us is celebrated to make the world a better place for us to live.* Go to Google, type 'World Creative and Innovation Week' and get more information on these celebrations.

Defined in simple terms, innovation is the implementation of creative ideas, concepts or methods in order to add value to the organisation, usually through increased profits, reduced operational costs or both. Innovation is a natural wonder creating greater value than what is initially perceived. Creativity is the seed from which it grows and enhances the performance of a process, person, team or organisation. *Therefore, innovation is the result of developing and implementing creative ideas and solutions.*

What is creative thinking then? Creative thinking is 'the process we use when we come up with a new idea. It can be accidental or deliberate.' You might have woken up out of a deep sleep with a great solution to a problem you'd been struggling with, or you are taking a shower and all of a sudden 'the answer' pops into your head. That happens to all of us. We come up with our most creative ideas by complete chance when we're not consciously thinking about them.

It seems easy to say we want to innovate, but it is like going over Niagara Falls in a barrel with all the misery and disorder that precedes innovation. Leaders' challenge is to help people make meaning of such a journey. To innovate is to intentionally let go of the 'way things are' and welcome 'the way they could be.' Albert Einstein said, 'The problems that exist in the world today cannot be solved by the level of thinking that created them.' It involves challenging the established habits of thought, norms, expectations, assumptions, standards and beliefs in order to embrace something 'unknown'. This journey is a period of stress, uncertainty, risk and unpredictability. There is no clear way forward and trial-and-error experimentation becomes the order. This is a period that requires a rapid learning cycle and taking smart risks as you learn your way forward.

Creativity brings into being something that did not exist before. It could be a product, a process or a thought. Some misconceptions about creativity are

- The smarter you are, the more creative you are
- The young are more creative than the old
- Creativity is reserved for the few—the flamboyant risk takers

- Creativity is a solitary act
- You can't manage creativity

You don't have to be a rocket scientist to be creative. It is wrong to assume that only highly intelligent people are creative. Research shows that once the IQ exceeds about 120, which is just little above average, intelligence and creativity are not at all related. That means, even if you are an average intelligent person, you still have potential to wield amazing creative powers. However, some bad habits make you kill your own creative instincts. These could be changed if you are willing to work at them. Here are eight of the worst habits I found on http://www.copyblogger.com/creativity-killers/ that you need to get rid of.

1. **Creating and evaluating simultaneously**
   While driving your car you cannot press accelerator and break at the same time. Similarly you should not engage in different types of thinking simultaneously. Creating involves generating new ideas, visualising, looking ahead and considering possibilities. Evaluating includes analysing and judging the ideas and sorting them into good and bad or useful and useless. You must treat creation and evaluation differently. Come up with lots of ideas first and then judge their worth later. Do not evaluate ideas too soon, and allow yourself to generate more ideas.

2. **Over-reliance on experts**
   It is wise to listen to gurus and experts, but unwise to follow without questioning. Tom Connelly said, 'He who asks a question may be a fool for five minutes, but he who never asks a question remains a fool forever.' Expert is a person who gets expertise from his past experience and may not be creative enough to predict future success of new ideas. Some of the most successful people in the world did what others told them would never work. They knew something about their own idea that others did not know. Every path to success is different.

3. **Fear of failure**
   Success and failure are the two sides of the same coin. Matches should be played to win and not for not losing. No one wants to make mistakes or fail. But if you try too hard to avoid failure, you are likely to miss success as well. It has been said that to increase your success rate, you should aim to make more mistakes. In other words, take more chances and you will succeed more often. Those few really great ideas you come up with will more than compensate for all the dumb mistakes you make.

4. **Ambiguity scare**
   Most people like things to make sense. Unfortunately, life is not neat and tidy. There are some things you will never understand and some problems you will never solve. Most great creative ideas emerge from a swirl of chaos. You must develop a part of yourself that is comfortable with mess and confusion. You should become comfortable with things that work even when you do not understand why.

5. **Lack of confidence**
   You must have confidence in your abilities in order to create and carry out effective innovations. Though experience enhances your confidence level, familiarity with how creativity works also helps. When you understand that ideas often seem crazy initially, that failure is just a learning experience and that nothing is impossible, you are on your way to becoming more confident and, therefore, more creative and innovative. Instead of dividing the world into the possible and impossible, divide it into 'what you have tried' and 'what you have not tried'. There are a million pathways to success.

6. **Discouragement from other people**

   Even if you have a wide-open mind and the ability to see what is possible, most people around you will not. They will tell you in various and often subtle ways to conform, be sensible and not rock the boat. Ignore them. The path to every victory is paved with predictions of failure. Once you have a big win under your belt, all the 'no sayers' will shut their noise and see you for what you are—a creative force to be reckoned with.

7. **Overload of analysis and information**

   It's called 'analysis paralysis', a condition of spending so much time thinking about a problem and cramming the brain with so much information that you lose the ability to act. It is said that information is to the brain what food is to the body; but just as you overeat, you can also over-think. Winston Churchill said, 'Perfect solutions of our difficulties are not to be looked for in an imperfect world.' You need to develop the ability to know when to stop collecting information and start taking action. Acting on a good plan today is better than waiting for a perfect plan tomorrow.

8. **Getting trapped in false limits**

   We are all a product of our experience and tend to think only about our expertise and experience. You know the story of the blind men trying to describe the elephant by touching it. If you are a mechanical engineer, you will not think about electrical engineering. These limitations are false and self-imposed directly or indirectly. Only when you force yourself to look past what you know, you come up with the breakthrough ideas you are looking for. Therefore, be open to anything, step outside your comfort zone, think out of box and consider how things work in unrelated areas. What seems impossible today may seem surprisingly doable tomorrow. Why a steel making company cannot be as clean as a pharma company?

If you recognise some of these problems in yourself, don't fret. In fact, rejoice! Knowing what's holding you back is the first step toward breaking down the barriers of creativity.

WAY FORWARD TO LEADING INNOVATION IN ORGANISATION

You may end up joining any of the following types of organisation or companies.

- Companies which are not innovative and do not claim to be so.
- Companies which talk about innovation on the surface, but discourage in practice.
- Companies which talk and walk innovation, are already well on its way to being an innovative leader—if it is not there already!

In all cases, it will be a great challenge for you to be creative and innovative. In the first case, you need to introduce innovation and generate realisation and interest in innovation. There could be resistance from the conservative type of people, but not difficult to overcome. The second case is more serious, where everybody will accept that innovation is the key to success but put all sorts of obstacles, including the budget constraints, for you to fail. Your people skills will be put to test in such a situation. The third case should be a smooth selling but poses a different kind of challenge. Here, the people will be creative and innovative and you have to come up to their level or exceed their level.

Your knowledge and understanding of creativity, creative thinking and innovation processes will be fully tested. The following should help you to successfully promote a culture of purposeful innovation in the organisation you work with.

- **Innovation is a group process**
  Innovation is not an individual thing. Though there are individual creative thinkers who come up with clever ideas that become the basis of innovations, the idea by itself is not an innovation. It is only the beginning. In business, ideas need to be evaluated for viability, developed into concepts and turned into a project before its coming into reality. For example, a new product idea will involve developing prototypes, seeking feedback, testing functionality, setting up production facilities, seeking suppliers and much more. Each of these steps requires participation of people with different expertise, all of whom contribute to the innovation process.
- **Define your innovation goals**
  You need to have clear innovation goals to shoot for. Innovation goals tend to be similar to strategy and business goals and, therefore, usually are a simple matter of reformulation as a part of the strategic planning process. Typical innovation goals might be

  - To increase the product shelf life by 100%
  - To reduce the field failures of our product by 50%
  - To improve process efficiency by 5% per year

  Once you have clarified these goals, you will find that innovation initiatives are a breeze to set up.
- **Mobilise appropriate resources**
  If innovation is the number one priority of your company and you are going to aim for breakthrough innovation, then you need to provide adequate budget for its development and implementation. You need to set up an innovation process, put a team in charge, procure innovation tools and provide training. All needs money. Ideas with the greatest innovation potential are, by necessity, radically different to business as usual. This means they are also risky and, therefore, need to be provided proper resources.
- **Work on your innovation culture**
  For creativity and innovation to thrive, you need to have a organisational culture that nurtures creative thinking, sees mistakes as on-the-job training and embraces every step of the innovation process. Proctor & Gamble in its plant has a nice banner which says, 'We do not punish people for making mistake; however, we do if they repeat it.' Most great innovations are built upon mountains of mistakes. You can congratulate the team responsible for their efforts, evaluate what went wrong, learn lessons and try again. But where mistakes cost people jobs, no one will dare to try anything radical—and that will kill innovation. No mistakes means no learning and no learning means no innovation. Very few companies understand this.
- **Establish diverse teams**
  Diversity of membership brings a broader range of knowledge, experience, thinking and creativity to any team. You should, therefore, ensure that project teams, problem solving teams and all teams that are expected to contribute to your innovation process are as diverse as possible.
- **Create environment for innovation**
  Foster an environment of imagination, exploration, acceptable risk and 'what ifs'. Give people time to think, toys to spark off and diverse partners to play with. The resource needs and costs of

innovation rise over time. Resources that drive early innovation, breakthrough and imagination are mainly emotional and psychological support.

- **Collaborate**

  Establish collaborative alliances internally and externally with research institutions, professional associations, technology institutions and others, and take advantage of their experiences and expertise. You can even look for collaborations, technology tie-ups nationally and internationally. Use make or buy decisions judiciously to have optimal mix of local and bought out technologies. Attend seminars and network with technologies and professionals. Obtain memberships of professional bodies and technology centres, and subscribe to different journals and magazine to keep yourself updated on global innovative practices and developments.

- **Implement**

  Innovation is not about idea generation, creativity or training programmes. It is about implementing creative ideas in order to add value. If your company is reluctant to implement highly creative ideas, then your innovation process will be only a creative thinking exercise. Moreover, if employees note that highly creative ideas are routinely not implemented, they will not bother sharing or developing such ideas.

- **Evaluate and improve**

  Your innovation process can also improve through innovation! You need to review the process and the results on a regular basis. Also, use your innovation process for generating, developing and implementing ideas for improving that innovation process!

Some of the creative aspects of my contribution are

- A chemical company in Trinidad, West Indies, wanted to improve productivity and reduce the cost of its bottle packaging operations. The application of very simple productivity improvement techniques resulted in productivity improvement by 58% with 12% less manpower.
- A cable manufacturing company in India wanted to build a new warehouse to meet its storage requirements. By increasing the capacity utilisation of the existing warehouse by 43%, huge investment on a new warehouse was avoided.
- A steel tube manufacturing company in India was facing customer complains about late deliveries and huge inventories. Using Lean principles, on-time delivery was improved to 94% and the process cycle time was reduced by 30% resulting in reduced inventory levels.
- A sheet glass company in India with automated production machinery was using over 200 people for just handling glass from the machine floor to warehouse. The manning requirement was reduced to 94 using simple techniques of work system design and with nearly *zero* investment.
- More variety in tooling results in more inventories and more tool changes. The application of value engineering techniques in an electric hand tool manufacturing company in India helped the number drill sizes reduce from 64 to 19.
- A reputed transformer manufacturing company in India had a problem of long cycle time, repetitive movements and inefficient work steps in assembly and welding of radiators. Work study approach achieved 55% reduction in transformer radiator assembly and welding time.
- Steel industry needs huge manpower and, thus, adds significant cost to a ton of steel produced. Scientific manpower utilisation studies resulted in 20% reduction in manning levels in a Steel Plant in Trinidad, West Indies, and reduction in the cost/ton of steel produced from $270.00 to $220.00.

- Space utilisation is a key factor in designing factory layouts. It not only reduces the cost of space, it also reduces the needs for handling materials. Systematic layout planning resulted in 50% space utilisation improvement of a batch-type heat treatment plant.

Finally, once again George Bernard Shaw; 'People see things those exist and ask the question WHY? I imagine things which don't exist and ask the question WHY NOT?' That is creativity which promotes creative thinking and brings innovation.

Work–Life Balance

9

As a student you did not have to worry about the aspect of balancing your personal life with your work life. You only had your academic and social life to be thoroughly enjoyed. Yes, there was pressure of classes, assignments and examinations, but they were by your choice. Attendance was compulsory, still you might have managed; assignments were tough, still manageable; examinations could be managed with guides and most likely question banks. Your wake-up time, sleeping time, lunch time, dinner time, nothing was really demanding on you and your sacrifice of convenience.

Now, as an employee you start your career and that creates another life which is called work life. Somebody else, your employer is now going to eat away a part of your life for his business success. He is going to hold you fully or partly responsible for his business success or failure; he is going to ask explanation from you for his business results. He is going to make you spend extra hours in office and maybe make you work at home and weekends. Soon you will realise that your life has become so mechanical and there is hardly any time left for your personal life. Today's executives are so much stressed out that it impairs them physically, mentally, emotionally and ... totally. We will talk about stress management in a subsequent chapter. However, I believe that if we could avoid stress, there is no need to manage it. It is your life and it is your choice.

You must have heard the term 'workaholic' which means that the work life gets more importance over your personal life. You need to nicely balance your both lives so that you enjoy your life in both worlds. You will realise its importance more when you get married, have a family and you are not able to balance the family life and the work commitments.

This does not mean that you can expect the work–life balance to

- **Be equal**
  Scheduling an equal number of hours for each of your work and personal activities is usually unrewarding and unrealistic. Life is and should be more fluid than that.
- **Have a fixed ratio; it is variable**
  The right balance for you today will probably be different for tomorrow. As you go higher up in the organisation, the imbalance is likely to increase. The balance will be different when you get married or when you have children and so on.
- **Have a formula**
  The best work–life balance is different for each of us because we all have different priorities, different professions, different employers and different lives.

I found some interesting material on work–life balance on www.worklifebalance.com. It describes two basic concepts for clearly understanding the work–life balance. They are achievement and enjoyment. Both are very deceptive in their simplicity. Both look for an answer to a key question 'Why?' Why do you want a better income…a new house…the kids through college…to do a good job today…to come to work at all?

Achievement is an easier concept of the two and easy to comprehend and measure. But enjoyment is a very complex aspect, subjective and personal. As part of a relevant work–life balance definition, enjoyment means pride, satisfaction, happiness, celebration, love, sense of well-being … all the joys of living.

Achievement and enjoyment are the two tracks of the life engine. The balance of life gets derailed if focus is more on any one of the two. While both complement each other in the work–life balance, they could compete each other and create conflicts resulting in a work–life imbalance situation.

I remember what I missed when I used to be on consulting assignments for longer durations. I had to celebrate the success of my son's 12th standard examination on a bottle of beer sitting alone in a hotel in Bhubaneswar. It was not easy. One of my relative is living in Delhi for the past 15 years while his family is in Pune. It is difficult to say 'who' is sacrificing 'what' for 'whom'? and finally also 'why?' Trying to live a one-sided life is why so many, so-called, successful people are not happy or not as happy as they should be.

Life delivers the value and balance we desire when we are achieving and enjoying something every single day. Our life has four quadrants, namely work, family, friends and self. They are like stakeholders putting demands on us. A good working definition of work–life balance is meaningful daily achievement and enjoyment in each of our four life quadrants.

Now ask yourself and keep asking yourself,

- When was the last time you achieved AND enjoyed something at work?
- What about achieved AND enjoyed with your family and friends?
- And how recently have you achieved AND enjoyed something just for yourself?
- Have you ever thought of taking 20 minutes on the way home from work and doing something just for yourself?
- And when you get home, before you walk in the door, think about whether you want to focus on achieving or enjoying at home tonight. Then act accordingly when you do walk in the door.

MANAGING WORK–LIFE BALANCE SITUATION AT WORK

At work you can create your own best work–life balance by making sure you not only achieve, but also reflect the joy of the job and the joy of life every day. If nobody pats you on the back today, pat yourself on the back and help others to do the same. When you are a person that not only gets things done, but also enjoys doing it, it attracts people to you. They want you on their teams and they want to be on your team. Try some of the following option if you see that your work–life balance is getting disturbed.

- **Negotiate a change with your current employer**
  Research your employer's policies and then approach your boss with a plan showing how you will be more valuable and productive if you can modify your current work situation. Progressive employers recognise the value of good employees and are willing to find ways to help employees deal with short-term or permanent changes caused by family situations. Such changes may include flexitime, job-sharing, telecommuting and work from home or part-time engagements.
- **Find a new career**
  Some careers are more stressful and time-consuming than others. If you need more time for yourself or your family, now may be the time to explore careers that are less stressful and more

flexible. My brother-in-law chose to work with Government in USA to take care of his primary interest of music. He became successful and happy at both.

- **Find a new job**

  Some of my students were hired by an IT company and made to work in shifts. Most of them have changed their jobs by now. Similarly, you simply need to take a less stressful job within your chosen career. This change may involve working with your current employer to identify a new position or a full new job-search or even becoming an entrepreneur or freelance consultant.

- **Slow down**

  Life is simply too short, so take steps to stop and enjoy the things and people around you. Schedule more time between meetings; don't make plans for every evening or weekend and find some ways to distance yourself from the things that are causing you the most stress.

- **Better manage your time**

  Avoid procrastination. Most of the stress comes from simply being disorganised and procrastinating. Remember, the word urgency does not exist. We create it. Learn to set more realistic goals and deadlines and then stick to them. You'll find that not only are you less stressed, but your work will be better.

- **Share the load and delegate**

  It is not always true that you are the only one capable of doing something. Get your partner or other family members to help you with all your personal/family responsibilities. Taking care of the household, children or parents should not be the responsibility of just one person. This is particularly true if you are in a joint family.

- **Let things go**

  Don't sweat the small stuff and learn to let things go once in a while. So what if the dishes are not washed everyday or that the clothes are laundered every day. I am sure you did not do it during your college days. Learn to recognise the things that don't really matter in your life and allow yourself to let them go at times. That does not mean that you should be disorganised and undisciplined.

- **Explore your options**

  Get help if you are feeling overwhelmed with family responsibilities and if you can afford it. Find a maid for household work, a sitter for your children, explore options for aging parents and seek counselling for yourself. In most cases, you have options, but you need to take the time to find them.

- **Take charge**

  Sometimes it's easier to allow ourselves to take charge and develop a prioritised list of things that need to get done. You will enjoy the satisfaction of crossing things off your list once they are done.

- **Simplify**

  It is human nature to take on too many tasks and responsibilities, try to do too much and to own too much. Find a way to simplify your life. Change your lifestyle. Learn to say no. Get rid of the clutter and baggage in your house—and your life.

In the end, the keyword is balance. You need to find the right balance that works for you. Celebrate your successes and don't dwell on your failures. Life is a process and so is striving for a balance in your life.

10 Time Management

Time management is predictable control an individual can exercise over a series of events. No matter how organised we are, there are always only 24 hours in a day and at the end of the day, generally, we get a feeling that we still have a lot left behind. As a student you had more flexibility of completing the tasks. The corporate world puts enormous pressure on employees to complete the tasks within agreed time frames and that brings stress if that is not achieved. Remember, time is the one resource which:

- Is limited to 24 hours a day
- Can't be recovered if lost
- Can't be shared or borrowed from others
- Can't be deposited in a bank and made to grow
- Can be either utilised or wasted

Time doesn't change and we cannot change the time. All we can actually manage is ourselves and what we do with the time that we have. Many of us are prey to time-wasters that steal time we could be using much more productively. Tracking daily activities is the first step to effective time management. It helps you to identify the value adding and non-value adding activities which you actually do. You're likely to waste valuable time in your work on account of

- Telephone interruptions
- Inefficient delegation
- Extended lunches or breaks
- Cluttered workspace
- Poorly run meetings
- Socialising on the job
- Misfiled information

- Poor planning
- Procrastination
- Paperwork
- Waiting/delays
- Net surfing/emails
- Drop-in visitors
- Not setting/sticking to priorities

You may end up wasting anywhere between 40% and 70% of your useful time on account of the earlier-mentioned time-wasters. These result in your working late and even bringing work at home. I have worked with the MD of a company who always came to office at sharp 9.00 am and left the office at sharp 6.00 pm. He could successfully work on the time-wasters mentioned earlier. I have also seen other extremes who worry about the office on 24/7 basis. If you remain in the office because something might fail or your boss may call you, or you have nothing else to do outside or at home, you get into the bad habit of late working. Then you tend to work to kill time and not necessarily to complete the tasks.

Time management needs a high level of commitment to bring into practise. It might be initially frustrating, but you would soon realise its importance and value to your performance and productivity. The following three-step approach will help you to manage your time effectively.

1. **Create time management goals.**
   Remember, the focus of time management is actually changing your behaviours, not changing time. A good place to start is by eliminating your personal time-wasters. Start a log and write down your goals and progress for each goal. Go through your goal log each week to make sure you are on the right track. Keeping a log on your computer is the most convenient way of tracking you time management success. It also tells you the proportion of time you spend towards achievement of your goals and other activities. Initially, this ratio could be very frustrating.

2. **Implement a time management plan.**
   The objective is to change your behaviours to spend maximum time towards achieving whatever goals you have set for yourself, such as increasing your productivity or decreasing your stress. So you need to not only set your specific goals, but identify the right activities and track them over time to see whether or not you're accomplishing them. It is more important to do the right things than just doing things right.

3. **Use time management tools.**
   Whether it is a day timer or a software program, the first step for managing your time is to know where it's going now and planning how you're going to spend your time in the future. A software program such as Outlook, for instance, lets you schedule events easily and can be set to remind you of the events in advance, making your time management easier.

Practise the following simple tips to use your time more effectively and eliminate the time-wasters.

- **Be sure your systems are organised.**
  Are you wasting a lot of time looking for files on your computer or searching for information? Is your filing system slowing you down? Take time to organise a file management system. Redo it, so it's organised to the point that you can quickly lay your hands on what you need. Don't be paper shufflers; pick a paper only if you decide to act on it and get rid of it as soon as possible. Have on your desk, the only items you are dealing with.

- **Plan your week ahead.**
  Spend some time at the beginning of each week or end of the previous week to plan your schedule. Taking extra time to do this will help increase your productivity and balance your important long-term projects with your more urgent tasks. All you need is 15 to 30 minutes each week for your planning session. Your work–life balance also could be improved through such a planning.

- **Write things down.**
  Do not rely on your memory to keep track of activities and information. Using a to-do list to write things down is a great way to take control of your tasks and keep yourself organised. Always carry the diary which the company generally provides to its executives. You never know when you are going to have a great idea or a brilliant insight. You can capture your thoughts quickly. If you wait too long to write them down, you forget.

- **Prioritise ruthlessly.**
  Start your day with prioritising the tasks from your to-do list for that day. Prioritising helps you focus and spend more time on items that really matter to you. UREGENT–IMPORTANT is one of the prioritisation systems. Note that all activities which are urgent may not be important and vice-a-versa. Urgency and importance are subjective and could be determined by your boss, you or your subordinates. You may also use MUST–SHOULD–COULD system of prioritisation. Out of your tasks for the day, which ones you MUST do which ones you SHOULD do and which ones you COULD do if time permits.

- **Set time limits for tasks.**
  Estimate the times for each of the activities including your rest periods. Sometimes you may have to allocate the time where estimation could be difficult. For instance, reading and answering emails can consume your whole day if you let it. Instead, set a limit of one hour a day for this task and stick to it. You need to schedule time for setting and evaluating your goals, planning and reviewing. Plan only for 80% of the time you have, as some foreign elements do keep creeping in.

- **Learn to delegate.**
  Once I asked one of the very senior executives, 'How much time you must have spent today on activities which you believe your subordinates should have done?' His answer was '80%'. There is no need for you to do everything. Let other people share the load. You need to use the delegation very carefully and should never lose control on the output of the tasks. Delegation without control is abdication or in simple words, 'passing the buck'. While delegating you need to ensure that:

  – Instructions given are complete, clear and understood.
  – Task times are estimated and agreed upon.
  – Progress is tracked periodically.
  – Good jobs are acknowledged and appreciated.

  Though you delegate the job or activity, final responsibility and accountability for success and failure is yours.

- **Don't waste time waiting.**
  It is good to avoid waiting for yourself and others. Work with prior appointments only as far as possible. However, you will still be faced with waiting somewhere for someone or something. You don't need to just sit there and twiddle your thumbs. Always take something to do, such as a report you need to read or just a blank pad of paper that you can use to plan your next project. Use technology to work for you wherever you are and your smart phone will help you stay connected.

- **Think before acting; learn to say no.**
  You tend to say 'yes' to everything that comes in your way and regret later for accepting it. Before committing to a new task, stop to think about it before you give your answer. Sometimes people are in habit of doing other people's work because of a 'hero' mentality. Instead, focus on your own tasks and goals and teach others how to do their own work. Many people over-commit and get overloaded with too much work. They say 'yes' when they really should be saying 'no'. Learn to say 'no'. You will free up time to spend on things that are more important to you. You may not be able to refuse at all times but try your best to say 'no'.

- **Continuously improve yourself.**
  Make time in your schedule to learn new things and develop your natural talents and abilities. For example, you could take a class, attend a training programme or read a book. Continuously improving your knowledge and skills increases your marketability, can help boost your career and is the most reliable path to your success. Also look for ideas where your existing work and work systems gets simpler, faster and more efficient.

- **Give up something unnecessary.**
  Evaluate regularly how you are spending your time. Many activities we keep doing because we have been doing it for years or for 'just in case'. The best is to stop doing an activity that is no longer necessary, relevant and value adding and spend time doing something more valuable.

Sometimes you skip shaving because you wake up late and need to do something important before you leave for office. Consider what you want to give up in order to maintain your current activities.

- **Eliminate procrastination.**

Do it now. Don't unnecessarily keep postponing. It was OK in college days when you kept postponing submissions until the last date of the deadline. Procrastination brings urgency which has a risk of mistakes and poor quality. If a job is too big, chop it into manageable chunks. Schedule nasty jobs for specific times and reward yourself on completion. If you have to eat a frog, don't look at it too long; if you have to eat two frogs, eat the big one first.

- **Self-discipline.**

Self-discipline is a must for effective time management. Is what you are doing at this minute moving you towards your goals and objectives? If not, don't do it. Plan for the average or for the maximum. Select your prime-time for high-yielding jobs such as early mornings or late evenings. Avoid interruptions and distractions. Remember, time is a non-renewable resource.

- **Don't be a perfectionist at all times.**

Some tasks don't require your best effort. Sending a short email to a colleague, for example, shouldn't take any more than a few minutes. Learn to distinguish between tasks that deserve to be done excellently and tasks that just need to be done.

- **Avoid 'efficiency traps'.**

Being efficient doesn't necessarily mean that you are being productive. Efficiency and effectiveness are two different things. You need to be effective while being efficient. Avoid taking on tasks that you can do with efficiency that actually don't need to be done at all. Just because you are busy and getting things done doesn't mean you are actually accomplishing anything significant.

The TIME is like a MAGICAL BANK for us. Each morning we awake to receive 86,400 seconds as a gift of life and when we go to sleep at night, any remaining time is NOT credited to us. What we haven't lived up that day is lost forever. Yesterday is forever gone. Each morning the account is refilled, but the bank can dissolve your account at anytime ... WITHOUT WARNING. SO, what will YOU do with your 86,400 seconds? Aren't they worth so much more than the same amount of money? Think about that and enjoy every second of your life, because time races by so much quicker than you think. So take care of yourself, be happy, love deeply and enjoy life!

11 Managing Stress

It seems like stress is just an unavoidable part of today's fast-paced, competitive world. But is it really? Stress is body's instinctive response to external environmental cues, as well as to one's inner thoughts and feelings. You do have some control over how stress operates in your life. What you can do is, change and reduce your exposure to those stressful situations. Stress and stress management are directly related to personal well-being and specifically to workplace well-being. The key to de-stressing in any moment is getting away from or removing yourself from the stress creator or stressor. Developing new habits, which remove you and distract you from stressors and stressful situations, is essentially how to manage stress in a sustained manner.

STRESS AFFECTS HEALTH AND PERFORMANCE

Stress is believed to trigger 70% of visits to doctors and 85% of serious illnesses (UK HSE stress statistics). It is proven to make people ill and cause a number of ailments such as heart disease, hypertension, strokes, ulcers, diabetes, muscle and joint pain, insomnia, miscarriage during pregnancy, allergies and even premature tooth loss. Stress significantly impairs brain functions such as memory, concentration and learning, all of which are central to effective performance at work. Stress can also lead people resorting to bad vices such as smoking, tobacco and liquor. Some health effects caused by stress are reversible and the person can become normal when stress is relieved, while others are irreversible and at worse terminal.

There are seven common types for stress, which are described in Table 11.1 with their causes.

IDENTIFICATION OF STRESS SYMPTOMS

Stress can be scientifically assessed clinically by measuring levels of Cortisol and DHEA (dehydroepiandrosterone), two hormones produced by the adrenal glands. However, before one reaches the clinical laboratory, there is need to rely on some other signs, symptoms and indicators. These should prompt investigation as to whether stress is present. You can use this list of indicators and others as a simple initial stress test.

- Sleep difficulties
- Loss of appetite
- Poor concentration or poor memory retention
- A drop in performance
- Uncharacteristic errors or missed deadlines

Table 11.1

Sr. No.	Type of Stress	Caused by
1.	Physical	Physical environment such as heat, humidity, intense exertion, manual labour, lack of sleep, travel
2.	Chemical	Drugs, alcohol, caffeine, nicotine and environmental pollutants such as cleaning chemicals or pesticides
3.	Mental	Perfectionism, worry, anxiety, long work hours, fatigue, financial or career pressures, challenges with life goals
4.	Emotional	Bullying or harassment, anger, guilt, loneliness, excessive time away from home and family, sadness, fear
5.	Nutritional	Food allergies, vitamin and mineral deficiency
6.	Traumatic	Accidents, injuries or burns, surgery, illness, infections, extreme temperatures
7.	Psycho-spiritual	Feeling powerless and lack of autonomy, continuous unreasonable performance demands, ineffective communication and conflict resolution, lack of job security, troubled relationships, spiritual alignment, insufficient reward for performance and responsibility

Source: Adopted from CARE2 website: http://www.care2.com/greenliving/7-kinds-of-stress.html

- Anger or tantrums
- Violent or anti-social behaviour
- Emotional outbursts
- Alcohol or drug abuse
- Nervous habits

Life is as it is short enough. With illness all around us, why make matters worse? Commit to change before one day change is forced upon you. If you recognise signs of stress at your workplace, do something about it. If you yourself cannot deal with the situation, refer to someone who can. The following stress reduction ideas and techniques are based on simple principles. These won't change the situation causing stress, but they will, more importantly, enable you to change your reaction and relationship to the stressful situations.

Use of humour
Humour is one of the greatest and quickest devices for reducing stress. The popularity of laughing clubs substantiates this. Humour brings laughter that produces helpful chemicals in the brain. It distracts you from having a stressed mindset and thereby diffuses the stressful feelings. You may even think of watching your favourite comedy movies or shows.

Brisk walk and self-talk
You must have seen star batsmen getting away from crease and doing self-talk in between every ball. The purpose is to get out of the impact of previous delivery and getting ready for the next one. Go for a short quick and brisk walk outside the office building. Breathe in some fresh air, smell the atmosphere and stimulate your senses with new things. You can chant mantras or even songs or poems while walking. Doing something physical and reinforcing it with self-talk opens up the world again.

Rehydrate

Drink around 6–8 glasses of water a day. All your organs, brain included, are highly dependent on water to function properly. If your body is starved for water, you will function below your best and get stressed, physically and mentally. Dry atmosphere of air-conditioned offices increases people's susceptibility to de-hydration. Keep some water ready at your desk at all times. You do not need expensive mineral water. Filtered (Aqua Guard) tap water is fine. If the tap water heavily smells of chlorine, keep it in fridge for couple of hours and chlorine dissipates naturally. You can add a slice of lemon or lime for luxury.

Catnap or powernap

Take a quick nap for 10–30 minutes. It is nature's way of recharging and re-energising. Unfortunately, we are conditioned to think that sleeping during day is lazy and unhealthy. It requires realisation that doing so is acceptable and beneficial. Most companies, nowadays, provide facilities for meditation, afternoon rest, etc., so that you phase out the stress and strain appropriately during a hard day's work. If your work situation is not quite ready to tolerate a short daytime nap then practise a short session of meditation with deep breathing at your desk. It works wonders.

Make a cuppa

A cup of tea works wonders in stressed times. Any tea will do. Experiment with different natural flavourings using herbs and spices. Fresh mint is excellent for the digestive system. Nettles contain natural relaxants. Orange zest is super. Ginger root is brilliant. Many herbs, spices and fruits make great flavoured tea and they have real therapeutic properties. You have options of sugar or honey and with or without milk.

Keep a hotpot in your office if not provided one in the pantry. Making tea also takes your mind off your problems; smelling and drinking tea relaxes you.

Crying

May sound ridiculous, but it is true. Have you cried any time recently and did you feel greatly relived after that? Unfortunately, crying is considered as bad, shameful and childish. This attitude prevents people from crying and it is a sad reflection on our unforgiving society. You need to be really brave to cry unashamedly. Whatever may be the science, a good bout of sobbing and weeping does release tension and stress. How and where you choose to use this most extreme of emotional impulse is up to you. Shedding a few tears can be a very good thing now and then. Just give it a try and you might be surprised.

PREVENTION IS BETTER THAN CURE IN STRESS MANAGEMENT

It is better to be physically and mentally strong to resist stressful situations. You should not wait to be impacted by ill effects of stressful situations; you are prepared to face and work with all situations at all times. It is a question of changing your habits. Here are some positive guidelines for you to follow which will help you and others to reduce stress susceptibility and remove stressors.

- **Eat right; improve diet**
  A balanced healthy diet is essential for the efficient functioning of all body systems including the brain. Adequate intake of minerals and vitamins are essential for a healthy body and brain.

The Vitamin B Group (B1, B2, B3, B6 and B12) is particularly relevant to the brain, nervous system and stress susceptibility. Vitamin C gives a healthy immune system and speeds healing and Vitamin D maintains a healthy body condition. Some simple points about your diet:

- Avoid processed foods for their bad chemical contents. Look at the packaging to see what you are putting into your body.
- Use butter and not margarine. Butter contains natural fat while margarine contains hydrogenated fat.
- Eat lots of fresh fruit and vegetables. Fish is good. But beware of those available in fast-food centres, which are cooked in hydrogenated cooking oil.
- Beans are good, but high salt and sugar content in canned baked beans are not. Look at the contents on the label.
- Canned and bottled fizzy 'pop' drinks are bad. They contain various chemicals, including aspartame, which has been linked with nervous system disorders.
- Too much coffee is bad. Interestingly, espresso coffee contains less caffeine than filter and instant coffee, because it passes through the coffee grounds more quickly.
- Tea is good for you. Especially green tea.
- Avoid pills and tablets as far as possible. Next time you have headache, don't take tablets, go for a run or walk in fresh air to relax naturally.

- **Stop, reduce toxin intake**
  Toxic materials such as tobacco and alcohol might seem to provide temporary relief and excitement but they are working against the body balance and contributing to stress susceptibility.
- **Exercise hard**
  Physical exercise is immensely beneficial in managing stress. It increases blood flow to the brain, releases hormones and stimulates the nervous system. Exercise burns up adrenaline and produces chemicals in the body such as beta-endorphin, which has a proven positive effect on our feeling of well-being and freshness. Exercise relaxes tense muscles and tight connective tissues in the body, and provides distraction from your stressful work. Exercise, like a better diet, is not difficult to adopt if you have personal commitment. It makes the difference.
- **Adequate sleep and rest**
  Sleep and rest are essential for a healthy life balance. Having a good night's sleep is vital for a healthy mind and body. Nature has created night for sleeping and the day for working. Follow the nature. It is said that 'early to bed and early to rise makes you healthy and wise.' As students, you had very undisciplined sleeping habits. You need to change them. Avoid late night staying awake for any reason and ensure 6–8 hours of good sleep depending upon the physical and mental exertion that you go through at work. Excessive international travelling brings the issue of jet lag which takes a couple of days to adjust. Frequent shift changes also have sleep adjustment problems.

  Limited napping during the day is also healthy. It recharges and energises, relaxes and helps to wipe the brain of pressures and unpleasant feelings.
- **Explore and use relaxation methods**
  Try yoga, meditation, self-hypnosis, massage, a breath of fresh air or anything that works and can be done in the particular situation. You may also seek out modern computer aids including free downloads and desktop add-ons for averting stresses specifically caused by sitting for long uninterrupted periods in front of a computer screen.

- **Have good mind control**
  Increase self-awareness of your moods and feelings, anticipate and take steps to avoid stress build-up before it becomes more serious. If you are stressed, try to be detached, step back and look from outside at issues that cause stress. Don't try to control things that are uncontrollable. Instead adjust response and adapt. Share worries with someone else because loneliness is a big ally of stress. So, sharing is essential.

- **Manage your anger**
  Getting angry is one of the worst habits you can have. Stress leads to anger and anger further results in stress. Anger management is only possible when you accept and commit to change. Some people take pride in their anger and fail to appreciate the effect on self and others. Angry behaviour is destructive and negative.

  As with stress, you need to understand the cause of your angry tendency. If the problem is temporary, then short-term acute stress may be the direct cause and where it is persistent, frequent and ongoing, long-term chronic stress is more likely to be the cause. If your anger leads you to violence at times, it is a clinical problem and so must be referred to a suitably qualified advisor or professional.

If you are suffering from stress and not obeying these simple rules, you will continue to be stressed, and moreover you will maintain a higher susceptibility to stress. Establishing commitment to change and identifying the causes of stress is generally sufficient for many people to make changes and improve. Note also that managing stress does not cure medical problems. Therefore, relieving stress is not a substitute for conventional treatments of illness, disease and injury. The challenge is not just knowing what is good and bad, it is a matter of commitment and personal resolve.

Remember, you have one body for the whole of your life—look after it totally! Best way to eliminate stress is to prevent it.

Being Effective in the Organisation

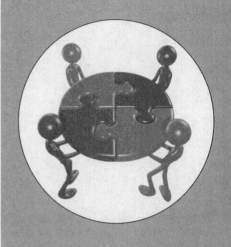

3

Being Effective in the Organisation

The 50 New Rules of Work

12

The list of the 50 new rules of work has been received from the Higher Education Forum (HEF) of India, of which I am a life member. HEF has requested that this may be shared with others so that they benefit from this list. I have, therefore, included the same in this book. Budding managers and future leaders should read, understand, internalise and act on just one rule per day. Make each of the following rules as a matter of habit.

1. You are not just paid to work for your comfort, you are paid to be uncomfortable and to pursue projects that scare you.
2. If you take care of your relationships, the money will take care of itself.
3. Lead yourself first. You can't help others reach their highest potential until you're in the process of reaching for yours.
4. To double your income, triple your rate of learning.
5. While victims condemn change, leaders get inspired by change.
6. Small daily improvements over time create stunning results.
7. Surround yourself with assertive people with courage to speak truthfully about what's best for your organisation and the customers you serve.
8. Don't fall in love with just your own publicity and popularity.
9. Every moment in front of a customer is a moment of truth (you either live by the values you profess or you don't).
10. Copying your competitor will only make you the second best.
11. Become obsessed with the user experience such that every touch point of doing business with you leaves people speechless, no, breathless.
12. If you're in business, you're in show business. The moment you get to work, you're on stage. Give them the performance of your life.
13. Be a master of your craft. And practice + practice + practice ....
14. Be physically, emotionally, socially and intellectually fit.
15. Read magazines you don't usually read; talk to people whom you don't usually speak to; go to places you don't commonly visit and explore to keep your mind fresh, hungry and brilliant.
16. Remember, what make a great business—in part—are the seemingly insignificant details. Obsess over them.
17. Being just good isn't good enough.
18. Brilliant things happen when you go the extra mile for every single customer.
19. An addiction to distraction is the death of creative production. Stay focused.
20. If you're not failing regularly, you're definitely not making much progress.
21. Lift your teammates up as against tearing your teammates down. Welcome critics. The key is to see the best in people.

22. Remember that a critic is a dreamer gone scared.

23. Leadership's no longer about position. Now, it's about passion and having an impact through the genius-level work that you do.

24. The bigger the dream, the more important the team.

25. If you're not thinking for yourself, you're following—not leading.

26. Work hard. But build an exceptional family life. What's the point of reaching the mountaintop if getting there alone?

27. Job of the leader is to develop more leaders.

28. The antidote to deep change is daily learning. Investing in your professional and personal development is the smartest investment you can make.

29. Smile. It makes a difference.

30. Say 'please' and 'thank you'. It makes a difference.

31. Shift from doing mindless toil to doing valuable work.

32. Remember that a job is only just a job if all you see it as a job.

33. Don't do your best work for the applause it generates but for the personal pride it delivers.

34. The only standard worth reaching for is: best in world .

35. In the new world of business, everyone works in Human Resources.

36. In the new world of business, everyone's part of the leadership team.

37. Words can inspire. And words can destroy. Choose yours well.

38. You become your excuses.

39. You'll get your game-changing ideas away from the office and not in the middle of work. Make time for solitude. Creativity needs the space to present itself.

40. The people who gossip about others when they are not around are the people who will gossip about you when you're not around.

41. It could take you 30 years to build a great reputation and 30 seconds of bad judgement to lose it.

42. The client is always watching.

43. The way you do one thing defines the way you'll do everything. Every act matters.

44. To be radically optimistic isn't soft. It's hard. Crankiness is easy.

45. People want to be inspired to pursue a vision. It's your job to give it to them.

46. Every visionary was initially called crazy.

47. The purpose of work is to help people. The other rewards are inevitable by-products of this singular focus.

48. Remember that the things that get scheduled are the things that get done.

49. Keep promises and be impeccable with your word. People buy more than just your products and services. They invest in your credibility.

50. Lead without a title.

Professional Etiquettes and Mannerisms

13

We have inherited the office mannerisms and etiquettes from British who ruled us for over 150 years. Starting each day with 'good morning' and ending with 'good night' were the expectations and practices in early days, and may be 30 years ago, officers were always seen in ties and suits. The Americans brought the 'Hi' concept, with more informality and friendliness in the business environment. Calling everybody by the first name became a practice. The IT industry further liberalised the office decorum with shorts, jeans and Tee shirts.

It does not mean that we can do without the etiquettes and manners that are supposed to be displayed as a matter of professionalism. They are key aspects of one's personality and also greatly impact the honour and respect one receives from people. It is not important whether you use Indian, American or British accents while talking, but what and how you talk demonstrate your mannerisms and etiquettes. Dr Thomas Clerk, President of CommuniSkills and Professor of Management at Xavier University, defines two basic rules of practicing etiquettes and mannerisms.

- **Golden rule:** Treat others as you would like to be treated.
- **Platinum rule:** Treat others as they would like to be treated.

People begin to evaluate you even before you speak a single word, based on your appearance, style, manners and etiquettes. The evaluation continues throughout your interaction with them and even when you leave the interaction. It may be an interview, a sales call, a meeting with client or even a retail sales interaction. Let us review and understand the key aspects that go into such evaluations.

HANDSHAKING

Handshaking is the first non-verbal communication which generally takes place. It usually takes place twice: once at the beginning of meeting and then towards the end. Both handshakes could be different, depending upon the outcome of the interaction during the meeting. If you give someone a handshake next time, practise a proper handshake using the following:

- Extend your right hand to meet the other person's right hand, with your arm at a slight downward angle and your thumb pointing towards other person's arm.
- Wrap your hand around the other person's hand when your thumb joints come together.
- Grasp the hand firmly and squeeze gently once. Avoid limp as well as bone-crushing grasps.
- Hold the handshake for 2–3 seconds. (Not more ... please)
- Pump your hand up and down (two to three times). (Not more ... please)

The type of handshake conveys a certain meaning of non-verbal communication.

Types of Handshakes	What It Means/Communicates
Normal handshake	'I'm honoured to meet you'
The lingering handshake: The end of handshake pauses or lingers.	Openness; sincerity; could be 'clingy'.
The push-off: The tendency to push hand towards other person during the handshake.	Wants to establish power.
The pull-in: The tendency to pull other person's hand during handshake.	A controller who wants things done certain way.
The two-handed shake.	'We're great buddies.'
The bone crusher: Too much pressure applied on the other's hand.	'That's the end of your life'; trying to prove strength.
The topper: The other person's hand comes first and takes upper level while shaking hands.	'I'm in charge, I'm the Boss.'
The finger squeeze: The tendency to squeeze fingers towards the end of handshake.	'It's me—the ever-victorious!'
The palm pinch: The hand does not reach beyond the palm.	'It's okay; it's okay'.
The twister: The tendency to twist the grip during shakehand.	'We may be coming into this as equals, but in the end I'll be on top.'
The dead fish: The force of handshake lacks.	Weak person, no energy, no interest, pessimistic.

A predictable handshake is an indication of a predictable person. Firmness in handshake indicates reliability. Maintaining eye contact while handshake means honesty and sincerity and a smile indicates friendliness.

DRESS AND GROOMING

Many companies provide uniforms to their employees, creating a sense of pride in being part of that organisation. It removes hierarchical issues and brings in a feeling of equality and dignity. It also puts additional responsibility on employees to behave properly when they are outside and facilitates identification in cases of mishaps.

The dress code defined by the company, if any, should be followed and, if not, one should dress up in formal clothes that are clean, comfortable to wear and nicely ironed. Shades, of clothes, that are synonymous with the business and corporate world should be chosen. No matter how relaxed your company is about the attire, always ensure that you go to work with tidy clothes. Shabby and provocative clothes should be totally avoided. There is really no compromise on this rule.

Men should keep their hair trimmed and nicely set. Women should put on minimal yet natural make-up. Shape your nails well and keep them clean. Polish your shoes neatly. It is okay to use a light perfume or cologne. Minimise use of jewellery in office, as it could be a distraction to your fellow employees. Avoid placing tattoos on visible part of your body. Use matching dress accessories such as the belt, socks, napkin and others.

GREETING AND INTRODUCTION

If you are being introduced by someone to somebody, either make a handshake or nod your head with a smile. If you are seated during introduction, stand up to meet or greet the person. If you have to introduce other people, start off with a lower ranked person and proceed towards the higher ranked ones. Do not enter the office and start greeting people with handshakes as you come across them, just a smile and a wish, 'good morning' or 'good afternoon', or now just a 'Hi' are sufficient in most cases.

FIRST WORDS

Visualise what you are going to say and do, and then mentally rehearse how you believe your audience will respond. Visualise what your audience's most preferred communicator would be saying and doing. Ask yourself, 'What would the other person like to hear me say first?' This will allow you to say something that will show you see things from the other person's point of view.

LISTENING

Good listeners are always admired by all. Therefore, be attentive and listen carefully to all your clients, superiors and subordinates. Furthermore, speak only when the other person finishes his part, rather than interrupting in between. You will learn more about listening in the chapter on communication skills.

CONVERSATION ETIQUETTES

- Use a polite and calm voice while interacting. Your tone should be low yet clear. Do not lose temper or use harsh words, even when the other person gets rude or offensive towards you. Good professional etiquettes do not permit being impolite to any of your colleagues or business associates.
- Always maintain eye contact with the person you are speaking to. Eye contact indicates honesty and confidence. Be careful, the eye contact does not mean staring at him/her all the time.
- Keep your conversation focused, short, crisp and to the point.
- Mind your own business and steer yourself clear of office gossip. Gossip is a waste of time and can even take a toll on your productivity. Avoid sharing office gossip, it hurts.

BUSINESS DINING ETIQUETTES

Lunches are the modern way to initiate or establish new relationships or business contacts.

- If you are the host, allow the guest to seat first. If you are a guest, be punctual and thank the host for the dinner.
- You can begin your discussion after the appetisers are served; you need not wait for the desserts to arrive in.

- Never open your mouth while chewing food.
- Never point your knife or fork towards the other person during the conversation.
- Don't drink heavily at an office party. Limit it to one mixed drink or a glass of wine.

OFFICE/CUBICLE ETIQUETTES

- Be punctual. Do not keep anyone waiting for you. Remember, everyone else's time is as important as yours. If you are late due to any reason, inform your supervisor or the person with whom you were supposed to meet.
- Keep your cubicle clean and organised. A messy cubicle is extremely unprofessional and can also speak bad of you.
- Respect privacy of other colleagues. Don't enter another person's cubicle unless you are invited. Ask for permission before barging into their cubicle. Also, don't read others' memos, emails or faxes.
- If you eat at your desk, take consent of people around you. Do not eat food that smells too much and do not leave mess at your table after eating. Make as less noise as possible while eating.
- Try to completely cut out personal calls during working hours and remember to turn off the speakerphones. It is also advisable to not use the Bluetooth in office while using cell phones.
- Don't interrupt someone who is on phone or appears deep in thought by using sign language or signals. When you prefer to be uninterrupted, avoid eye contact with the people.
- Don't discuss any controversial matter in your cubicle. Everything you say makes an impression about you.
- Avoid hair brushing, eyebrow plucking, flossing, make-up, etc. at the work desk. Do it in rest room before you arrive at the desk or during the lunch hour.
- Don't play music at your desk during business hours. If you have to, use a headset.

MEETING ETIQUETTES

When you are a participant, the following meeting etiquettes should be practised:

- Be sure to respond if RSVP is requested for a business meeting invitation.
- Be punctual or, even better, turn up a bit earlier. Don't be late and if you are late, step in quickly and quietly and take your seat with minimum interruption.
- Come prepared with a pen, a writing pad and all the relevant information/documents as per the meeting agenda.
- If you need to hold a presentation, make sure that handouts, PPT slides, etc. are ready and organised.
- Don't interrupt the speaker unless he/she has encouraged open discussions during the meeting. Don't interrupt other attendees as well.
- Don't talk during a meeting with other colleagues.
- Keep your cell phone in the silent mode. If you get a call during the meeting, do not look at your phone. You can either activate a voice mail or forward messages to another phone. If you have forgotten to turn off your phone, don't answer it in the middle of the meeting.

- When asking a question, don't just blurt out your question, raise your hand. Hold it until the end of the meeting or other specified time. Make sure you only ask one question at a time. Don't ask long questions. Break them into several questions.
- Listen carefully to all presentations, the participants' questions and the answers provided. You surely don't want to ask a question that has already been asked.
- Regardless of how heated the meeting may become, remain calm. Don't fidget, tap your pen, play with your fingers, read materials not concerning the meeting or any other act that might distract other participants.
- Attend the entire meeting. You can leave the meeting early only if it is absolutely necessary, unavoidable and you have prior permission.
- Give full attention to the meeting, don't text messages, check your emails, apply make-up, comb your hair, clip your nails, etc.
- Dress professionally for the meeting.
- If there is an established seating pattern, accept it. If you are unsure, ask.
- Be brief while speaking and make sure what you say is relevant.
- Ensure confidentiality of the information shared or points discussed during the meeting.

When you are hosting or conducting the meeting, the following meeting etiquettes should be practised:

- Create an agenda and circulate it to all participants in advance. Stick to the agenda.
- Set a time limit for the meeting agenda and end time.
- Be poised, polite and polished. Demonstrate your knowledge and understanding and conduct yourself professionally.
- If the meeting goes off-track, remind the participants of the agenda and suggest that unrelated matters be addressed at another time.
- If the meeting is to discuss problems, make sure you and the participants have done homework for some solutions to offer.
- Maintain eye contact most of the time.
- Respect the wishes of the meeting chairman and thank him at the end for conducting the meeting. Also thank people for attending the meeting and request feedback.
- Circulate the minutes of the meeting within 48 hours of the end of the meeting. If someone cannot attend the meeting, provide them with minutes of the meeting.

TELEPHONE ETIQUETTES

- Avoid calling anybody before 7:00 am and after 9:00 pm, unless in an emergency situation or predetermined call time agreed. Respect the time zones of different countries in the cases of overseas calling.
- Ensure that you have correct number. If you happen to call a wrong number, before you hang up, have the decency to say, *'I'm so sorry! I have the wrong number!'* Likewise, if a person calls you with wrong number, politely point out that they have called the wrong number.
- Your voice and tone reflect your character and personality, even on phone. Always speak in a pleasant tone and very clearly. Smile through your voice! What they hear will make a positive or negative impression.

- When someone answers the phone, don't abruptly tell them what you want. You will also appear rude, if you say *'Who is this?'* You phoned them, so introduce yourself first and state what you want politely. For example, *'Hello, my name is _____, I'd like to speak to _____. Is she/he available?'*

- If the person is not available, tell the receiver that you will call back later or request them to call you back. When finished, say, *'thank you and goodbye'* and ensure that you give them time to say goodbye too.

- Give people a chance to answer the phone. Don't just ring three times and hang up. It is annoying when a person stops doing something to attend the phone and the caller hangs up just as the phone gets to his ear

- Don't spend hours chatting and be brief and to the point on the phone. Have your point list ready before you begin your conversation.

- While answering your phone, be pleasant and polite. Just say, 'Hello.' Avoid saying, 'residence of _____' or '_____ speaking.' It is too dangerous to reveal your identity to strangers. Be safe!

- If the call is for someone else, say *'One moment please, I'll just go and call them for you.'* Put the receiver down gently. If the concerned person is unavailable, say *'I'm sorry, _____ isn't available right now. May I take a message?'*

- If you have to carry on two conversations at once, you should always excuse yourself from one and resume it later. Say, *'I'm sorry, can you hold on a minute? My boss is telling me something.'* If the other conversation lasts more than a minute, ask the first caller, *'Can I call you back? It may take a few minutes.'*

- In case, you want to attend something very urgent without sharing too much information, just say *'Can you hold on for a few minutes? I will be right back.'*

- When talking on phone in a public space, everything you say is not just your news. Keep your voice at indoor level or lower. Generally, people with good manners don't talk about embarrassing private issues in public.

- When on the phone, don't talk with others in the room. If someone tries to talk to you, simply point to your phone and they will get the message.

- Avoid using the computer while on the phone unless it is part of customer services. It is extremely rude and unpleasant when someone has to listen to a clacking keyboard.

- Refrain from using your cell phone when you are with others in a social meeting. It implies that the person you are with is less important and you would rather be with someone else and somewhere else.

- It is a bad practice to give missed calls to anybody.

EMAIL ETIQUETTES

- **Start with a salutation**
  Start your email by addressing the person to whom you are writing. If the email is meant for a friend, you can skip the salutation. For business messages, begin your email with 'Dear Mr Joshi' or 'Dear Professor Joshi', if you do not know the person. In case you are in a working relationship with the person, you can address by first name such as 'Dear Ashok'. Generally, last names are preceded by the title and the first name is not used in addressing a communication.

- **Use short paragraphs**

  Do not waste time waffling and get straight to the point. Divide your email into two or four short paragraphs. Discuss only a single idea in each paragraph. Use bullet points, in case you are listing several questions for the recipient to answer, suggesting a number of alternative options or explaining the steps that you would be carrying out. Use a double line break between paragraphs instead of an indent (tab).

- **Stick to one topic**

  In case there are several different issues to be discussed, do not put them in a single mail. Create separate mails for separate issues, as it can be hard for some people to keep track of different email threads and conversations, as the topics may get jumbled up.

- **Use capitals appropriately**

  - Never write a whole sentence or whole email in capitals.
  - Always capitalise 'I' and the first letter of proper nouns (names).
  - Capitalise acronyms (IIT, SAP, NDTV, etc.).
  - Always begin a sentence with a capital letter.

- **Sign off the mail**

  If you are writing an internal company email, put a double space after your last paragraph and type your name. If the email is more formal, close it appropriately.

  - If you know the name of your addressee, use 'Yours sincerely'.
  - For very formal emails, such as job applications, use 'Yours faithfully' when you have addressed it to 'Dear Sir/ Madam'.
  - In other situations, you can just use 'Best regards' or 'Kind regards'.

- **Use sensible email signature**

  Wherever appropriate, include your name, email address, telephone number and postal address. It will be easier for your correspondents to find your contact details each time an email is sent.

14 Building Relationships within an Organisation

Every business today is a relationship business. Successful managers go beyond the basics of communication and build effective relationships within and outside their organisations. The quality and impact of a manager's work and the profitability of the business depend upon relationships with customers, co-workers, competitors, suppliers, distributors, support services, subordinates, senior managers and even the boards. In this chapter, we will focus on the relationship issues within the organisations that include colleagues/co-workers, supervisor/boss and subordinates. These relationships generally vary according to status, intimacy and choice.

Meeting people is easy but developing relationship is not. It takes years to build a relationship that could be broken in seconds. We are not talking about e-relationships developed through Internet or social media forums such as Facebook. We are talking about the organisational relationships that can make or break your career with the organisation.

As a new entrant in any organisation, you need to take lot of initiatives in relationship building in order to be successful. The following measures may be helpful to you in that process:

- **Be relaxed**
  Having a relax mind during the process of communication, with whom you are interested in building relationship, is the key to build strong trust and relationship. When you feel comfortable with others, they will feel comfortable with you. If you appear anxious and nervous, others might sense it and avoid you. If you meet someone for the first time, show as if you have rediscovered a long-lost friend. A smile is always the key rapport builder. Communicating in a relaxed manner with energy and enthusiasm provides a strong foundation for lasting relationships.

  Stephen Covey says, '*Seek first to understand, then to be understood.*' So, approach people with open arms and a smiling face. Keep your body language positive. Put your arms at your sides, stand up straight and lean a little forward.

- **Listen**
  God has given two ears and one mouth. Therefore, listen more than speak. The first lessons in most communication courses are about effective listening. Most of us try hard to come up with clever things to say, but find it difficult to shut up sometimes and take a minute to listen.

  Proper listening involves listening to what is being said in words and what is not being said but expressed. Listen with heart and feel the emotions conveyed by the tone of the voice and rhythm of the speech. Understand the body gestures while listening. You will listen carefully when you place yourself in others' place. Listen intently and intensely to understand the meaning behind and between the words.

MAKING CLEAR THE EXPECTATIONS

Set clear expectations for yourselves and others. Don't expect other people to read what is in your mind. Articulate exactly what you expect from them and why. Create positive boundaries. All of us feel comfortable if we know how far we can go. Take control of the situation.

- **Connect with interest**
  It is important to show that you are interested in building relationship. They will be more inclined to connect with you if you show a level of commitment. Ask people about their lives and listen to what they say. When they ask the same from you, it is time to make the connection. Start by finding common grounds such as your background, interests or village, etc. Be open when it is your turn to respond to their questions.

- **Be sincere**
  You must demonstrate that you are sincere about the conversation and the relationship. Don't use the conversation to show off your knowledge or as a chance to complain about other people or your problems or promoting your own ulterior motive. They may not be interested. If you don't have anything worth to say, it is better to keep quiet. Be as neutral as possible. Start with something small such as a sincere compliment or even something as the weather and save the potentially controversial topics and heated opinions for later. Even at that stage, your sincerity to find solution should be made obvious.

- **Be open**
  Relationships are about opening up and connecting. You need to create an open atmosphere for the relationship to build. Take time to know new people in your life. Slowly open up by sharing your life and encourage them to share theirs. That builds trust. Sometimes, you may hit a wall, in which case you know the boundaries of openness in that relationship.

- **Feel empathy**
  Being empathetic means feeling or seeing the other person's perspective without seeing your own belief. It is *'Putting yourself in their shoes.'* In relationships, you must see the perspective point of the person who is sharing the problem rather than your own point. It leads to a two-way communication between the both. When you feel the other person's mistakes as yours, it leads to solutions. Treat his/her shortcomings and mistakes as you would want him/her to treat yours and show respect to the person. Genuine feeling of empathy builds and strengthens a strong relationship with trust.

- **Respond carefully**
  A response can be encouraging or discouraging. When you are emotionally charged, use your words carefully. Words can build or destroy trust with their meaning, intensity and impact. Before responding to a question, listen deeply and analyse the words deeply in your heart. Reply with your view and provide solution to the person carefully. When you respond back, use his/her words rather than your own that will create a feeling that you have listened to his/her words and problems, again building trust on you. Complimenting the person for the wisdom and insights he/she shared with you shows appreciation and encourages further dialogue.

- **Synchronise cooperatively**
  People synchronise their watches to ensure that individual actions occur at the same time to produce an intended outcome. Similarly, a true and trusting friendship and relationship will

happen when everybody's interest and activities lie in the same frequency. Not every human is having same interest; you need to find common interest of others and try to develop with that. Relationships also require ongoing cooperative actions to survive and thrive. The needs and values of individuals and relationships keep changing with time, and therefore it requires flexibility to adapt to those changes. They are part of 'give and take' that empowers strong and enduring relationships.

- **Act authentically**
  Authenticity is about being genuine and real. It is one's true or core self in his/her daily life. It involves integrity, honesty and living in harmony with one's values. Be yourself when you are with someone and avoid making false pretentions and appearances which you are not. You say what you do and do what you say. Ask for what you want out of your relationships and also find out what your relationship partners want. Being authentic creates mutual trust and respect.

- **Compliment generously**
  Complimenting does miracles. It gives you an assurance that your work is appreciated. Similarly, compliment others whenever possible. Look for and appreciate the positive qualities in others. Appreciating a person is similar to walking on top of a knife. Over doing it may give a feeling that you are teasing a person rather than truly appreciating his/her work. Therefore, be careful. Share his/her joys and sorrows too. Each and every person loves compliments. Expressing gratitude by words and actions will strengthen the bonds of any relationship.

WHAT GETS IN THE WAY OF RELATIONSHIPS?

A number of things that can get in the way of forming an effective relationship include:

- **A history of mistrust or stereotyping**
  We receive plenty of misinformation about people in different groups. There is often more difference between the members of a group than between groups. If we think *'All of them are like that'*, then we are stereotyping. Each one is unique and wants to feel uniquely valuable. Stereotyping reinforces people's negative feelings that can colour their attitudes.

- **Blaming others for a difficult relationship**
  Blaming another person or group creates distance and defensiveness, and does not help the relationship develop. If you are not happy about a relationship, you should think about what you need to do or needn't do, to make it better. You change your own behaviour easily than persuade others to do so.

- **Focusing on task, overlooking the feelings and needs of others**
  People come to work with feelings. Some organisations harness these feelings and help people use their energy, joy and laughter to good effect. If the tasks are driven regardless of the feelings, even the best people leave organisations. People are not machines. They need to be treated with respect and dignity, so that they contribute more and work better together.

- **Unclear objectives, roles and expectations of each other**
  If we don't know what we want from each other, misunderstandings are inevitable and the relationship suffers.

RELATIONSHIP BUILDING

Society is a web of relationships, requiring all parties to work together in order to create something that is good. If you understand what people want and why they want it, you can usually find a way to make progress together. Respect is the foundation for a strong relationship, which means respecting yourself as well as others. Ask yourself.

- What thoughts and behaviours will attract the kind of relationships you desire?
- What is one action that you would take today that would empower your current relationships?
- Write down all the qualities or behaviours that you desire for your relationships and select the power skills that will attract those qualities.
- Keep a log of actions you take and the progress you make.
- By turning these skills into lifelong habits, you will build relationships that are healthy, strong and mutually rewarding.

SAYING 'NO'

Saying 'NO' is one of the most difficult things one has to face in the interest of relationships. You may be always trying to be nice to others in the interest of relationships, but at the expense of yourself. Common reasons for your reluctance to say 'No' are:

- You are so good at heart and want to help, even at the cost of your time and convenience.
- You are afraid of sounding rude, especially to senior people where face-saving is important.
- You don't want to alienate yourself from the group, so you confirm to others' requests.
- You are afraid that the person might be angry with your rejection and might lead to confrontation and dissent, which could lead to negative consequences in the future
- You may be worried that saying 'No' means closing doors on future opportunities for the promotion and career advancement.

While saying 'No', the manner of your denial is more important to know rather than your actual denial. After all, you have your own priorities and needs, just like everyone else, and your saying 'NO' is about respecting and valuing your time, priorities, needs and space, and it is your prerogative. Some of the responses you can use when you have to say 'No' are:

- **'I can't commit to this as I have other priorities at the moment.'**
  Use this, if you have too many commitments and are too busy to accept the request. This is an indication to requestor to hold off on this as well as future requests. You may share what you're working on, so the person can understand better.
- **Now is not a good time as I am in the middle of something. How about we reconnect at other time?**
  This is a temporarily hold on the request, while you are also indicating your desire to help at some other convenient time. This way, the person doesn't feel blown off.

- **I would love to do this, but ...**
  It is a gentle and encouraging way, as it lets the person know that you like the idea (say this only if you really like it), and that makes him/her happy. The request and idea might be great, but you do not want to commit to it due to prior commitments or different needs or priorities.
- **Let me think about it first and I'll get back to you.**
  Use this, if you are interested, but you don't want to say 'yes' right away. This is more like a 'Maybe' than a straight-out 'No'. You may need time to think and commit to the idea. Do specify a date/time range when the person can expect a reply. A person, who is sincere about his request, will be happy to wait a short while.
- **This doesn't meet my needs now but I'll be sure to keep you in mind.**
  If someone is pitching an idea which isn't what you are looking for, let him know straight that it doesn't meet your needs. It helps the person know it's nothing wrong about his idea, but that you are looking for something else. Also, by saying that you'll keep him in mind, you signal openness to future opportunities.
- **I'm not the best person to help on this. Why don't you try X?**
  If you can't contribute much or don't have resources to help on the request, let it be known, they are looking at the wrong person. You may refer them to a lead or someone you know they can pursue. This way you help steer the person in the right place.
- **No, I can't.**
  This is the simplest and most direct way to say 'No'; it may harm relationships.

Don't think so much about saying no and just say it outright. You'll be surprised when the reception isn't half as bad as what you imagined it to be. Once you learn to say 'NO', you'll find how easy it actually is. You'll get more time for yourself, your work and things that are most important to you.

BEING ASSERTIVE IN RELATIONSHIPS

Being assertive is different from being arrogant and adamant. It is an honest, direct and appropriate expression of one's feelings, thoughts and beliefs. Assertiveness increases your ability to reach these goals while maintaining your rights and dignity. Assertiveness comes into play when:

- You express negative feelings about other people and their behaviours without using abusive language.
- You are able to exercise and express your strengths.
- You easily recognise and compliment other people's achievements.
- You have the confidence to ask for what is rightfully yours.
- You accept criticism without being defensive.
- You feel comfortable accepting compliments.
- You are able to stand up for your rights.
- You are able to refuse unreasonable requests from friends, family or co-workers.
- You comfortably start and carry on a conversation with others.
- You ask for assistance when you need it.

Some factors that keep you from being assertive are fear of change, refusal to admit your submissiveness, fear of ruining relationships and lack confidence in your ability.

Communication Skills   15

The ability to effectively communicate with other people is an important skill. Through communication, people reach some understanding of each other, learn to like each other, influence one another, build trust and learn more about themselves and how people perceive them. People who communicate effectively know how to interact with others flexibly, skilfully and responsibly, but without sacrificing their own needs and integrity.

Communication is a significant part of a manager's job. In today's team-oriented workplace, the development of good communication skills is an important key to success. In fact, this is one of the most important skills that the corporate world looks at while hiring its employees. To build competence in communication up front is, therefore, key to employability and sustainable career success. Some of the benefits of effective communication are:

- A more professional image
- Improved self-confidence
- Improved relationships
- Less stress
- Greater acceptance by others

In your employment, you will have to communicate with different kinds of people at different levels of the organisation. Some of you may find it easy to communicate while some may find difficult. Researchers have identified few types of people to communicate and they are as follows:

- **Placater**
  The Placater always talks in an ingratiating way, trying to please, apologizing and never disagreeing, no matter what. For example, Whatever you want is okay. I am just here to make you happy. The placater indicates a sense of helplessness. He/she feels I feel like nothing: without him or her, I am dead. I am worthless.

- **Blamer**
  The Blamer is a fault finder, a dictator and a boss and always acts as superior. He/she always says, You never do anything right. What is the matter with you? Or If it weren't for you, everything would be all right. While he/she keeps emphasising that I am the boss around here, internally he/she feels I am lonely and unsuccessful.

- **Computer**
  The Computer is very correct and very reasonable, with no signs of any feeling showing. He/she is calm, cool and collected, and tries to sound intellectual. The computer uses big words or jargons. For example, If one were to observe carefully, one might notice the work-worn hands of

someone present here. Externally he/she feels I'm calm, cool and collected, but internally, he/she will be saying I feel vulnerable.

- **Distracter**
  The Distracter never makes a direct response to anything. Anything he/she says is totally irrelevant to what anyone else is saying or doing. His/her statements make no sense and are totally irrelevant. Distracter may be saying at all times Nobody cares. There is no place for me.

Mutual trust and respect are the foundation for effective communications. With their presence, goals can be developed and all individuals and groups become committed. Communication systems and processes based on shared goals and developed cooperatively are those most supported, most adhered to and consequently most efficient.

TYPES OF COMMUNICATIONS

Communication can have the following varied forms:

- **Intrapersonal communication**
  People talk to themselves. It combines their thoughts, experiences and perceptions. Behaviour responses on all other types of communications essentially begin at this level. At this level, the individual forms personal rules and patterns of communication. Some forms of intrapersonal communication are:

  - Sense making, for example, interpreting maps, texts, signs and symbols.
  - Interpreting non-verbal communication, for example, gestures and eye contact.
  - Communication between the body parts, for example 'My stomach is telling me it's time for lunch.'
  - Daydreaming and many others.

- **Interpersonal communication**
  Interpersonal communication is between two individuals or with a small group of individuals. This requires skills to handle different people in different situations and making people feel at ease. Gestures such as eye contact, body movement and hand gestures are part of interpersonal communication. The forms of interpersonal communication vary from verbal to non-verbal and from situation to situation. Interpersonal communication involves face-to-face communication in a way that accomplishes the purpose and is appropriate.
- **Small group communication**
  Small group communication is also interpersonal in nature and occurs among three or more people interacting in order to achieve common goals, either face-to-face or through mediated forms. The small group may be a family talking at supper or a meeting in an organisation with just a few members.
- **Public communication or public speaking**
  The speaker sends messages to an audience, which is not identified as individuals. Unlike the previous levels, the speaker is doing most of the talking.
- **Mass communication**
  Mass communication occurs when a small number of people send messages to a large anonymous and usually heterogeneous audience using specialised communication media. It represents

the creation and sending of a homogeneous message to a large heterogeneous audience through the media. This communication is mostly one sided and sender focused.

- **Non-verbal communication**

  People send messages to each other without talking. They communicate through facial expressions, head positions, arm and hand movements, body posture and positioning of legs and feet. By being aware of non-verbal communication, one can interpret the signals of others or send signals to others. Awareness of non-verbal communication helps people to:

  - Project an image of confidence and knowledge.
  - Demonstrate power or influence.
  - Express sincerity, interest and cooperativeness.
  - Create trust.
  - Recognise personal tension in self and others.
  - Identify discrepancies between what people are saying and what actually they are thinking.
  - Change behaviour and environment to encourage productive discussion.

HOW WE GET, RETAIN AND USE INFORMATION

How much information we retain in the communication process depends on many factors. Do we remember most of what we read? Most of what we hear? Do we learn more if someone shows us? Research indicates that we spend on average 70–80% of our waking time in some form of communication. Of that time, we spend about 9% writing, 16% reading, 30% speaking and 45% listening. Typically, our retention of information has the following pattern:

- 10% of what we read
- 20% of what we hear
- 30% of what we see
- 50% of what we see and hear
- 70% of what we see and discuss
- 90% of what we do

7Cs OF COMMUNICATION

Irrespective of the type of communication and media used, the following 7Cs become important characteristics of any communication process:

Clarity:	Apply the KISS formula—'Keep it short and simple.'
	Choose precise, familiar and conversational words.
	Construct effective sentences and paragraphs.
	Achieve appropriate readability and listenability.
	Avoid too many abbreviations, slangs or jargons.
Completeness:	Answer all questions asked.
	Give something extra, when desirable.
	Check for the five Ws (What, Where, When, Who and Why) and any other essentials.

Conciseness:	Shorten or omit wordy expressions.
	Include only relevant statements.
	Avoid unnecessary repetition, long sentences, relative pronouns, abstract subjects and passive verbs.
Correctness:	Use the right and correct language.
	Include only accurate facts, words and figures.
	Maintain good writing habits—grammar, tenses, spellings and vocabulary.
	Choose non-discriminatory expressions.
	Apply all other pertinent 'Cs'.
Concreteness:	Use specific facts and figures.
	Put action in your verbs.
	Choose vivid, image-building words.
	Avoid relative words, indefinite phrases and abstract words.
Consideration:	Focus on 'you' instead of 'I' and 'we.'
	Take interest in the reader; show how the reader will benefit.
	Emphasise positive, pleasant facts.
	Apply integrity and ethics.
	Avoid negative words.
Courtesy:	Be sincere, tactful, thoughtful and appreciative.
	Omit expressions that irritate, hurt or belittle.
	Apologise when necessary.
	Use words and phrases that set a positive tone.
	Make the reply easy.

METHODS OF COMMUNICATION

The communication methods used in organisations primarily include verbal and non-verbal forms:

- Verbal communication includes listening and speaking.
- Non-verbal communication includes reading and writing.

All four of these basic methods can be learned and improved, provided you want to improve your communication skills. You must understand them and recognise their importance in the communication process. Then, you need to learn the skills and practise them to become a better and more effective communicator.

Listening Skills

We spend significant amount of time listening. Yet, listening is a skill, never taught to us, unlike writing, reading and speaking, neither in schools/colleges nor anywhere else. Probably, listening is the first communication skill we should develop. Listening is really where all good communication begins. Misunderstanding what other person is saying is one of the biggest obstacles to communication. We expect everyone sees the world in the same way as we do.

Hearing is natural, but listening must be learned. Listening is a mental process requiring effort. Let us first understand what are the barriers to good listening skills. Dan Bobinski calls them '7 deadly sins' that get in the way of good verbal communication.

- **Sin 1: Filtering**
  This is when a person's mind is sifting another's words and tuning in only when he/she hears agreement. Commonly, a Filterer replies to someone else's statements with 'yeah, but....'.
- **Sin 2: Second guessing**
  Someone who is second guessing usually misses important details because he/she is too busy imagining some hidden motives for saying what the other person is saying and trying to figure out what those hidden motives might be.
- **Sin 3: Discounting**
  Listener lacks the respect for a speaker. What the speaker is saying could be totally correct, but a Discounter will either internally or publicly scoff at what's being said. Unfortunately, he/she often misses the solutions to the problems, simply because he/she doesn't like the source. A milder form of discounting occurs when content is brushed off just because the person speaking is not a good speaker.
- **Sin 4: Relating**
  A Relater continually finds references from his/her own background and compares them to what the speaker is saying. He/she often appears self-centred, as everything he/she hears is publicly compared or contrasted to his/her own experiences.
- **Sin 5: Rehearsing**
  This blocks much listening, as he/she is waiting for the other speaker to finish his/her speaking so the rehearser can start talking again. While someone else is talking, the rehearser is thinking about what to say next.
- **Sin 6: Forecasting**
  When someone takes an idea from the speaker and runs ahead of the topic at hand in the future. Forecasting can stem from being bored with the subject matter or simply because one's mind automatically thinks ahead.
- **Sin 7: Placating**
  Worst of all listening sins, placating means agreeing with everything anyone else says, just to avoid conflict.

Active listening is a way of listening and responding to another person that improves mutual understanding and helps overcoming communication roadblocks. There are five levels of active listening:

- **Basic Acknowledgements**
  Basic acknowledgements include verbal, visual, non-verbal signs and vocal sounds that let the speaker know that the audience is listening with interest and respect, such as head nodding, leaning forward or backward, making eye contacts, 'uh-huh', 'oh really', 'no kidding, 'tell me more', 'I hear you', 'so...', 'I see' and 'yes'.
- **Questions**
  Asking questions supports active listening. An active listener asks questions in order to show the speaker his/her interest in what is being said and to gain better understanding of the speaker's point of view. Open-ended questions are preferable to close-ended questions, because they

provide opportunities for speaker to open up, to explore his/her thoughts and feelings. It is also important to ask one question at a time, for example:

– What do you mean when you say?
– Where else did you spend all that money?

Another questioning technique is called the one-point solution. When using the 'one-point solution' to ask a question, you can use several words, such as 'one' or 'best' or 'top'. Here are some examples of 'one-point solution' questions:

– What is the one thing you would suggest to increase our effectiveness on the job?
– What will your top priority action be out of different actions you recommended?
– When is the best time to conduct training?

- **Paraphrasing**
  Paraphrasing focuses on the speaker's content and summarises what was said in order to clarify and confirm correct understanding. The steps of the paraphrasing process are:

  – Let the speaker finish what he/she wanted to say.
  – Restate with your own words what you think the speaker has said.
  – If the speaker confirms your understanding continue the conversation.
  – If the speaker indicates that you misunderstood, ask the speaker to repeat: 'Could you say it again?' Example: 'So, you're saying that...' and 'If I understand correctly, you said...'.

- **Mirroring Feelings**
  Mirroring is reflecting back to the speaker the emotions he/she is communicating. Do not miss the emotional dimension of a conversation. Encourage the speaker to disclose feelings, may be joy, sorrow, frustration, anger or grief. The reflection of feelings will help the speaker understand his/her own emotions and move towards a solution of the problem. In order to understand and mirror feelings:

  – Observe the feeling words the speaker uses.
  – The speaker may not use feeling words at all. In that case, focus on the content and ask yourself: 'If I were having that experience, if I were saying and doing those things, what would I be feeling?'
  – Observe the body language, facial expressions, tone of the voice, gestures and posture.

- **Reflecting meanings**
  Once a person knows how to reflect feeling and content separately, it is relatively easy to put the two together into a reflection of meaning. It would be useful to use the formula: 'You feel (insert the feeling word) because (insert the event or other content associated with the feeling)'.
  For example, 'You are feeling bad because XYZ got a promotion...?'

- **Encourage**
  It is always advisable to encourage the speaker to say more.

  – 'Tell me more about...'
  – 'Would you like to talk about it?'
  – 'Want to have lunch and talk?'

- **Take notes**

  Never go for a meeting or presentation without a notepad and something to write. Taking notes always improves listening and allows you to have documentation for the future reference.

Improvements will occur only if you practise good listening skills. Try one of them for about three months; it takes at least that long to create a new habit. Then, practise asking questions to clarify what you hear. Success with one new habit will encourage you to try others.

Speaking

Managers are required to make speeches and presentations at various places and on different subjects. Within organisation, it may be selling of ideas, gathering of team support or giving directions or instructions to staff. Externally, it could be to customers, suppliers, financial institutions, investors and others. Speaking either in public or small meetings is integral part of managers' day-to-day activities and responsibilities. With access to knowledge and information from Internet, audience expect more content from speakers today. Here is a quick guide to improve you speaking skills.

Use of Language

Dr J. Mitchell Perry, a consultant for effective communications, states that if our voice is an instrument, then language is the music. We must practise with our voice, just as we would with any musical instrument and then master the language we put through that instrument. While most of us are articulate and comfortable with our mother tongue, in professional speaking, the rules change somewhat and we are judged as an authority based on our use of language.

The first thing an audience will notice, when the speaker begins, is the tone and inflection of the speaker's voice. A monotone dialogue is disastrous to a message; varying volume and pace of our speech are necessary. By increasing and decreasing the volume on important words, speeding up or slowing down the tempo of our conversation and effective use of pausing, a speaker can force the audience to adjust their listening process to match the new pace. The listeners remain more attentive, which improves the chances that they will understand what is being said.

The Message

What is being said is equally important as how it's being said. Vast reading and good vocabulary make you comfortable with a variety of subjects and words. A broader vocabulary obviously does not mean attempting to astound the audience with verbiage and verbosity, but an articulate and eloquent speaker commands more respect than one who appears to be stuck in the middle-school English class.

Be Judicious with Fillers

Most of us use some words or phrases without realizing how distracting they can be to our message. Most of us easily recognise the 'you know' and 'umm' space fillers, but other words such as 'always' and 'never' may evoke subconscious negative responses to the idea we are trying to convey. Other phrases such as 'why don't you', which implies someone isn't doing something correctly now and requires action on their part, and 'to be honest', which implies the speaker hasn't been honest up to this point, can evoke a similar reaction.

Be aware of what is being said and keep changing to words that engender support and understanding or deflect hostility so that the audience feel more responsive and eager to listen to the message.

Image

A speaker's physical appearance is of equal importance. While our skin colour, gender and height cannot be changed, we can still make a good first impression with overall image and personality.

Physical appearance, such as clothing selection, hair and even the appearance of our hands, affects how we and thereby the authority of our message are perceived. The type of clothing and grooming must be appropriate to the setting and the audience. By dressing inappropriately, speakers create an impression that they are not part of the audience and establish a negative image for themselves.

Adapt to International Environment

Operating effectively within the international environment is becoming increasingly important in today's environment. Successful managers must be able to manoeuvre effectively in this culturally and ethnically challenging environment. You need to understand the etiquettes and mannerisms of greeting, both physically and verbally, acceptance of gifts and appropriate dinning manners. Use good judgement and common courtesy before engaging in international business relations. Be sure to do some informal research on foreign nations being visited; conversely, become familiar with the customs and culture of any foreign visitors or dignitaries before their arrival.

Get Early Attention of the Audience

Listeners pay close attention when a person shares his/her own relevant experiences or ask a relevant question to make a beginning, for example:

- Two weeks ago as I was driving to work a car pulled out in front of me. ...
- You might have read in the paper this morning about the flood that. ...
- How many of you feel our society spends too much on healthcare?

Once you grab attention of the audience, you are on your way to a successful speech.

Be Energetic in Delivery

Speak with a variety of pace, tone and volume in your voice. Slow down for a dramatic point and speed up to show excitement. Pause occasionally for audience response such as laugh or clapping. If possible, keep moving within the space rather than sticking behind the lectern all the time. Take a step towards the audience if you want to encourage and enthuse them. Gesture to show how big or wide or tall or small an object is that you are describing. Show facial expression as you speak. Smile when talking about something pleasant and let your face show other emotions as you tell about an event or activity.

Structure Your Speech

Restrict your main points of speech to two or three. Preview them in the beginning of the speech. Provide appropriate substantiations for each point with definitions, testimony, illustrations, examples, experiences or statistics. Use visuals when you want your audience to understand a process or concept or understand a financial goal. Line graphs are best for trends. Bar graphs are best for comparisons and pie charts are best for showing distribution of percentages.

Tie Your Points Together with Transitions

Use an internal summary by simply including the point you just made and telling your next point. Example, 'Now that we have talked about structure, let's move on to the use of stories.'

Tell Your Own Story Somewhere

Audience will connect with you if you include a personal experience that is relevant to your speech content. That way your audience gets emotionally linked to what you are talking about. When you tell the story, start at the beginning and move chronologically through the narrative, including answers to the '5W' questions: 'Who', ' What', 'When', 'Why' and 'Where'.

If you are delivering a persuasive speech, in addition to your own stories, include testimony of experts whom the audience respects and whose views reinforce your points. Add a key statistic when possible to show the seriousness of what you are discussing.

Look at the Audience as You Speak

If it is a small audience, you can look at each person periodically and cover the whole audience easily. If it is a large audience, focus on a small 'clump' in the audience and gradually move from one clump to another. One way to ensure good eye contact is to look at your audience before you start to speak. Go to the lectern and pause, smile, look at the audience and then start your speech. This, however, should not last more than few seconds before you start speaking and must look natural.

Reading a written speech is not really a good public speaking practice. It causes losing all important eye contact and enthusiasm during the delivery of the speech. Sometimes, you may have to do that though. Whenever you have no other option, do that, but do not lose sight of these two key issues. A good practice is to use note cards with key points or words on them. The word or phrase should trigger the thoughts in your mind and then you can elaborate on those points. If you are including a quotation or complex statistics, reading from your note card actually lends credibility to what you wish to say. You may, however, write your entire speech for the rehearsal purpose.

Include a 'wow' factor. Something in your speech should get the audience in 'Wow!' expression. It could be a story, a dramatic point, an unusual statistic or an effective visual that grips the audience to your speech. With a 'wow' factor early in the speech, you have something to look forward to and have an impact on your audience. You'll become more enthusiastic once you experience the 'wow' factor with your audience.

Use of Humour

Humour helps you to be perceived as an amiable person. It is hard for people to disagree or be bored if they are smiling at you. Unless the topic of your speech is humour based, keep your humour limited, as it might divert the session from the main topic and even upset the audience at times. Tell a short embarrassing or funny story from your life experiences or even a joke. Don't poke fun at your audience; the object of that fun or humour should be you yourself and somebody not in the audience.

Finally, Leave the Audience with Something to Think About

People remember best what you say last. A summary of points you made or a statement such as: 'What I want you to do as a result of this presentation is ...' reinforces the purpose of the presentation or the speech. You may end up your speech with a thought-provoking question such as '... so having heard all this, would you still continue smoking ...? I leave it to you to decide.'

The ability to speak in a group setting, conveying a message, is an essential skill in the business environment. A good introduction, two or three main points with support for each, appropriate transitions and a conclusion will organise your speech in a way that the audience can follow you easily. Developing public speaking skills is a lifelong experience. But the points discussed here will get you started in becoming the speaker you want to be and the speaker your audience wants to hear. The practice is the key in public speaking.

Reading

Managers shuffle papers, read reports (soft or hard copies) and books more than ever before in this competing environment. Their reading becomes very specialised at times to keep up to date with technology and other business developments in the world. The volume of information available to read is tremendous and that justifies the need for understanding reading approaches, processes, skills and strategies.

Efficient reading means the ability to extract information, meaning and understanding from a written communication, which could be a report or a book, as rapidly and completely as possible. Our reading in schools and colleges was more oriented to education and learning. We were hardly required to make sense or interpret what was being read. No specific actions or decision were required to be taken based on what was read. Business reading is more purposeful and action oriented. It needs specialised skills to interpret, understand and comprehend the written contents in shortest span of time.

Thoughtful consideration to and practicing the following factors should help improving reading efficiency.

Comprehension

Comprehension is the most important purpose of efficient reading. It is the process of extracting information and meaning from a large amount of text. It is the ability to understand precisely the subject matter or message or learning from what has been read. You need to develop ability to concentrate while reading, to grasp, remember and retain ideas. There are three actions to help you in the process of comprehension.

- Determine the basic theme or purpose of the text being read.
- Determine the writer's point of view and examine his/her supporting evidence.
- Evaluate the written text based on your understanding of it and assess the relevance and appropriateness of the text to the point being made.

Reading Speed

Reading speed is another important aspect of efficient reading. You must be able to read rapidly to get the message quickly because time is a valuable commodity. Numerous courses are available on speed-reading or rapid reading. The experts who developed these courses believe that most of us have the potential to improve our reading rate threefold if we learn how to speed-read and practice.

A great deal of effort and concentrated practice are required to increase your reading efficiency. It is up to you to dedicate yourself to the task. It is important to note that the increased reading rate has to be without the loss of comprehension. Remember, if the speed indicates reading efficiency, the comprehension indicates the reading effectiveness. If you are really sincere about increasing your reading rate, there are five basic steps:

- **Increase the span of recognition**
  Your eyes move and then pause one or more times as they cross a line of written material. That's the time the reading takes place. The number of stops you make in reading a line of text called 'fixations' is determined by the span of recognition. The higher the span of recognition, the lower is the number of fixations, and therefore faster reading. In simple terms, try reading the entire line of text together, rather than reading word by word. Practise reading daily with a single fixation per line.
- **Decrease the fixation time**
  Having reduced the number of fixations as above, the next thing is to reduce the time per fixation. Force yourself to read at an uncomfortable rate and you will soon reduce the fixation time. Time yourself using a stop watch and try to read each succeeding page of a book at a faster rate.
- **Decrease the number of regressions**
  You regress when your eyes move backward to the left side of a page to fix on a word. The ability to read an entire sentence at one go would naturally reduce the regressions. Regression is not necessarily bad and needed to analyse a confusing statement or to re-examine an unfamiliar work to improve comprehension. It is important to note that with a lack of concentration while reading, regression increases. Therefore, concentrate on your reading. *Eliminate sub-vocalisation.*

In childhood, we were asked to read aloud to make sure that we focus on what we were reading. Consequently, when we started to read silently, we tended to say each word to ourselves. This is called sub-vocalisation. Sub-vocalisation limits the reading rate. A faster reader uses only eyes and brain to read silently. A continued practice at speed greater than 400 words per minute will do much to break the sub-vocalizing habit.

- **Increase vocabulary**
  A poor vocabulary diminishes the comprehension and increases the tendency to regress. The best way to increase your vocabulary is to read more extensively and find new applications of old words in different contexts as well as use of different new words. Keep the dictionary handy while reading. As you read more and more, words become an active part of your reading vocabulary and enhance your comprehensions as well as reading efficiency.

Remember that the reading rate also varies with the type of reading. It is higher when you read 'light' rather than 'heavy' material.

Using Discrimination

Finally, it is important to decide early whether to read or not to read something. Most reports, magazine articles or books have less useful content, relevant and appropriate to your needs. You have to determine the worth of what you read in advance. The trick is to find it quickly. For this purpose:

- Scan the table of contents for a rough idea of what it is all about.
- Scan it quickly to know the writer and how he writes.
- Read carefully those sections that appear to contain the information in which you have interest.

If you make a decision not to read an article, report or book, you have gained time and not filled your mind with useless information. This gives you more time for important and interesting reading. Then you determine the most efficient manner to gain knowledge or information. If the material must be understood thoroughly, you read with attention to detail. If the material must be read to gain general information, you read rapidly. This saves time and still provides the information needed.

Reading improvement is a continuing process. For leaders of our modern, complex organisations, efficient reading is imperative. To become an efficient reader, try to overcome the above barriers. You can do so by following the suggestions made here. You can then increase your reading efficiency still more by adjusting your reading rate to your reading objective and the reading material. Good reading habits and strategies help managers handle their tasks more efficiently.

Writing

No matter what your job is, you will find the need to write at one time or another. To produce good writing, you have to make the information fit the document and style that best communicates to readers. Technical and business writing consists of special documents such as memos, reports, manuals and instructions. It usually requires several stages of text development:

- Brainstorm on the contents and key messages of the communication.
- Cluster your ideas into topics.

- Outline your topics, including subtopics.
- Write a rough draft.
- Revise by editing your work.
- Proofread carefully.
- Produce the final draft.

Crisp and correct writing is essential to successful business communication. Some basics of a good writing are listed below.

- **Keep writing simple**

  Write the reader's language. This principle relates to one of the key elements in the communication process, knowing your audience or knowing your reader.

  Avoid wordiness. Shorten wordy phrases and keep writing simple. It is not difficult. After you write a letter, memos or instructions for a procedure, look critically at unnecessary words and phrases. When one or two words can substitute for five or six, do it. For example:

Instead of writing	Write
We made a decision ...	We decided ...
With reference to ...	Concerning ...
Cooperate together ...	Cooperate ...

The point is if we use the language natural to us, it will seem natural to others. Avoid jargons familiar to you and your professions but a foreign language to others. The people in IT profession should particularly remember this. If you need to use technical language, explain it to your reader in words he/she can understand.

- **Keep writing positive**

  Be reader friendly by putting readers in perspective as much as possible. Minimise use of negative language, words and phrases. Use positive language instead. For example:

  Negative: *We can't issue the permit until you complete the application.*

  Positive: *We can issue the permit when you complete the application.*

  Negative: *Drivers won't be able to use the main street during the paving project.*

  Positive: *Drivers will use the short detour during the main street paving project.*

  Negative: *You are not eligible for the discount.*

  Positive: *Members are eligible for this discount. To become a member, please complete and submit this form.*

- **Provide facts and do not blame**

  Avoid: *You did not include a check in your recent mortgage payment mailing.*

  Write: *We did not find a check in your recent mortgage payment mailing.*

- **Keep writing accurate**

  The reader is likely to remember errors in written communication than the message. Good grammar, correct spelling and punctuation reflect a professional writer and one who respects the reader. Whether you are not so good in spelling or grammar, ask someone to proofread your writing. Even the best writers have editors who check their work. Accuracy shows that you care about your image and that you respect your reader. Use a dictionary to verify spelling or use a computer spellcheck.

- **Be polite**

  Politeness means being courteous, civil, considerate and respectful to the reader. Politeness is achieved by using proper language when addressing the reader. The appropriateness of the language used is indicative of the relationship that exists between the writer and the reader.

  If the writer and the reader have a formal relationship, courtesy titles such as Mr, Mrs, Ms or Dr are used. These titles should be used for all communication outside the organisation. If the writer and the reader belong to the same company or organisation, then politeness of language depends upon their respective positions in the hierarchy. Superiors can more easily address subordinates on a first-name basis, ignoring courtesy titles. Subordinates should have a personal relationship with superiors before addressing them without using courtesy titles.

  To end, use either 'Sincerely yours' for a more formal letter and 'Sincerely' for less formality. The terms 'Thanking you for your kind attention' or 'yours faithfully' are more appropriate in government communication. The use of 'best regards' and 'keep in touch' is appropriate when the communication is addressed to a person.

- **Be fair**

  Global companies are aware of the diversity of the world marketplace and the importance of being inclusive of groups that comprise their customers. Avoiding all types of discrimination in company language makes good business sense because it appeals to as many customers as possible. Therefore, it is a good practice to avoid making assumptions to include information about race, religion or ethnicity apart from when it is relevant to the purpose of the message.

Guide to Document Revision

1. Revising to improve the content and sentence structure.
2. Proofreading to correct grammar, spelling, punctuation, format and mechanics.
3. Evaluating to analyse whether the message achieves its purpose.

Sentences and Lines per Paragraph

A paragraph is a set of related sentences, indicated by indenting the first sentence or by leaving a blank line or spacing between paragraphs. A professional writing needs to be as simple and straightforward as possible. Therefore, keep sentences short and use active voice. Paragraphs are most effective when they are crisp, clean, short and to the point. Good business paragraphs develop one idea at a time.

In business letters and memos, one-sentence paragraphs are common in the first and last paragraphs. However, in reports, one- and two-sentence paragraphs make the report seem too choppy. The number of lines in a paragraph is the best judge of its proper length. Paragraphs in letters and memos are easiest to read if they do not exceed four to five printed lines. In reports, paragraphs of seven to nine lines or even little more are acceptable. Extra long paragraphs appear difficult and uninviting to read.

Check the words per sentence in your document for conciseness. If your average sentence length is too long, reduce its length by avoiding wordiness, passive sentences or by breaking long sentences into two or more sentences or making a bullet point list.

Short sentence length also makes your writing choppy. Check to see how many sentences have fewer than 10 words and combine some of your short sentences into complex or compound sentences. For example:

Original: *The Company usually does not give semi-annual increments. However, all employees will receive a raise in June.*
Revision I: *Although the company usually does not give semi-annual raises, all employees will receive a raise in June.*
Revision II: *The Company usually does not give semi-annual raises, but all employees will receive a raise this June.*

Readability

Too many passive sentences should be avoided in a business writing. A business letter or memo is considered good if about 80% of the verbs used are active. In other words, only one out of five sentences could be passive. If your work contains more than 20% passive sentences, revise the sentences using active verbs. In general, the active voice is more effective in business communications than the passive voice. For example:

Passive: *The decision was made by the manager at the last moment.*
Active: *The manager decided at the last moment or The manager took this decision last minute or It was the Manager's last-minute decision.*

Note that the active voice makes the sentence shorter and action oriented, with full clarity on who did what and when. To make passive verbs active, ask yourself who did which action when. Move that person or thing to the beginning of the sentence as the subject and change the verb as necessary.

A working knowledge of passive voice is necessary when considering the tone of your message. The passive is often used to improve the tone of a communication by de-emphasising 'who' took the action if that is not important and pleasant. For example:

Poor: *You did not complete all the items on the form.*
Better: *All the items on the form were not completed. (Better tone)*
Poor: *The construction company finished the building on Wednesday.*
Better: *The building was finished on Wednesday.* (This example is better, assuming that it is not important or it is implied who finished the work.)

Parallelism

Parallel structure applies to words joined by a conjunction, joined by a conjunctive pair, appearing in a series and in a listing. For example:

'The whole day was spent returning phone calls, reading mails, and dictating correspondence.'

When reading this report, you will

- *Learn the costs involved in old inventories.*
- *Appreciate the new computerised accounting system.*
- *Understand the new elements in the zero-based approach.*

Titles and Numbers

Names of books, magazines and newspapers should be underlined or put in italics. For example:

'*Fortune* and *Business Week* are important information sources.'
'*The Wall Street Journal* had an article on that topic recently.'
Numbers included in text vary according to their value and location.

- Numbers opening a paragraph or at the beginning of a sentence are written as words.
  'Three hundred bankers rushed to Wall Street today.'
- Numbers one to ten (1–10) are entered in text as words.
  'I have three job offers currently.'
- Numbers above 10 are placed in text as digits except when they open a paragraph.
  'She left her son ₹4 lakhs in cash and securities.'

Regional Usage/Slang

Regionalisms should be avoided in formal writing. For example, in USA, it is a common practice to omit 'to be', as in, 'The job needs done.' Since there is no verb in that phrase, it is not a complete sentence. In business writing, use 'The job needs to be done.'

Proofreading

- Proofread everything, including titles, subtitles, words, punctuation, capitalisation, indented items and numbers.
- Concentrate on each word. If necessary, read your document backwards to check spelling. Then, read sentences and paragraphs out of order. This helps you read what you actually have written instead of what you believe you have written.
- Cover the document with a piece of paper so you can read only one line at a time. This will help you overcome your eyes' tendency to move on too quickly.
- Read aloud to someone who will follow along on another copy of the document.
- Examine all numbers and totals. Recheck all calculations and look for misplaced commas and decimal points.
- Make sure all quotation marks, brackets, dashes and parentheses come in pairs.
- Double check all highlighted material.
- Keep a list of all repeated errors. See if you find a pattern that will help you proofread future documents more effectively.
- Ask co-workers to proofread your document and to initial it when they are confident they have uncovered all mistakes.

Product Evaluation

- Ask yourself, 'Does this communication achieve its purpose?'
- Obtain feedback from others about the quality of the communication.
- Encourage feedback from the receiver about the quality of your communication.

Guidelines for Writing Professional Reports

- Define the main point.
- Define the goals and objectives.
- Collect the evidence needed to support the main point.
- Organise the report.
- State the conclusions and recommendations.

Report Structure

- Title
- Executive summary
- Introduction
- Materials and methods
- Results and discussions
- Conclusions
- Recommendations

Presentation Skills

Planning and Writing Your Presentation

If your presentation has a clear, succinct message:

- You'll be able to remember it better.
- You'll be less nervous when you come to present it.
- Your audience will be able to understand it better.

The best way to create a clear, succinct and well-designed presentation is to take a structured approach for planning and writing it. Some key steps for achieving excellent presentations are:

- **Establish the purpose of the presentation**
  There are lots of different types of presentations. You might be trying to sell something; you might be trying to persuade your audience about something or influencing them or you might be simply trying to inform them about something. The first thing to do is to establish the purpose of your presentation. What do you want to achieve from your presentation.

- **Write it down**

  Having got the purpose clear, it is important to write that down. It is, therefore, clear in your mind and you are able to refer back to the purpose while developing the presentation.

- **Build an audience profile**

  Think about your audience. Put together an audience profile, covering the type of people who will attend your presentation. Where are they coming from; what level of expertise do they have; are there any decision-makers in the audience; what is their attitude towards the topic that you are presenting on; do they have any preconceived ideas or expectations about what you will be presenting, etc. Brainstorm as much as you can about your audience. The more that you understand the audience the more you'll be able to adapt your contents and the presentation style.

- **Establish the key message of your presentation**

  Think about your key message. Every presentation should have one key message that everything else ultimately links to. The key message should have a very strong benefit for the audience to listen to you. Brainstorm the main benefits your presentation brings to the audience. Ask yourself what's in it for them. Answer to this question would enable you to identify your key message. Write it down.

- **Develop and structure the content of your presentation**

  Putting content into a strong clear structure is very important to help you stay on track and also to help the audience to follow the presentation clearly. Think in terms of Beginning, Middle and End. Split your middle part appropriately into sections, and each section can have three or four further points you want to make and expand on, to reinforce things. Keep your audience, purpose and key message at the back of your mind while creating the content for your presentation. If you have a strong structure, you are likely to keep focused holding the audience with you at all times.

- **Edit your presentation content**

  It is important to edit your draft, taking into consideration the language used to help you keep the audience's interest. Identify ways of grabbing their attention and ways of actually helping them to listen to you. Don't use long winded sentences or words that may not be relevant to the audience or that they might not even understand. So, edit the material and adapt the language that you are going to use.

Use of Visual Aids

Today, most presentations involve use of PowerPoint Slides. But slide after slide of bullet points with lots of different transition effects can turn off most audience. This becomes worse when the presenter is just reading bullet points on the slides or has his/her back to the audience much of the time! Visual aids can be a great way of enhancing a presentation visually, when they are used sensibly and with a clear purpose. You need to relate your visual aids to your audience and to the type of presentation you are designing.

For example, if it is just a small intimate presentation, you may just use a few sheets on a flipchart. This is also more appropriate for an interactive presentation/discussion, as audience can then partly own the flip chart with you, and hence buy into overall process more easily. If it is a bigger and more formal presentation, it is expected that you use a software tool such as PowerPoint. But remember, it is there to enhance your message and not just your prompts!

Designing Visual Aids

If you are designing slides using PowerPoint, then you need to make sure that they enhance the message and at the same time do not take over from you as the presenter or your message.

- Keep them as visual as possible as against full of text. Wherever possible, use images, graphs, diagrams, etc., that will help your audience understand what you are talking about. Connect with it emotionally if that's what you are trying to achieve. Images can be a great way of doing that.
- Keep bullet points to a minimum, say six or eight maximum. Where possible, add some visual effects on the same slide. Keep things simple and don't end up spending up 80% of your time on slides and 20% on the actual presentation content!

Managing Your Visual Aids

It's also important to think about how you are going to manage your visual aids.

- Where to place them in the room?
- How to work around them physically?
- How visible will they be to the audience?

All such practical things are best thought of ahead of when you are actually standing there ready to present.

Effective Use of Visual Aids

- Use the KISS rule (Keep It Simple and Succinct), regarding your use of visual aids.
- Don't overdo things.
- Don't use too many different transition effects.
- Don't use too small font sizes.
- Keep the number of slides to a minimum.
- Keep it as visual and text free as possible.

There are also other tools such as handouts that you can use, and they might well be more suited to your presentation than a software tool and data projector. Again thinking about your audience, purpose of presentation and contents, you can decide what is going to be most suitable tool. If you need to give the audience more information to support your message, then you may want to produce some handouts for the audience to take away and possibly use as future reference.

Do not forget to have backups for your presentation, as anything can go wrong with the visual aids. The data projector or PC stops working or your PPT version is not compatible with the PC in the room. One simple way is to make sure that you at least have some hard copies of your slides. If you're not sure if the presentation PC has the latest version of PowerPoint, on a safer side, save your file in the format used by an older version. Alternatively, it might be worth taking your own laptop along—just in case. Be prepared! Ask the organiser beforehand wherever possible.

Preparing to Present

It is important to feel confident about making a presentation. People do get nervous at times before and during the presentation if they are not used to making presentations often. Being ready for the presentation is therefore a very important step. When you are nervous, you tend to speed up your speech in an anxiety to get it over. Calmness and confidence help you to control all aspects of your speech. While planning is an important ingredient of the speech preparation, there are other useful techniques that would help you to take control of your presentation.

Breathing is a simple technique that can really help to calm and slow you down. Meditation is another way to enhance your focus, calmness and concentration. Creative visualisation is one more technique where you visualise that the presentation has just taken place and that it was successful. Spend time imagining that success and how you feel at that time. Imagine the voices and other sounds that you hear at the end of the presentation and what the audience faces look like and what else you can see in the room. Take time to imagine all of the positives about the presentation that made it a success. Forcing the mind to focus on the positive can help turn things around and will help build your confidence.

These techniques can help you to maintain a positive mental attitude towards your presentation and help you remain in control if any negative thoughts start to creep into your mind.

Rehearsing the Presentation

Experience is one of the best ways to get rid of your nerves. The more presentation experience you have, the more confident you will feel. So, rehearse your presentation again and again. Get your friends, colleagues and even family members during rehearsal and get their reactions and feedback.

Delivering the Presentation

A good delivery of your presentation gives you added confidence. If your preparation of presentation is good, then there is every chance that the delivery should also be good. The difference is: it is the audience that would determine the success of the presentation delivered. The audience starts judging you and your presentation even before you start to speak and they continue to do so till the end of your presentation.

First Impression

First impression is very important. *There is no second chance to make the first impression!* You need to look confident and be able to demonstrate the knowledge of the subject of the presentation early. The audience starts taking you seriously from this point onwards. If you take too long to 'warm up' into it you may well 'lose' your audience before you get to your key message. Building rapport with the audience is very essential in making a good impact. The way you use your voice, body language and space in engaging with the audience would determine the success of your presentation.

Speaking Confidently

Confidence is essential for you to get your message across clearly when you speak. Correct pronunciations, right pace and appropriate pauses also add to the speaking effectiveness. It is important to speak clearly without slurring your words together, as this will make you sound hesitant.

Sounding Interesting

The ability to make the speech interesting is important. Although you might be passionate about what you are saying, if this doesn't go across well to your audience, they won't be convinced. You need to display enthusiasm, use more expression in your tone of voice and avoid a monotone style. You may also emphasise certain keywords that will help influence the audience regarding real meaning of your messages.

Injecting pauses into speech helps to create an impact as well as helps to control your speed. It also gives the audience an opportunity to digest what has been said and respond appropriately. You can use these techniques to help change the dynamics of your presentation, keeping the audience interested throughout your presentation.

Looking Confident

The ability to look confident is important, especially as you might be feeling nervous that can unfortunately have a rather negative impact on your overall presence. The ways in which you use your posture, gesture and eye contact can help you to control any bad habits created by nerves and create a much stronger presence. Make sure that you are standing evenly on two feet with a strong but relaxed posture.

Take a few seconds before you start to speak to take in your audience. This will help you feel more in control and more confident and you will be less likely to fidget or look uncomfortable. Make sure that you also feel comfortable in the space that you are presenting, so that you look like you have ownership of the space and that you can move around appropriately. It also helps if you can walk around the space before your presentation—before the audience arrive to help you get used to it.

Engaging with the Audience

Eye contact is very important to help you engage with your audience. If you just stare at them blankly, you won't get the right connection with them. So, you need to use confident eye contact so that you really connect with individual members of the audience while you are speaking with them. And although it might sound a bit daunting to look directly at audience members, it actually has the opposite effect and helps you to feel more confident.

Presentation Stamina

It takes a lot of energy to speak in front of an audience, even if it's just for 5 minutes. It is therefore important to use the voice and body language techniques we have discussed above and to practise them so that you build up your vocal stamina. You don't have to wait until your next presentation; you can practise the vocal and body language techniques on the telephone or in a meeting. Once you are used to using these techniques, you will maintain the energy you need to keep your audience interested throughout your presentation, no matter how long you are talking for.

Answering Presentation Questions

Questions are an integral part of your presentation and require the same preparation as the presentation content. There are different ways of taking questions from the audience, depending on the type of presentation. If you are giving a more interactive presentation, you may be taking questions throughout the presentation and it can become more of a discussion with the audience. If it is a more formal presentation, you may have a Q&A session at the end of the presentation.

The Importance of Preparation

Irrespective of the type of presentation, it is not complete without questions from the audience. You don't want to just rely on being able to think on your feet on the day and hope that it all goes well. You can do some specific preparation to face questions, just as you do with your presentation.

Audience Baggage

It's good to think about the audience again and what attitude or pre-conceived ideas or opinions they may have when they come to the presentation. This is called 'Audience Baggage'. If you consider the Audience Baggage beforehand and think about the types of questions the audience may ask, you are likely to be more prepared.

Preparing for Difficult Questions

It's good to write down some of the most difficult questions the audience may ask. Then, take the time to decide how best to answer these. Write down your answers. Then, practise answering them out aloud. If you're unhappy about your response, rework it. The responses that you have prepared will then help you if you are actually asked these (or similar) questions on the day by giving you a set of phrases and words you have already formulated in your mind that you can now draw upon.

Controlling the Audience

You want to be in control of your audience and not let anyone take over in the question section. It is important to understand the questions first before responding. Often, we go into panic mode when we hear the question rather than staying calm and taking time to listen to the question to make sure that we fully understand it. So, taking time to listen and understand the question first is a good calming technique and will help you stay in control.

Avoiding Audience Traps

The ability to deal with difficult questions and being able to respond with ease, without losing face, are very important in order to maintain your confidence. It's therefore important that you are succinct in your responses and say what you want to say rather than what the audience might try and trap you into saying. The more you have prepared beforehand and anticipated difficult or trap questions, the more you will be able to handle them effectively on the day.

Ending Confidently

It's also important that you know how to end the question and answer session confidently. It can be sometimes hard to bring the session to an end if people have got more questions to ask. The last thing you want is to lose control of things right at the end, so plan how you want to end the Q&A session beforehand. Make sure you stick to the time allocated and have a closing statement or strategy at hand, ready to use when you want to end the session.

The ability to take questions effectively is all about good preparation and planning, so that you have the ability and confidence to be able to tackle any question that you have thrown at yourself.

16 Working in Teams

A team is a small group of people with complementary skills who are committed to a common purpose, performance goals and approach for which they hold themselves mutually accountable. **T**ogether **E**ach **A**chieves **M**ore is the TEAM. Have you ever been a member of a high-performing and smooth-running team in the past? If yes, it is an experience that you will never forget. Probably you trusted one another, worked cooperatively, enjoyed the task and achieved the goals higher than anyone may have imagined.

CHARACTERISTICS OF EFFECTIVE TEAMS

A team could be considered effective if it has:

1. **Clear goals:** Goal clarity is critical for all team members to move in the same direction. Lack of goal clarity results in loss of motivation and enthusiasm to work together.
2. **Defined roles:** A clear role definition justifies the presence of a member on the team in terms of specific contribution he/she is supposed to make. It becomes more important in the matters of crisis management. The role issues also come up during problem-solving, when new roles need to be identified. 'Who does what' or 'Who is responsible for what', such questions are better answered with role clarity.
3. **Open and clear communication:** Communication is the key to make decisions or take specific actions for which the teams exist. All 7Cs of communications, discussed earlier, apply to effective team working. Open and clear communication also helps building trust, minimise conflicts and rework and generally contributes to healthy interpersonal relationships.
4. **Effective decision-making:** Teams are formed primarily to make decisions, solve problems or take actions. Common understanding of the problem at hand, its boundaries and a broad framework to work with helps effective decision-making. Effective decision-making is essential to a team's progress. Shared knowledge of various decision-making processes, solution optimisation techniques certainly help teams to make best decision or right action with consensus.
5. **Balanced participation:** Team expects all members to participate and in a non-dominating manner. The type of participation can be different from different members depending on their roles and expertise. Balanced participation ensures that everyone on the team is fully involved and that each team member is part of the decision and/or action taken or proposed to be taken by the team. It also means that everyone's opinions are sought and valued by others on the team.
6. **Valued diversity:** A diversity of thinking, ideas, methods, experiences and opinions brings synergy to the team performance. Irrespective of the members' individual backgrounds, competencies and capabilities, the effective team recognises the strengths each member brings to the team.

7. **Managed conflict:** Constructive conflict ensures that problems are resolved in an unbiased and unprejudiced manner. It means that the team has discussed and given appropriate considerations to members' points of view about an issue and has ensured that conflicts, if any, have been managed in a healthy manner.

8. **Positive environment:** A team must strive on a climate of trust and openness. A positive environment means that the team members understand each other, respect roles and competencies of each other and openly share their thoughts, doubts and feelings without fear or doubt. The risk factors of making decisions also are shared with full understanding. Openness promotes involvement, commitment, creativity and productivity.

9. **Cooperative relationships:** Team members have full realisation of need for individual and collective skills, knowledge and expertise to produce something together. There is a sense of belongingness and a willingness to make things work for the purpose for which the team is formed.

10. **Participative leadership:** A team being a group, situation participative leadership works best in its functioning. The team leader needs to take its members along with him rather than driving them on his chosen path. In effective teams, it will be difficult to identify the leader as the team progresses its work in a cohesive manner on a path of consensus.

FORMS OF TEAMS IN ORGANISATIONS

The kind of team of which you might be required to be a member in your organisation would depend upon the team goal assigned by the management. A team can be a temporary group or on a permanent basis to achieve a common objective or task. Here are the two most common types of work teams you may have to work with:

- **Project team:** *A project team* (sometimes referred to as *Steering Committee or task force*) is established to accomplish a particular project. Typically, this team is dismantled when the project ends. The project teams are generally comprised of people with requisite qualifications and experiences needed to meet the purpose of their formation. The roles and contributions of each of the team members are also defined with reasonable clarity. A cross-functional team is made-up of employees from different departments or areas of the business to extract their expertise needed to solve complex issues.

- **Self-directed work team:** A self-directed work team is not appointed by the management but formed voluntarily by individuals coming together to solve a problem. They being voluntary in nature have a high level of commitment and goal orientation. The phrase self-directed or self-managed team doesn't mean that it doesn't need a leader. The leader, in this case, is generally the person who builds the team. It just means that the team is responsible and accountable for its decisions as opposed to proposing action that will need approval of someone outside the team.

TEN QUALITIES OF AN EFFECTIVE TEAM PLAYER

Teams need strong team players to perform well. Just having strong technical knowledge and skills does not make anybody a good team player. Some of qualities and attributes an effective team player must possess are:

- **Reliability**

  Being reliable means others can count on you for results and promises. The confidence other team members have in you to complete the tasks and accomplish your fair share of work and responsibilities. Consistency in reliability over the entire duration of team's existence is another important factor.

- **Constructive communication**

  Teams need people who can effectively communicate in various forms of communication. All 7Cs of communication discussed earlier apply to any good team player. Such a team member does not shy away from making a point but makes it in a positive, confident and respectful manner.

- **Active listener**

  As discussed earlier, listening is an important skill to be learnt and practised. Teams need players who can absorb, understand and consider ideas and points of view from other people without debating and arguing every point. He may have to receive criticism at times without reacting defensively. Team members need to listen first and speak later so that a meaningful dialogue results.

- **Initiative and drive**

  Good team players come prepared with homework for team meetings and fully participate in discussions. They are fully involved in the work at hand. They take initiative to help make things happen and volunteer for assignments. They present a *'can-do'* attitude and continuously think, *'What contribution can I make to help the team achieve success?'*

- **Sharing attitude**

  Good team players willingly share information, knowledge and experience. They believe in learning from each other in the process. They are very communicative and comfortable talking with one another and keeping other team members in the loop with information and expertise that helps get the job done and prevents surprises.

- **Cooperative and helping nature**

  Co-operation is the act of working together to accomplish a job. Good team players have cooperative and collaborative approach towards work and believe in helping each other in case of problems. Even if they have differences with other team members on certain issues, they always figure out ways to work together to get work done. They respond to requests for assistance and take initiative to offer help.

- **Flexibility and adaptability**

  Teams often need to deal with changing conditions and often effect changes themselves. Good team players adapt to changing situations. They don't complain or get stressed out because something new is being tried or some new direction is being set. Good team player also shows flexibility in considering different viewpoints and even compromising when needed. They are firm in their thoughts, yet open to what others have to offer.

- **Commitment to the team**

  Good team players are highly committed individuals to the team goals and processes. They care about what the team expects and contribute to its success without needing a push. Committed team players look beyond their own work and care about the team's overall success. Winning instinct as a team is one of the great motivators for a good team player.

- **A Problem-solver**

  Teams deal with problems. Good team players are willing to deal with problems with a view to solve them. They are problem-solvers, not problem-dwellers, problem-blamers or problem-avoiders. They don't simply rehash a problem or look for others to blame or avoid dealing with them. Team players get problems out in the open for discussion and then collaborate with others to find the solutions.

- **Respect and support to others**
  Good team players treat fellow team members with respect and courtesy. They show understanding and seek or lend appropriate support to others. Their support to other team members is unconditional. In a nutshell, effective team players deal with other people in a professional manner.

DEALING WITH DIFFERENT TYPE OF PEOPLE IN TEAMS

Not only in teams but when you get employed in the organisation you will come across different types of people and you may have to adjust your approach of dealing with them.

- **A dictator**
  A dictator bullies and intimidates others. He is blunt and can go to the extent of insulting others. *Never antagonise such people more by countering. Allow them to finish and then say, 'I can see this is a big problem for you. Let's see what we can do to solve it!' If it doesn't work ask them to leave by saying, 'I can't listen to you when you are using that tone of voice Mr...'. Say their name loudly. It helps.*

- **The know-it-all**
  These people consider themselves as experts on everything. They can be arrogant and they have an opinion on every issue. When they're proved wrong, they become very defensive or try to counter attack.
  Acknowledge their accomplishments and suggest a common ground for you both to work together. For example: 'Your idea is very good and it very much relates to with my systems and expertise, we could make a difference!' Let them get a feeling that great minds think alike!

- **The YES people**
  They agree with anything, promise any deadline and yet rarely deliver. While they are always sorry for failures, you cannot trust them to do what they say.
  The challenge is to make YES people keep their word and deliver. Tie their promise to a sense of personal integrity: 'Do I have your word on this?' 'Can we minute it?'

- **The passives**
  These people are sort of disinterested in everything that happens around them. They present blank faces, dead expressions and weak handshakes. Avoiding conflict and controversy at all costs being their motto, they never offer ideas or opinions.
  Set a system of recognising and rewarding people who voice their opinions and take initiative. The passives may notice and take action. Sometimes these people may share their opinions and comments in a private setting.

- **The NO people**
  These people are both negative and pessimistic. They are quick to point out why something won't work. They are inflexible and do not like change.
  Do change management in small pieces and prove its worth to them. Never use negative communication to them—keep it positive.

- **The complainants**

  The complainants are of the opinion that nothing ever goes their way and would complain about everything happening around them. They might be right at times but their negativity can turn people off.

  Patiently listen to their complaint. Do not allow them to reinforce their thinking about a situation. Have them examine the other person's behaviour and motivations to understand their position better.

- **Angry people**

  A person gets angry when things are not going in his way. Some people get disappointed or frustrated while some would get angry. Angry people cannot see the things in wider perspective because even a slightest mismatch could make them lose their temper.

  'If you are patient in one moment of anger, you will escape a hundred days of sorrow'—Old Chinese proverb. When faced with angry person, stay calm and focused on the situation and the outcome you want. Don't get distracted by the other person's anger. Patient hearing is the best medicine for cooling the angry person down.

Happy people make happy teams and happy teams get great results for organisations.

Managing Conflicts

17

Life is full of conflicts and compromises. Right from which dress to wear for party, who should cook in the hostel room, which career to choose or who should drop child to the school are some of the normal life situations where conflict could be involved. Conflicting situations are generally created when you have more than one option to choose from or when you have to deal with more than one opinion, thought and approaches. As in personal life, it is quite common to have conflict in organisations. It is nothing to be ashamed of or embarrassed about. In today's environment of competing interests and diversity of needs, managers need to have skills to resolve conflict constructively. This chapter aims to help you to better identify and understand conflict, how to resolve it and how to establish a climate of cooperation.

The fiercely competitive environment has generated increasing stress, tension and reduced the energy available to work on the mission, goals and objectives of an organisation. The performance and progress suffers as organisations become concerned with survival. Tensions and conflicts tend to build up in a climate of constraint, unrealistic expectations and inadequate resources. Some of the noticeable symptoms of existence of conflicting situations in an organisation are:

- Tensions
- No desire to communicate
- Work not done properly
- Disastrous meetings
- Anger occurs quickly and easily
- Failing productivity
- Slipping morale
- Absenteeism
- Slamming doors
- Shouting

When you join as a new member of the organisation, such conflicting situations can have a huge impact on your progress within the organisation and career. Irrespective of the nature of conflicts and the parties involved, it takes energy away from an effective leadership and management of the organisation. Let us first get our minds clear on some of the key issues related to conflicts.

- **Conflicts are unavoidable.** Conflict is often seen as negative and something to be avoided. It is not important whether or not we have conflict; it is what we do with it that makes the difference.

    There are methods and approaches to resolve conflict. They work in some situations and may not work in others. Not all conflicts could be resolved. How we respond to a conflict can determine whether it is prevented, resolved or allowed to escalate into an all-out dispute.

- **Conflicts results out of not recognising or meeting individuals' needs.** Regardless of differences in religion, race or culture, people everywhere share the same basic need for acceptance and being understood—a need unfulfilled is the root of virtually every conflict.
- **Conflict needs to be managed constructively.** Little is attained without constructive management of conflict. It is necessary to view differences of opinion as opportunities to learn rather than obstacles to overcome.
- **Conflict can be constructive or destructive.** Conflict is constructive when it results in clarification; understanding each other's needs and building cooperation and trust. It is destructive when it diverts energy, polarises groups and deepens differences. Parties take either or positions, believing theirs is the only right way and develop negative feelings towards each other
- **Conflict is neither good nor bad.** It is a part of human nature and human interaction. Conflict can provide opportunities to learn new skills, develop problem-solving abilities and infuse energy. If unresolved, conflict grows. It is, therefore, important to recognise symptoms and address conflict early.
- **Conflict contributes to the health of organisations.** Healthy organisations immediately address people differences and promote open discussions. If the conflict is not open for discussion, people discuss it in informal situations, building misinformation, positions and factions. Emotions get too high and people get entrenched in their positions if the conflict is not openly dealt with.

SOURCES OF CONFLICT

Conflicts can emerge from various sources, such as sharing material goods, principles, territory, communication, policies, process and/or personalities. We can categorise them as instrumental conflicts, conflicts of interest and personal/relational conflicts.

- Instrumental conflicts concern goals, means, priorities, procedures and structures.
- Conflicts of interest involves distribution of means such as money, time, staff and space, or factors that are important for the distribution of these means like importance, ownership, power, competence and expertise.
- Personal conflicts are about questions of identity, self-image, relationships and prejudices/biases. Relational conflicts may centre on loyalty, breach of confidence, perceptions/values, facts and feelings, simple misunderstanding, poor communication, unfulfilled expectations, lack of respect or betrayal of friendship.

Resolving is not always easy. Parties can sabotage efforts and cause conflict to escalate. It is important to identify the source of the conflict and analyse before deciding the strategy for its resolution.

LEVELS OF CONFLICT

There are a number of clues that can help us to understand the level of conflict and what to do about it. The key is early intervention before it leads to a really difficult situation.

- **Discomforts:** Nothing is said. It may be difficult to identify the problem, but things just don't feel right.

- **Incidents:** This takes the form of a minor outward clash; no real significant internal reactions take place.
- **Misunderstandings:** The parties begin to have negative images and perceptions of each other. It is still relatively easy to fix at this stage.
- **Tensions:** Negative attitudes and stances are added to negative images and perceptions. Tend to become fixed overtime and hard to resolve.
- **Crisis:** Behaviour is affected, normal functioning becomes difficult, extreme gestures are contemplated, if not executed. Here personal and social conflicts become really serious.

METHODS OF CONFLICT RESOLUTION

Table 17.1 describes the five most commonly used methods for resolving conflict and when each method is appropriate or inappropriate to use. Different situations require different methods. The usefulness of each method depends on the context, issue, goals to achieve and the relationship between parties. However, collaboration is preferred, if possible, because it results in a win–win for both or all parties.

Addressing conflict early allows the individuals involved to control the outcome and their own destiny. Negotiation offers most control over the conflict and the outcome because the parties work together to resolve the conflict. If the parties cannot work together to resolve the conflict, they may use

Table 17.1 Methods for Resolving Conflicts

Methods	Impact when used	Appropriate when	Inappropriate when
Power or compete (FIGHT)	One's power, position or strength settles the conflict. I'm okay, you're not OK.	When power comes with position of authority, this method has been agreed upon.	Losers are powerless to express themselves, their concerns.
Collaboration (FACE)	Mutual respect and agreement to work together to resolve results in I'm okay, You're OK.	Time is available; parties committed to working together as we versus the problem, not we–they.	Time, commitment and ability are not present.
Compromise or negotiation	Each party gives up something in order to meet midway, often leaving both parties dissatisfied. We are both sort of OK.	Both parties are better off with a compromise than attempting a win–lose stance.	Solution becomes so watered down that commitment by both parties is doubtful.
Denial, avoidance (FLIGHT)	People just avoid a conflict by denying its existence. I'm not okay; you're not okay.	Conflict is relatively unimportant, timing is wrong, a cooling-off period is needed.	Conflict is important and will not disappear, but will continue to build.
Accommodating, smoothing over (FREEZE)	Differences are played down and surface harmony is maintained. You're okay, I'm not okay.	When preservation of the relationship is more important at the moment.	If smoothing over leads to evading the issue when others are ready to deal with it.

Source: Participant Workbook, Workshop on Conflict Resolution, Prepared by Judy Kent & Anne Touwen, 2001, International Federation of University Women, 8, rue de l'Ancien-Port, 1201 Geneva, Switzerland.

mediation, that is, a neutral third party who helps the conflicting parties. The mediator does not resolve the conflict but guides the parties to develop their own solution(s). If mediation does not work, arbitration becomes the next option, that is, an arbitrator is appointed to decide the outcome, thus taking the decision out of the hands of the conflicting parties. If arbitration does not work, the final process for resolving the conflict is the judiciary, in which a judge or jury decides the outcome.

Some of the skills which would help you to manage conflict resolution are:

- **Assertive communication**

  We have dealt with assertiveness in the chapter on building relationships. Just to refresh, each person has the right to be treated with respect, the right to have and to express feelings, opinions and 'wants', the right to be listened to and taken seriously by others. Too often in conflict situations, these rights get ignored. Assertive communication is a result of assertive behaviour, that is, clearly expressing what you feel and saying what you want. It is self-enhancing because it shows a positive firmness. Assertive behaviour is revealed when you:

  - Allow others to complete their thoughts before you speak.
  - Stand up for the position that matches your feelings or the evidence.
  - Make your own decisions based on what you think is right.
  - Consider yourself strong and capable, but generally equal to other people.
  - Own responsibility with respect to your situation, your own and others' needs and rights.

  There are three simple steps to communicating assertively:

  1. Describe the situation or idea as clearly and specifically as you can.
  2. Express how you feel about the situation. (Note: Use 'I' or 'My' statements to refer to how you are feeling and what you are thinking.)
  3. Specify what you want. Include a specific deadline.

  For example, someone has pushed in front of you in a line for a bus. If you choose to respond assertively, the following dialogue is appropriate:

  Describe the situation: *'Excuse me. There is a line-up here of people who all want to get onto the next bus. Some of us have been waiting for over an hour.'*

  Express how you feel: *'I find it frustrating that you just push into line without concern for others and their needs to get to work on time.'*

  Specify what you want done: *'I think it is only fair that you go to the end of the line and wait your turn with the rest of us.'*

  This is just a simple example to demonstrate how to use the assertive behaviour. Now think and practise about assertive behaviours in the following cases:

  - Someone you respect has expressed an opinion with which you strongly disagree.
  - Someone in your organisation has a specific complaint that they won't let go, even though it has been dealt with several times.
  - A friend has betrayed your confidence or hurt you.

– A person in your organisation is constantly talking about another member behind her back. This is divisive and destructive to your organisation.

- **Active listening skills**
  Active listening is essential to a successful conflict resolution. We have dealt with active listening in the chapter on communication skills. Just to refresh, here are some characteristics of active listening:

  – Listening is, understanding what is said and what is not said and not just lending ears.
  – Listen for the whole message by paying attention to body language.
  – Do not prejudge because of previous history, appearance, accent or other irrelevant characteristics.
  – Do not interrupt.
  – If you disagree, do not become aggressive. Restate the speaker's comments, present your point of view and return the dialogue to the speaker by asking for a reaction to your views.

- **Negotiation and mediation skills**
  Negotiation involves discussions between two or more parties around specific issues for the purpose of reaching a mutually satisfactory agreement. The issue is not whether you negotiate, but rather how effective you are. The aim of negotiation should be win–win. Win–win negotiation is an approach to negotiating that stresses common interests and goals. By working together, parties can seek creative solutions and reach decisions in which all parties can win. Negotiation is a skill that can be improved with practice. We will deal more with negotiation skills in the next chapter.

ROLE OF MEDIATION IN CONFLICT MANAGEMENT

You could be asked to be a mediator in various types of disputes. Mediation is the intervention of an acceptable and impartial third party in a dispute. Mediation brings people together to talk about their conflict and accept responsibility for finding a solution together. Before you accept to be mediator, ensure that the following are in place:

- Voluntary participation by all parties
- Face-to-face discussions
- Each party has the same opportunity to speak, to present facts and perceptions and to be heard
- All relevant information is shared
- The agreement, having been reached jointly, is accepted by both the parties

Role of the Mediator

- An expert, who helps people to resolve a conflicting situation
- Listens to all opinions during the dispute
- Helps to clarify parties' statements and positions
- Is impartial and unbiased
- Does not have any decision-making responsibility

- Helps each party understand the issue and the other parties' perspective
- Does not blame anyone, is neutral and objective
- Does not present his/her personal opinion
- Compiles all information in a way that leads to possible success
- Writes a mutually acceptable agreement that is specific to the issues to be resolved

Skills Required for a Mediator

- Active listening: using both verbal and non-verbal behaviours to express your attention to what is being said and showing that you understand the content.
- Looking for facts: Once both parties have described the situation, ask open- ended questions that do not contain any judgement or criticism.
- Identification of controversial points: state the obvious points of controversy and describe under-lying emotions or possible interpretations to both the parties. It is often difficult for conflicting parties to say these points.
- Be able to reframe and rephrase controversial points in such a way that the tension and blaming are reduced.
- Facilitate agreement by assisting parties in identifying solutions to controversial points and pri-oritise for action.

Table 17.2   The Mediation Process

Steps in Mediation	Key Points for Implementing the Step
1. Preparation	Basic rules of communication: • Only one person speaks at a time; others are quiet and they listen. • If the parties argue, abuse or beat each other, the mediator has the responsibility to stop them—the mediator protects all parties. • Confidentiality: What transpires during mediation is confidential and not to be spoken with others unless both parties agree to do so. Separate meetings: • When the mediator decides or one party requests, it is possible to have separate meetings with each party.
2. Reconstruction of the conflict	Task of the mediator: • Agree on sequence of parties speaking (according to the parties' wishes). • Listen actively to the telling of their story. • Write down complaints, questions and positive statements about the parties. • Clarify what each party wants to achieve (that is, what are the interests and needs). Procedure: • Every party takes a turn in describing briefly the conflict. • Mediator briefly summarises the main points, by framing the conflict in a neutral manner.

(Table 17.2 Contd)

(Table 17.2 Contd)

Steps in Mediation	Key Points for Implementing the Step
	• Mediator checks to ensure the main points have been correctly understood (test the reality). • If the conflict has more than one problem, write them. Propose the order in which the problems should be discussed. • Name the positive points of the mediation, for example (willingness to cooperate, attendance at the meeting and commitment to a common cause). • Name the emotional problems (anger, disappointment and distrust). Be honest and frame comments with no biases.
3. Definition of points of dispute and agreement	Objectives: • To look at each other as human beings. • Move from focus on the past to focus on the future. • Work on understanding the other's position. • Move from personal attacks to resolving a common problem. Techniques for the mediator: • Paraphrase—tell the essence of the story in your own words. • Appreciate—the feelings of each party and their willingness to resolve the dispute. • Reframe demands and requirements into neutral language. • Summarise—provide a synopsis of points made and agreements to date. Tips on procedure: • If necessary, take a break. • Verify with the parties whether their understanding of the dispute agrees with your framing of the dispute. • Propose to resolve the easiest and most 'neutral' dispute point.
4. Creating acceptable options for agreement	Steps: • Start with the simplest problems and facts. • Brainstorm potential solutions or options (without evaluation). • If necessary, establish objective criteria with all parties in order to evaluate options for solutions. • Define the importance of these criteria in order to select the best options. Tips for the mediator: • Make sure participants cover all parts of the problem. • Encourage all parties to create solutions. • Ensure parties to participate equally in the number of proposals developed. • Build linkages among different proposals. • Verify which solutions suit both parties. • Let the parties chose solutions that suit them. • Guide the parties to choose one solution. • Fine tune the proposed solutions together.
5. Forming an agreement	Agreement should be SMART: • Specific (concrete) • Measurable

(Table 17.2 Contd)

(Table 17.2 Contd)

Steps in Mediation	Key Points for Implementing the Step
	• Attainable (feasible) • Realistic • Timely Procedure for an Agreement: • Write the proposal in neutral language and read it aloud. • Record individual points on the draft agreement separately. • Avoid general or vague points. • Describe concrete behaviours, activities and timelines that parties are supposed to perform. • Avoid getting trapped in 'legalese' or 'lawyer-speak'. • Have both parties sign the agreement. Closing the meeting when agreement is reached: • Praise participants of the parties on this meeting. • Designate deadline for another meeting with the parties, if necessary. • Summarise the progress, result and any next steps. • Adjourn the meeting. In case of no agreement: • Positively summarise what was achieved and what occurred. • Identify remaining difficulties and options. • Agree upon next steps, if any and your openness to continued involvement. • Praise participants for their participation.

Source: Participant Workbook, Workshop on Conflict Resolution, Prepared by Judy Kent & Anne Touwen, 2001, International Federation of University Women, 8, rue de l'Ancien-Port, 1201 Geneva, Switzerland.

Effective Negotiation Skills

18

Negotiation involves discussions between two or more parties around specific issues for the purpose of reaching a mutually satisfactory agreement. Everyone is a negotiator. It is an everyday occurrence. Life is an endless series of interactions that require negotiation. This is a skill which you need to use probably many more times than you realise. How many times have you been in one or more of the following situations?

- Negotiating a two-wheeler or an expensive cell phone with your parents
- Negotiating your package with the prospective employer
- Negotiating rent of your accommodation
- Trying to close a sale deal with a customer or purchase deal with a supplier
- Trying to get approval for extensions on your work deadline
- First access to the shower in the hostel
- Compliances with rules and regulations
- Negotiating terms from a supplier

The stakes may be different in each case, but the common thread running through them is the need for negotiation skills. Negotiating is an activity that all managers engage in to some degree day in and day out. Negotiation can take place anywhere, formally or informally. Sometimes it can take place abruptly, when you are least prepared and be concluded in a matter of seconds. The issue is not whether you negotiate, but rather how effective you are as a negotiator. It is definitely a skill worth learning. This skill is also applicable to conflict management as discussed in the earlier chapter. Even if you feel you already have the negotiation skills, there are always ways to develop and continuously improve them. This chapter aims to give you some tips for becoming a more efficient negotiator.

WHAT NEGOTIATION MEANS

Most people think of negotiation only when people sit at a table and hold intense discussions in some formal way. Negotiation has also been considered as talking tough and seeing how much you can get. This is a negative attitude to negotiation. Successful negotiators do not try to 'win at all costs'. Win–win negotiation is an approach to negotiating that stresses on common interests and goals. By working together parties can seek creative solutions and reach decisions in which all parties can win.

It is important to note that the formal type of negotiation is often an exception, not the rule. Most negotiations you participate in will involve day-to-day operations of your business and will focus more on building long-term relationships than on making a deal. You need to increase your awareness of what you are doing and learn to use both your intellect as well as your intuition during the negotiation process.

THE GOAL OF NEGOTIATION

The purpose of all businesses is to remain in business and grow. In order to achieve that you need to establish good relationships with other businesses. This means acting with fairness and integrity. The 'Principle of Negotiation' should therefore be the foundation for all business negotiations. Some of the characteristics of good negotiations are:

- Win/win
- No tears
- No arguments
- No fisty cuffs
- No sulking

APPROACH TO PROFESSIONAL NEGOTIATION

The best approach to negotiate is to be cooperative and look for areas of agreement that can benefit both sides. Of course, it is important to protect your own interests in such a way that you feel satisfied with the outcome of the negotiation. Good negotiators are the people who understand how to build key relationships, how to identify what people need, how to give them what they need and how to get what they want in return, all in a way that seems effortless. Do not view negotiation as only competitive endeavour to make a killing in order to emerge the 'winner'.

Negotiation should therefore be viewed as a relationship building process with your company colleagues, with customers, suppliers and others. In this sense, negotiations never really end. One piece of negotiation is often the beginning of the next phase of negotiation. It is critical to understand that negotiating is not following a pre-packaged set of principles and applying them to all situations. That might work if everyone could be counted on to behave rationally and predictably, but people always don't. To negotiate well, you must be prepared to use a variety of approaches. Negotiation, like most other skills, gets easier with time. With practice, you develop your own personal style and become comfortable with your own limits. As in so many other things in life, experience is the best teacher when it comes to effective negotiations.

Even though we talk of win/win outcome in business negotiations, usually the feeling is that one side gains more than the other. This may be true, but the challenge for a good negotiator is to work towards a fair and balanced resolution for both the parties. It often makes good strategic sense to make some concessions now for a gain later. For example, a discount now to a customer might help in retaining the customer or the client. One of your key aims in business should be to retain customers because they have a 'lifetime value' beyond the immediate sale. A deal that leaves the other party feeling that they have been fairly treated, promotes positive word of mouth that helps generate a future business.

Many business people fear being seen as a 'soft touch' or a 'pushover' in negotiation situations not involving customer or clients, such as unions or suppliers or foreign collaborators. Sometimes it is necessary to be very firm, particularly if you sense the other party is not interested in cooperative negotiation. People do respect a fair but firm negotiator.

Negotiators should have a long-term and sustainable outlook. For example, in driving a very hard bargain, you may gain temporary financial advantage for your business, but you may also lose a customer or supplier.

THE NEGOTIATION PROCESS AND TECHNIQUES

Do Your Homework

Information is the first power source of the negotiation. The more thorough your preparation, the stronger your negotiating position. Trying to negotiate from a position of ignorance or lack of comprehension of the real issues is a recipe for failure.

Work Out Your BATNA

Always start by working out your 'Best Alternative to a Negotiated Agreement' or BATNA. This allows you to walk away from the negotiations if you cannot achieve at least this, minimum acceptable, outcome through the negotiation process.

Work Out Stakeholders' Interests

Make sure you've considered all the stakeholders of the issue in the negotiation process. These may not all be obvious at first. Try to identify and list the interests of the stakeholders and how these might affect the outcome. Knowing the real interests of the important stakeholders allows you to stress the benefits of the deal for them. Try to work out their BATNA as well. The balance of power often depends on the relative strengths of each party's BATNA.

Separate the Position from the Person

Watch out for the issue of becoming too closely involved with the person or the person's ego. Emotionally charged issues can be the hardest to resolve. If possible, try to separate such issues from the person. A simple example of an emotionally charged issue is an employee coming to you for a salary raise. An outright rejection of the issue might lead the employee to interpret this as a rejection of his or her personal worth.

Listen Carefully for Real Interests

Good negotiators listen more than they speak. The more carefully you listen, the more you learn about the other party's real interests. The negotiator, who fully understands what the other party really wants (different from what they say they want), gains an advantage in the negotiation process. Find the issue which really gives the other party sleepless nights. It may not always be the price. It could be the quality, delivery, timeliness of service or some other factors which could be the real points to put forward in the negotiation.

Anticipate Demands

Put yourself in the other person's shoes to anticipate what they might demand and prepare appropriate responses in advance. For example, your subordinate walks into your office to ask for a pay rise. A flat 'No' is likely to affect his or her morale. However, with prior anticipation, your response could be: 'Yes, let's look at that'. 'Why don't you prepare a one-page review of your achievements and contribution to the business so far? We can meet on Friday to discuss it.' At the Friday meeting, you might then set some objectives: 'I agree you've made a positive contribution. Here are the goals we need to reach for me to grant/recommend to management a raise for you'. You could then list the targets as well as training or skills to be acquired by your subordinate. The subordinate has had a fair hearing and now knows exactly what he/she needs to do to get the raise. Using 'US' and 'WE' encourages cooperative approach and avoid 'YOU' versus 'ME' confrontation which sets one against another.

Breaking a Deadlock: Find Common Ground

Identify and resolve some easier issues first. If negotiations have ground to a halt over the major issue (such as the final price or some issue that is highly emotionally charged), you might look at the minor issues and get agreement first.

You might say, 'Well, let's leave that question aside for the moment and deal with some other issues. Would early October delivery suit you?'

Your tactic here is to gain agreement on some smaller issues to build rapport with the other party. By demonstrating a spirit of friendly negotiation, you make the other party feel: 'Well, this person is not so difficult after all'. You can now move back to the main sticking point in a far more cooperative atmosphere: 'It seems we have been able to resolve these other issues without too many difficulties. Let's have another look at the price issue'. Often by agreeing on one issue many other issues just fall into place.

An alternative is to say, 'Look, we have had our differences over this issue. But let's put that behind us and think positively. How do you think we can now move forward?' If the other party comes up with something constructive, nurture the constructive suggestion to build rapport. If the negotiation really seems to be broken down and if there's a real personality conflict then using a mediator could be the way forward.

Sometimes simply ask the question, 'What would it take from me for the deal to work for you?' You may be pleasantly surprised at how reasonable the demands are and how easily you can meet them.

Use Visuals

Communication is often easier if there is something visual for people to see. Particularly in technical negotiations, diagrams on a whiteboard, charts and documents provide common understanding, facilitating the negotiations.

Concede to 'Get'

The negotiating parties often like to end up with the satisfaction of winning an advantage over other. A concession can often close the sale or clinch agreement. For example, if the other party wants an unrealistic discount and you are determined to keep your margins, you could say: 'Our margins on this product/service are so tight that we really don't have room to go further. However, I can offer you an extended warranty/free home delivery/bundle in some extra features.' Negotiation is often about trading concessions and it is good customer relations approach to offer a something in return for one made by the customer: 'I really appreciate your willingness to wait an extra week for the delivery and in return we'd like to offer free delivery'.

Know When to Keep Silent

There are times in most negotiations where it pays to keep silent. When the other party becomes angry or emotionally upset, this tactic helps to modify their approach. Avoid becoming emotionally involved. Becoming angry or upset in negotiations is a sure road to deadlock or failure because you tend to focus on the individual rather than the issues. Try instead to focus on the real issues and to be as rational as possible.

Look Past the Personality

You might find the other party personally offensive or objectionable, but the issues are what really matter. Successful negotiators look past the person to identify the core of the problem.

CHARACTERISTICS OF SUCCESSFUL NEGOTIATORS

People get better at negotiation with practice. Successful negotiators

- Are facilitators not blockers.
- Do their homework on the issues.
- Work out their BATNA and the other party's likely BATNA.
- Have strong people skills.
- Listen more than they speak.
- Can interpret the real issues that concern the other parties (not necessarily the surface positions).
- Can 'read' body language as an aid to interpreting true positions.
- Are firm but fair.
- Look to build long-term relationships, not force confrontations.
- Look for options or ways to build mutual gain.
- Look for common ground on minor issues to build rapport that will help with the major issues.
- Are willing to trade concessions.
- Use objective criteria (facts and figures) to support a rational argument.
- Avoid getting into slanging matches.
- Can look past the personality in favour of the actual issue.
- Think laterally and realise there's always another way.

FACTORS INFLUENCING SUCCESS OF NEGOTIATIONS

The factors influencing the success of negotiations are:

- Pacing: fast or slow?
- Formality: high or low?
- Oral or written agreements: which are more binding and inclusive?
- Bluntness of communication: direct or indirect?
- Time frame of the outcome: short term or long term?
- Who negotiates: equals or most competent?

Creative Problem-solving

19

Do you see yourself as a problem-solver? May or may not be. But in reality we are constantly solving problems. And the better we are at it, the easier our lives will be. Problems arise in many shapes and forms. They can be simple or complex problems, for example:

- Your friends suddenly drop in for dinner tonight without warning.
- Traffic jam on your normal route forces you to take an alternate route.
- You need to fix a project that is running behind schedule.
- You are not happy about the current job, so what is to be done?
- You have scored II-class in graduate examination and you are looking for a good job.

Everyday, you will be faced with at least one problem to solve. It actually gets easier when you realise that there is nothing 'scary' about them. It is just about making a decision or choice. No matter what job you are in, where you live, who your partner is, how many friends you have; you will be judged on your ability to solve problems. So the more problems you can solve, the happier people are with you.

WHAT IS A PROBLEM?

A problem is the difference between the actual state and the desired state. Clarity of the problem is determined by the clarity of the knowledge of what precisely one wants and what one has. Greater clarity of the problem helps in finding a better and effective solution. My simple definition of problem is:

> What it should be ≠ (is not e qual to) what it is

Problem could be about a situation, a method, time, place or person. If we extend the above definition of a problem, it would be like this:

> Where it should be ≠ (is not equal to) where it is
> When it should be ≠ (is not equal to) when it is
> How it should be ≠ (is not equal to) how it is
> How the person should be ≠ (is not equal to) how the person is
> Who should be doing it ≠ (is not equal to) who does it

A problem is actually an opportunity for improvement. Somebody coined the word 'probortunity'— an acronym combining the words 'problem' and 'opportunity'. A probortunity is a reminder to look at problems as possible opportunities for improvement. Whenever you face a problem try seeking answers for the questions such as:

- Is there more than one probortunity?
- Is it my personal probortunity? Is it the organisation's probortunity?
- Is it an actual probortunity or just an annoyance?
- Is this the real probortunity or merely a symptom of a larger one?

A problem also could be a result of recognition of a present imperfect situation and the belief in the possibility of its being better. The belief that hopes can be achieved gives one the will to strive hard for them. Hopes challenge one's potential, and challenge is another definition of a probortunity.

CREATIVE APPROACH TO PROBLEM-SOLVING

- **Focus on the solution—not the problem**
  It has been proved that your brain cannot find solutions if you focus on the problem. This is because when you focus on the problem you're effectively feeding 'negativity' which in turn activates negative emotions in the brain. These emotions block potential solutions. That does not mean you should ignore the problem. First, acknowledge the problem and then move to a solution-oriented mindset where you focus on the 'solution' instead of lingering on 'what went wrong' and 'whose fault it is'.
- **Have an open mind**
  Try and consider all possible solutions even if they seem ridiculous at first. It's important for you to keep an open mind to boost creative thinking, which can trigger potential solutions. Creative thinking is the foundation for most problem-solving techniques. No idea is a bad idea! Never ridicule yourself for coming up with 'stupid solutions' as it's often the crazy ideas that trigger other more viable solutions.
- **View problems neutrally**
  Try not to view problems as 'scary' things! A problem is really just a perception of your current situation. All a problem is telling you is that something is not currently working and that you need to find a new way around it. So, try and approach problems neutrally without any judgement. Any judgemental or biased approach may hamper potential solutions from popping up!
- **Think laterally**
  'Lateral thinking' is coming at a problem from a different (perhaps non-standard) direction. It is also described as 'Out-of-box thinking'. Try to change your approach and look at things in a new perspective. You try flipping your objective around and looking for solution that may be polar opposite! Even if it feels silly, a fresh and unique approach usually stimulates a fresh solution.
- **Use language that creates possibility**
  Lead your thinking with phrases like 'what if …' and 'imagine if …'. These terms open up our brains to think creatively and encourage unique solutions. Avoid closed, negative language such as 'I don't think …' or 'This is not right but …'.
- **Simplify things**
  As human beings we have a tendency to make things more complicated than they need to be! Try simplifying your problem by generalising it. Remove all the detail and go back to the basics. Try

looking for a really easy, obvious solution—you might be surprised at the results! And we all know that it's often the simple things that are the most productive.

CREATIVE PROBLEM-SOLVING PROCESS

- **Identifying the problem**

  The first step in the creative problem-solving process is assessing the situation to identify the problem. That sounds simple enough, but sometimes you might be uncertain about what the problem is; there might just be a feeling of general anxiety or confusion about what is getting in the way of your objectives. More often than not we end up dealing with symptoms and not the problem. Remember, well-defined problem is half the solution!

- **Exploring the problem**

  Having identified the problem, you should analyse it to see what the root cause is. Often people get caught up in symptoms or effects of a problem and never get down to the real cause. They get mad at someone's attitude, anger or actions, which are not the cause of the problem. The key here is to focus on analysing the problem for the real cause without being affected by the emotional issues. Seeing answers for questions such as the following will help explore the problem:

  Ask who?

  – Who says that this is a problem?
  – Who caused or is causing the problem?
  – Whom does it or will it affect?
  – Who has done something about the problem?

  Ask what?

  – What happened or will happen?
  – What are the symptoms?
  – What are the consequences for others?
  – What circumstances surround the occurrence of the problem?
  – What is not functioning as desired?

  Ask when?

  – Did it or will it happen?
  – Why did it happen?
  – When did it first occur?
  – Will it happen again?

  Ask where?

  – Where is the problem occurring?
  – Did it or will it have an impact?
  – Where did it have an impact?

Ask why?

- Why is this a problem?
- Did it or will it occur?
- Why did it occur?
- Why was nothing done to prevent the problem from occurring?
- Why did no one recognise and do something about the problem at the earliest?
- Why is a response needed now?

Ask how?

- How should the process be working?
- How are others dealing with this or similar problems?
- How do you know this is a problem; what supporting information do you have?

Once the cause is found, plans can be made to fix it. Analysing the replies to above questions should lead you to the root cause of the problem. If there is not enough information, you should figure out how to research and collect it. At times you may have to simulate the problem situation to get the data and analyse it.

- **Set goals**

  Having explored and analysed the problem, the next step is to write a goal statement that focuses on the desired state of the process. Making and writing down a goal statement helps to clarify the focus and provides direction to solving the problem.

  The desired state is what should occur as a result of the solution. This whole process is about closing the gap between the current situation or the problem and the goal. Writing down the problem ensures common understanding of the problem amongst the problem-solving team.

- **Look at alternatives**

  Now that the problem has been analysed, the development of possible solutions could begin. This is a creative as well as practical step where every possible solution is identified. The idea is to develop as many alternative solutions as possible.

- **Select the best solution**

  With wide variety of possible solutions available, it is time to select the best solution to fix the problem, given the circumstances, resources and other considerations. Here the managers try to figure out exactly what would work best given the nature of the problem. There are always a number of things that can affect a solution such as money, time, people, procedures, policies, rules and so on. All of these factors must be thought about. Managers should prioritise the solutions by their effectiveness. This is a process of elimination. Eventually, managers should narrow down the choices to one best possible solution which will promise the best or optimal outcomes.

- **Implementation**

  Implementation is a crucial part of problem-solving process. Managers must have an action plan to implement the solution and communicate it to those directly and indirectly affected. Communication is most effective when it precedes action and events. Managers who implement the solution should have answers to the following type of questions:

  - What should be communicated?
  - What is the reason for the decision?

- Whom will it affect and how?
- What are the benefits expected for the individual, the department and the organisation?
- What adjustments will be required in terms of how work will be done?
- What, specifically, is each individual's role in implementing the decision?
- What results are expected from each individual?
- When does the action called for by the decision go into effect?

Transparency in communication helps overcome any resistance to implementation that otherwise might be encountered.

- **Evaluation**

This is the final step in the problem-solving process. Managers should review the effectiveness of the solution against the desired outcomes. Did the solution work? If not, why not? What went right and what went wrong? What adjustments do they have to make to ensure that the solution works better? This stage requires careful analysis that improves upon the best solution.

The review of your progress can help a manager identify any problem. Steps may need to be revised or new steps added. One may need to consider a different solution, if the current one, he/she has been working with, is not helping.

PROBLEM-SOLVING TOOLS AND TECHNIQUES

William G. Huitt lists out the following problem-solving techniques, which focus more on logic and critical thinking, especially within the context of applying the scientific approach:

- **Means–ends analysis**

In means–ends analysis, the problem-solver compares the present situation with the goal, detects a difference between them and then searches memory for actions that are likely to reduce the difference.

- **Backward planning**

The strategy of working backwards entails starting with the end results and reversing the steps you need to get those results, in order to figure out the answer to the problem.

- **Categorising/classifying**

It is the process of grouping objects or events together on the basis of a logical rationale. There are two kinds of categorising: grouping and classifying. Grouping is putting together objects on the basis of a single property. Files might be grouped on the basis of 'urgent' and 'not urgent'. Grouping is useful in revealing similarities and differences that otherwise might go unnoticed. Classifying involves putting items together on the basis of more than a single property at a time.

- **Challenging assumptions**

It involves the direct confrontation of ideas, opinions or attitudes that have previously been taken for granted. Why it did not work last time ...? The purpose is to identify the fallacies, consistencies and inconsistencies in the problem-solving process.

- **Evaluating/judging**

It involves the comparison with a standard and making a qualitative or quantitative judgement of value or worth. Good evaluations of problem-solving are generally based on multiple sources of assessment information.

- **Inductive/deductive reasoning**

  Reasoning is the systematic and logical development of rules or concepts from specific instances or the identification of cases based on a general principle or proposition using generalisation and inference.

- **Thinking aloud**

  It is the process of verbalising about a problem and its solution while a partner listens in detail for errors in thinking or understanding.

- **Network analysis**

  It is a systems approach to project planning and management where relationships among activities, events, resources and timelines are developed and charted. Specific examples include Program Evaluation and Review Technique (Plus-Minus-Interesting [PMI]) and Critical Path Method (CPM).

- **Plus–Minus–Interesting (PMI)**

  It involves considering the positive, negative and interesting or thought-provoking aspects of an idea or an alternative using a balance sheet grid where plus and minus refer to criteria identified in the second step of the problem-solving process.

- **Task analysis**

  It is the consideration of skills and knowledge required to learn or perform a specific task.

In addition to the above, you are advised to learn and practise the following tools to help you analyse the data and finding solutions to the problems:

- Cause-and-effect diagram
- Pareto chart
- Flow charts
- Histogram
- Check sheet
- Scatter diagram
- Brainstorming

You will find these tools described in any book of total quality management.

Some of the constraints and barriers to creative problem-solving are:

- **Resistance to change**

  People are often reluctant to change from the time-honoured way of doing things. Resistance to change can prevent people from taking chances and from considering new possibilities.

- **Habits**

  Old habits die hard, as they say! Habits limit our vision of what can be accomplished and may stand in the way of solving a problem. Habits may go undetected by an individual and may be a tremendous deterrent to correcting a problem. For example, receptionist who is having difficulty in completing his or her work may be unaware that the habit of taking personal calls is taking the bulk of work time.

- **Individual insecurity**

  Individual insecurity may deter individuals from taking risks or from pursuing behaviours that may require them to take a stand. Individual insecurity may come from past experiences or from an overall lack of self-confidence or fear of failure.

- **Past history**

  Knowing what happened before, what worked and did not work, can inhibit an individual's desire to try new methods of problem-solving or decision-making. Past history is frequently an excuse for not making changes. The individual, who may not wish to approach a situation in a new way, may remind others that a similar idea failed in the past.

- **Fear of failure**

  The fear of failure may be unreasonable, but it greatly deters the confrontation of problems. The unknown can be a frightening thing. When something new is attempted, the possibility exists that it may work well or not at all. In either instance, changes may occur. While some people thrive on recognition, others shy away from it. These fears may cause people to avoid the possibility of success or failure altogether.

- **Jumping to conclusions**

  When problems must be solved and decisions made, it is easy to jump to conclusions. When someone jumps to conclusions, assumptions are made about what might or might not work and the possible results; assumptions may frequently take on negative perspectives.

- **Perceptions**

  As we have stated, perceptions are the ways that we see things based on our experiences. We may be unable to see something from another perspective because we are so blinded by our own perception.

20 Power and Politics in Organisations

People generally do not like the words, power and politics but enjoy using them when opportunities arise. The presence of politics in organisations, big or small, is a universal phenomenon. Power may be at times a necessary evil to be exercised in matters of emergency and crisis. As long as both power and politics are fairly played and exercised, they do not create any nuisance value. Both power and politics are considered as necessary evils for the 'normal' functioning of companies. Both are used to influence thoughts, feelings and behaviour of other persons. If power is used to influence others' behaviour in a formal setting, it means one has the authority or right to do so. However, if the power is used to influence others' behaviour in an informal setting it could be politics. Therefore, while dealing with the power and organisational politics, we need to understand both as influencing mechanisms.

Power is inter-personal (or inter-group) relationship in which one individual (or group) can cause another individual (or group) to take an action that he would not otherwise take. It involves changing the behaviour of other person. Person A has power over person B if B believes A can force B to comply. Some of the symbols of having power are:

- Ability to get placements for favoured employees
- Exceeding budget limitations
- Procuring above average raises for the employees
- Getting items on the agenda at meetings
- Access to early information
- Having top managers seek out their opinion
- Control of critical resources

Some signs of powerless behaviour of managers are as follows:

- Overly close supervision
- Inflexible adherence to rules
- Tendency to do the job themselves instead of delegating and developing others
- Staff resistance to change
- Seeking protective turf
- Focus on budget cuts, punishment and top-down communication

Some signs of powerless behaviour of staff are as follows:

- React passively
- Overdependent on boss
- Blaming others

- Kissing up
- Passing the buck
- Covering your rear
- Creating conflict
- Building clicks
- Scheming

Politics is about those activities taken within organisations to acquire, develop and use power and other resources to obtain one's preferred outcome in a situation where there is uncertainty of outcome. Power is a force or store of political influence through which events can be affected. Although, power is closely related to leadership and authority, people in the organisations derive power from different sources.

Reward power
Influence based on the ability to reward (money can be a source of power).

Coercive power (punishment power)
Influence based on the ability to punish (might makes right!).

Legitimate power (authority)
Influence based on the legitimate right of someone to influence others (often embedded in position, always complex).

Referent power (charisma)
Influence by example, peer pressure power (I want to be like him…! A role model).

Expert power
Influence based on the ability to convince others to follow your good advice.

Information power
Possessing more information than others give power.

Connection power
Nearness to the top management gives power (nearness to Sun!).

THE NATURE OF POLITICS IN ORGANISATIONS

Politics is aimed at changing the way people see your performance and behaviour in the context of the formal and informal power system. Some examples of politics are:

- Making sure that people know that you came early to office today.
- Informing your boss about fight between you and your colleague or two of your colleagues.
- Telling you about the firing your colleague got from your boss.

Political environment in an organisation could range from fairly straightforward and relatively simple to incredibly complex and ruthless. The extent and gravity of political environment would depend upon:

- **Size of the organisation**
  Generally, larger the organisation, the more extensive is the political environment. You will find more gossip, grapevine communication and groupism.
- **History of the company**
  Politics is one of the indications of the culture of the organisation. Once it gets stuck, it remains there as inseparable element of its culture.
- **Extent of the formal power system**
  In an organisation, where formal systems and structures are missing, informal systems take over their management styles and the decision-making processes. Politics prospers more in informal situations. Clearly defined roles, structures, policies and procedures, to some extent, limit the informal environment and therefore the politics.
- **Character of the top boss**
  Is the top boss very hands-on or more 'strategic' or detached? Does he tolerate some of the most destructive political techniques such as bad mouthing or the setting up of internal competitions? Or does the boss turn a blind eye to politics and simply claim 'it doesn't go on here'?
- **The concentration of power players**
  Power players are skilled at playing their own games. They lay traps and exploit the political moves of others. A large concentration of them usually means a more politically dangerous and a destructive environment.
- **The level in the company**
  As people climb up the hierarchy, two things happen: it becomes harder to accurately measure their effectiveness and performance in their jobs and there are more people targeting them for political manoeuvring. As a general rule, higher level in the company means more political risk.

There is often a temptation to view informal power systems in a strictly negative sense, but doing so ignores the fact that they exist as part of a disciplinary system to regulate employee behaviour. Informal systems help to get the organisation to agree to decisions and to get people working towards common goals, which is not practical if relied fully on the formal power systems.

For organisations, informal systems are necessary and so the politics, which is nurtured by the informal power system. It is next to impossible to get rid of the politics in organisations. Politics works in the environment of opinion, perception, ambiguity and opportunism. Politics is a wilful attempt to bend perception for an individual's own purposes. If someone tells you their organisation has no politics, they are simply ignorant.

RESPONSES TO THE POLITICAL ENVIRONMENT

If we accept that politics is present in virtually every organisation, the question is no longer politics 'yes' or 'no', it really is how a person responds to it. Researchers have noted three different reactions to corporate politics.

Avoiders

These are people who either don't grasp the organisational politics or hate dealing with it in a passionate way. They say, 'I hate politics so much, that maybe if I just pretend it doesn't exist and it will go away.

I should just put my head down and work hard and maybe it won't impact me'. These people never seem to understand the game or its rules. Remember, if you want to win, you have to at least learn the rules.

To reach a higher level in the company, you will undoubtedly have to bend those rules to serve your purposes. If you are not one of these people, you should probably resign to working only on the bottom rungs of the corporate ladder. If you start climbing while ignoring the political environment, you're probably going to fall off the ladder. When that happens, you will either be fired or if you are a good worker, you will be pigeonholed. Ambition to climb and political avoidance don't mix well. If you are looking for both, shift to a smaller company or start/buy your own.

Neutrals

Neutrals generally see and understand the political realities and over time become used to navigating through them. Being generally ethical, they lack the ability to lay out politics of their own.

Neutrals often find politics distasteful and the political behaviours of others unfair. Therefore, they often ignore it until they have already sustained some damage. But some of them could be very effective power players in their own way.

Anyone who wants to climb the corporate ladder needs to become at least a competent neutral and the sooner the better. Even if it is distasteful, neutrals need to keep company politics at the back of their minds. Without constant vigilance, they are just as likely to become a victim as an avoider.

Power Players

Power players attempt to manipulate the political environment to their own or someone else's advantage. They are the ones who lay traps and drop additional mines for the rest of the company to trip over. There are two types of power players who have widely varying approaches to manipulation of the political environment.

Street Fighters

These power players are the political terrorists of the company. They tend to be overt with their tactics, but can deposit some pretty powerful ammunition targeted at specific individuals or small groups. Over time, street fighters make a lot of enemies and there is often quiet cheering if they have their own tactics boomeranged. You should never underestimate a street fighter as they can be perceptive, adept and ruthless.

Manoeuvrers

Manoeuvrers are the top-class politicians. They are the top explosives experts. They have the most advanced weapons making and disguising skills and like to use them covertly. Unlike street fighters, manoeuvrers often have extensive networks of allies they can tap in to work their political manipulations. A significant concentration of manoeuvrers exists at the top levels of large corporations.

Manoeuvrers are usually strategic in their actions and tend to see politics more as a game they play to win. You might personally offend a manoeuvrer and suffer no consequences, if taking you on is not in his best interests. In other cases a skilled manoeuvrer can make your chances of long-term organisational survival slim.

Whether an avoider, neutral or power player, you will feel impact of the corporate political environment. You may govern yourself by your personal sense of right and wrong, but ignorance of the organisational politics will never work in your favour. Some of the skills you need to develop to sail through the organisational politics are as follows:

1. **Understand people.** It is critical to understand who are the allies and enemies. You should build connections with as many groups as possible without giving them the impression that you fall into their camp exclusively. You must learn the positions the power players have staked out for themselves on important issues before you start expressing loud opinions. When in doubt, keep your mouth shut.

2. **Think through your relationships.** Maintain relationships unless the stakes are very high. If you do, make sure you know your exposures. Sometimes you're forced to take sides in a dispute, but usually there are ways of doing this tactfully without offending others. When you can't, make sure you know who you are taking on and how they might come back at you. Anticipating the counter-attack might give you time to prepare defences.

3. **Understand the value criteria (results, loyalty, sacrifice or whatever) and its measures.** If, for example, the organisation values personal sacrifice and they measure it by how much vacation you don't take each year, then you need to carefully manage perceptions along this dimension. It is surprising how many organisations seem to watch the clock and penalise employees that don't give extra time to the company. Knowing what you are giving up and what it might do to your prospects of career advancement is essential to making wise decisions.

4. **Be careful about what you put in writing; it could be used against you by others.** Avoid emotional emails which could have a damaging effect. Don't think this admonition stops at the company walls. If you write something obnoxious on Facebook, you can expect someone from work to find it and use it. Be particularly careful if you feel emotional about the topic of your writing—emotional writing can often be picked apart, out of context, by your enemies.

5. **Lend support before you need it.** Think of your political alliances. When you support others, you add to the balance. When you need support, you reduce that balance. Particularly, be careful about the relationship aspect above. Once you burn a bridge, virtually no amount of support will be enough to offset your past sins.

6. **Make sure, risks are limited in number and tilted in your favour.** When you take risks, do your best to make sure they ultimately result in wins. You might be able to survive one failure, but not three or four simultaneously. A number of missed promises or overestimates of performance can add up to one big bomb. When you have to take a big risk, make sure it is as close to a sure thing as possible. Better to back off of something you said previously than to be backed into taking on a big risk.

7. **Presentations count a lot.** Top management will have limited opportunities to see you, learn about you and assess your capabilities. Make sure you put your best foot forward when these opportunities come up. Master the subject matter, take time to make your presentation perfect and deliver it well. Bonus points are given for coming up with fresh or new ways to look at the old problems.

8. **Don't hide bad news.** But be very careful about how you reveal it. The 'bad news sandwich' works the best with some good news on each side. If you must make a confession, get the admission up front in a conversation. It also helps if you have an action plan for how to handle any issues, just make sure you're prepared to execute it.

9. **Don't badmouth your enemies.** You will probably have competitors or enemies, whether they are people you don't like, who don't like you or who see you as an impediment to getting what they want. If you badmouth them, it is highly likely to get back to them and you effectively raise your importance as a target. That might not matter if they are an avoider, but if they are a street fighter—better watch out.

10. **Keep complaints to yourself.** If you are unhappy with some aspect of the company, don't discuss it with other employees. It gives rise to rumours or may offend others. Remember those things valued by your organisation. Of course, a light dose of criticism accompanied by a realistic plan to make improvements can get you far, just be prepared to make it happen.

   If you are aspiring to be a power player the following advanced skills and tactics should help you. Be careful. Use them only once you have proven yourself skilled at managing the neutral tactics. Recognise that some of these tactics may be offensive and be aware of your own moral compass as you consider active involvement in each.

11. **Actively manage your reputation.** You want to be seen as smart, hardworking and innovative or whatever the company thinks as important. Be well aware of how you are seen by others, even if it means seeking the advice of a keen observer or a mentor.

12. **Cultivate a mentor.** Look for one who is a skilled politician of the type you aspire to be and not just somebody higher up the ladder. Many skilled politicians, in the later part of their career, seem to develop a desire to help younger co-workers. Perhaps it's all the years of not being able to talk about their political manoeuvring to anyone …?

13. **Ask for what you want.** You can't expect the organisation to figure out where you want to go and put you there. Ambition is generally admired as long as you don't appear to threaten or be a threat to the person you are talking to. Carefully make your long-term desires known.

14. **Set the bar credibly low.** Hitting your targets is important in almost every organisation. How the target is set is important. Eighty percent of your wins or losses will be determined, not by how hard, smart or fast you work, but instead by where the bar is set. Managers are taught to set high targets for their subordinates, build in cushion of their own and push down blame. So, take every opportunity to make sure you score wins, rather than losses by influencing the setting of targets at reasonable levels.

15. **Provide some original thinking.** Original thinking can greatly enhance your reputation. While what is valued by corporations does vary, having smart people on the team is always desired. The ability to introduce new ideas to the company is critical to being seen as 'smart'. Avoiding stupid mistakes helps too. The ideas need not be original in total, just new to the company.

16. **Promote yourself.** This, however, requires the lightest of touches. It's a fine line between tooting one's own horn and being seen as an obnoxious self-promoter. Better if you can enlist someone else to promote you.

17. **Distance yourself from failure.** There is an old saying that 'success has many fathers, but failure is an orphan'. Many large organisations seem to have an almost pathological need to identify and punish the persons responsible for failures. As soon as you see a ship is sinking, be the first rat to jump.

18. **Expect betrayal.** Business relationships are often relationships of convenience and it may become convenient for somebody to sacrifice you at some point. You, therefore, need to deepen

your relationships beyond just the office with some of your best and strongest supporters. Even then, a friend in need (need not be) is a friend indeed.

19. **Invest in scapegoats.** Try maximum to insert someone between yourself and high-risk projects or tasks. If failure occurs on the project you can sacrifice that person. It might not save you in every case but the technique is widely used by managers. This is perhaps the most morally repugnant political behaviour but it does work if it is within your moral comfort zone.

20. **Use power sparingly and strategically.** Power player tactics are often seen as offensive by the organisation at large. Overindulgence in them can make you a target by itself. Sparing use and covert use will get you much further than craftlessly lashing about.

Managing Your Boss 21

We dealt with the managing power and the political situations in organisations in the earlier chapter. When you join your first organisation or any subsequent new organisation, you come across an unknown personality to whom you are told to report. This is your supervisor or senior or more popularly termed as the boss. He/she is the person with whom you are likely to have the most important relationship in the workplace. He/she also has more influence on your career than anyone else. The boss–subordinate relationship is very different than the relationship between a parent and a child in that the burden for managing the relationship does not fall entirely on the boss. You need to take initiative and share this responsibility of promoting that relationship.

Your boss is the person who represents to you the culture of the organisation, style of functioning, decision-making, rewarding and recognition. Keeping your boss happy and interested in you is the key to your progress in the organisation and your career. If you could manage him properly, your boss could be a resource for you to climb the hierarchical ladder of the organisation. Moreover, even if you leave the organisation to take up other careers, your good relationship with the boss always helps you by way of referrals, recommendations and moral support.

Managing your boss need not be political manoeuvring or apple polishing. It is a process of consciously working with your superior to obtain the best possible results for you, your boss and your company. Following hints may help you to be effective in that process:

- **Accept your boss as it is**
  Management has given your boss an authority to direct and control your activities. He is your boss for a reason, because he is more experienced, more knowledgeable than you in the professional arena. Accept and respect him for that fact. Even if you consider yourself more intelligent and smarter than your boss, he is still supreme. You are stuck with him as long as you are in your current position. Therefore, becoming rebellious will only make the situation worse.

- **Don't expect perfection**
  Your boss is a human being just like you and therefore will have endless variety of quirks, eccentricities and odd habits. Be careful and do not annoy and upset your boss on such virtues. If you have a wonderful boss who is a pleasure to work with, celebrate! Be grateful everyday for as long as it lasts. If not, lower your expectations.

- **Get mindshare**
  First three months in a job, do what your boss says. Deliver on time. Volunteer when he needs someone for a task. Once he forms an opinion, no one can change it. This period is important for building mutual trust and relationship and you need to take all the initiative.

- **Study your boss' management style**
  Understand your boss's expectations in terms of results, work habits, communication style or anything else. If you are not clear, then don't try to guess—ask! Like 'Would you like me to...'

or 'would you prefer ...'. Any reasonable manager will gladly answer these questions and, in fact, will be pleased and surprised by your interest.

- **Bosses love solutions**
  Bosses don't like problems. They love solutions. So if there is an issue, go with solutions. You will soon build your reputation as a solution provider.

- **Try to make your boss look good**
  Produce quality results, meet deadlines, stay within your budget and respond to people quickly. Find problems that need to be solved and address them. Contribute new ideas and suggestions. Share useful information with your boss. Your own power will grow when your boss tells everybody how wonderful you are!

- **Make things easy for your boss**
  Try to understand the commitments your boss has given to his/her boss or his/her goals for himself, department or organisation. Share them wholeheartedly, participate, perform and contribute. Make things easy for your boss.

- **Promise less and deliver more**
  Never promise what you can't deliver. That is a risk for your reputation. Promise less and deliver more.

- **Never complain to others about your boss**
  Never complain about your boss to others, especially to people outside your department or to your colleagues or your subordinates. Trumpeting your unhappiness company-wide will only get you in trouble.

- **Give your boss sincere compliments from time to time**
  Managers hear lots of complaints, but few employees ever bother to give their boss a kind word. However bad your manager may be, you can still find some quality worth praising. Mention it at some appropriate point. Paying a sincere compliment is different to leaking or sucking up. There is also no harm in wishing your boss on his/her birthday.

- **Never try to please the boss**
  Never try to please the boss. Be professional. Execute your tasks well. Let your work speak for itself. Don't hang around his/her desk. Bosses actually dislike it.

- **Ask for help**
  Seek help from your boss when you encounter a problem. They love to help. That's when they feel they are valued.

- **Don't ask his/her opinion if you don't need one**
  Don't keep asking for his/her opinion unless it is absolutely necessary. Without wasting his/her time, bring the issues to focus, present your findings, state your actions, get his/her buy in and move on.

- **Partner with boss**
  Never look at your boss as an enemy. He is your partner on a journey called career. Look at him positively. Connect to him. Don't trigger his/her ego. Don't argue. Lend your shoulder to the wheel.

- **Boss is always right**
  Don't argue with boss in public. Talk to him tactfully in private, he will respect you for that. There is no harm in expressing diverse opinions. Remember the golden rule; 'If you are arguing with your boss with facts and figures, you could be right; if you are arguing with your boss on feelings, the boss is always right'.

- **Finally, remember, 'It's not your boss who protects your job, it's your boss' boss'**
  Look for opportunities to interact with higher level managers. If they know who you are and think well of you, then you will have enhanced both your political power and your job security.

The above hints are generally applicable. However, you need to assess the situation before you use any of them. Successfully managing above-mentioned points will make your time at work more pleasant and make it easier to accomplish your goals.

Technology Skills and Certifications

Introduction and Need for Technology Skills

22

Today's businesses are run on technology. It is not much of manufacturing technology or banking technology or mobile technology or computer hardware. It is about the role of information technology (IT) in managing businesses and making decisions. Discussing employability would be incomplete without discussing IT capability. You can't escape the use of technology today. Whether it's using your credit card at the grocery store, the automated teller machine (ATM) at the bank or the self check-in kiosk at the airport, technology is present. More and more employers are requiring that employees are familiar or should be familiar with a wide variety of computer and IT applications. Computer literacy is no more a matter of added qualification, it has become a need to gain respectable employment. The knowledge of IT and its applications provides you a competitive advantage and opens more doors for your career prospects.

In the fast-paced technology world, business requirements are changing and the technical skills needed for business are also changing rapidly. Your job may or may not require immediate use of computer skills. It is still worth to at least get introduced to this form of technology. The Internet is loaded with tools that will assist you in finding a job, keeping a job and advancing in a job. However, in practice what is needed is demonstration of the competencies in applying these tools into real-life situation. You can also meet and learn from sources around the world through the social media. If you have your own computer with an Internet connection, you can access information at all hours of the day or night at your convenience. To be technologically literate, you need skills in these areas such as exchanging emails, browsing Internet and using popular word processing software, spreadsheet applications and presentation software. These needs have now become very basic and you need to learn something beyond them to demonstrate your technological potential and superiority. New applications and techniques are appearing on the scene all the time. It is, therefore, important to understand the basic as well as relevant technical skills, which will be needed to be ensure that you are ready for the job.

Most of these technology areas are not part of syllabi of general graduate programmes. If you are pursuing IT-related graduation programme, you are little better off in this aspect than others. In any case, it is important to acquire the knowledge and skills of IT that are universal in nature and applicable across industry sectors.

Apart from the technology skills, there are two other areas where you need to look at if you want to enhance your career prospects. These are obtaining certifications and taking membership of professional associations, institutions and societies. A certification makes an individual more marketable. Unless the prospective employer is familiar with your institute and the quality of its students, it has no independent means of knowing how rigorous your programme or experience is. When a job candidate comes to an employer with recognised and accepted professional certifications, it gives the employer more confidence to hire. Particularly, for freshers, who are new to the employment market without a great deal of past experience, the combination of an academic degree and an industry-recognised certification puts them in a stronger position when looking for a placement.

Looking at the most emerging areas for employability in the current market like enterprise resource planning (ERP), supply chain, information technology, IT-enabled services, consulting, retail and financial services, most companies are multinational corporations (MNCs) or have foreign affiliations. Certifications make their employees globally compatible. It is assumed that certified professionals have greater ability to understand new or complex technologies and are, therefore, more productive and bring more insightful problem-solving to the workplace. Getting certified in your area of expertise or major interest gives significant advantages to you over others.

- Certification helps to prepare for many of the tasks and activities encountered on the job.
- Certification provides a substantial indicator of intellectual curiosity, an interest in learning and a drive towards accomplishment.
- Certification does provide indirect benefits, in the form of better annual reviews, higher increments, possible promotions and even occasional new job offers.
- Some certifications offer much more substantial earnings opportunities than others.

Memberships of professional associations and societies is another opportunity, you should look at. It gives tremendous advantages to enhance your career prospects, knowledge gain and networking. Most specialisations and industries have a professional body, normally an association or institute or institution or society, which people with relevant background, experience or qualifications can join. Some potential benefits of professional membership include:

- Professional recognition
- Information and advice
- Networking opportunities
- Magazines/journals
- Career development

Professional association and institutes generally charge for assessment and accreditation, if available, and there is also an annual membership subscription fee in addition to one-time entrance fee. However, the benefits generally far outweigh the costs incurred. You may even speak to your institute authorities to take a group membership of some of the relevant institutions specialised in your field of graduation. It is also cost-effective to begin as the student members and gradually upgrade your membership category. It is important for you to ensure that you gain value from joining a professional association or institution. Their websites generally have all the information for you to research before applying for membership.

The following chapters are aimed at providing you more information related to:

- IT skills
- The knowledge of ERP
- Certifications and memberships

The objective is just to create awareness and provide overview and not to educate you on any of the skills. You need to find relevant resources such as training institutions to get yourself more knowledgeable and qualified in some of the areas referred to in this section.

Basic Information Technology (IT) Skills

23

While every career is different, the basic computer skills you are likely to need are generally the same. By mastering some of those computer skills and applications, you could potentially position yourself for success in today's increasingly competitive job market. Courses often cover everything from email and familiarity with the Internet to applications like Word processing software, spreadsheets, database programs and presentation software programs. Acquisition of basic computer skills might help your transition into a more efficient and productive professional. Possessing these basic skills may not, however, give you an edge to climb the career ladder. Those special skills which can do that are discussed in the next chapter.

Here is a list of some of the in demand applications and technologies that are expected from today's new employees so that they are up to date with the latest trends and able to do something different for the company. You need not be experts in any of them; having some knowledge and foundation helps in developing further expertise while working with the organisations or opting to get certified based on the organisational needs. Students who are from information technology (IT) discipline at graduate or post-graduate level, however, will be expected to have higher expertise in these areas than those who have lesser prior IT background.

BASIC COMPUTER SKILLS

These skills are popularly referred to as computer literacy. These IT skills are considered as most basic skills which even a child is familiar with. While learning these skills is important, the competency in these skills entirely depends on your constantly using and practising them. Most of these skills do not need coaching classes. You can develop yourself to learn and use these skills using tutorials and/or buying very cheap computer books like '.... for Dummies!!' The most important is the practice.

Microsoft Office

Microsoft Office, or more popularly known as MS Office, is a suite of interrelated desktop applications, servers and services for the Microsoft Windows and Mac OS X operating systems. It was first introduced by Microsoft in 1989 for Mac OS. The version for Windows came out in 1990. Over the years, Office applications have grown substantially with shared features such as a common spellchecker, OLE data integration and Microsoft Visual Basic for Applications scripting language. Microsoft also positions Office as a development platform for line-of-business software under the Office Business Applications (OBA) brand.

At the time of writing this book, Office 2013 was the latest version of Microsoft Office. As the world becomes increasingly connected and cloud computing becomes more mainstream, online productivity software has been gaining momentum among small- and medium-sized businesses. The most popular online offerings include Google Docs from Google and Office 365 from Microsoft. It is important to be familiar with at least one office productivity suite and many students should expect to use these tools on an almost daily basis.

When it comes to Microsoft Office, students should be well versed with one or more of the following applications:

- MS Word
- MS Excel
- MS PowerPoint
- MS Outlook

Other Microsoft Office tools that are not essential but whose knowledge can vastly improve employability are mentioned as follows:

- MS Visio
- MS OneNote

Finally, for professionals who are likely to be in the programme management roles, MS project is an excellent resource for planning and managing project resources and schedules.

As mentioned earlier, you are not expected to be expert on the above programs. In fact nobody is. However, you should be able to use them reasonably well for you to be considered for an employment by a company. Those who can afford should attend coaching classes to learn MS Office or even obtain certifications from Microsoft. I would, however, recommend self-learning with hard practice as the best way to acquire MS Office knowledge and skills.

Microsoft Word

Microsoft Word is a word processor package that helps you to create, edit, format and print a document. It is quite flexible and easy to use. It is one of the most popular word processors for Windows. It has a number of user friendly menus and commands. It provides the facility to save the document automatically after pressing save commands. It has options of spell and grammar checking and mail merge, which are not available in other word processing softwares. It also lets you to add images, clip art, diagrams and different font or design choices. The main file formats are .doc (MS Word 97–2003) and .docx (MS Word 2007 onwards). Your curriculum vitae (CV) may be your first attempt to use MS Word effectively. Some of the MS Word features that you should be familiar with are as follows:

- You can create professional documents fast, using built-in and custom templates.
- You can easily manage large documents using features like creating table of contents, index and cross-references.
- You can work on multiple documents simultaneously.

- AutoCorrect and AutoFormat features catch typographical errors automatically and allow you to use predefined shortcuts and typing patterns to quickly format your documents. It checks the spelling of each word from top to bottom one by one and if there is a spelling mistake, the suggested changes or ignoring prompts appear as a spelling dialogue box. You have options of using various dictionaries.
- The print zoom facility scales a document on different paper sizes and allows you to print out multiple pages on a single sheet of paper.
- The nested tables feature supports putting one table inside another table.
- You can export and save your word documents in PDF and XPS file format.
- It has a facility to create tables automatically. You can create a table having any number of rows and columns having different size of cells.
- The mail merge facility enables the process of merging some form of address database with a form of letter to create a group of individual letters. Mail merge is used to print letters, envelopes, mailing labels, etc.

Microsoft Excel

Microsoft Excel, also known as MS Excel, is a spreadsheet and mathematics program that can make calculations and graphs based on the data entered. The file formats are .xls (for MS Excel 2003) and .xlsx (for MS Excel 2007). MS Excel has spreadsheets in which number of sheets can be added as per our requirements. Each sheet consists of rows, columns and cells. Every cell has different address. Sum, product, subtraction, division and many mathematical and logical functions are available with this application. You can also find other features such as tables, charts, clip art, etc. It is the most important software for all kinds of business applications where database is to be processed. Every manager needs to be familiar with various features of Excel. In fact for a manager, MS Excel is a must as he is required to make decisions based on analysis and logical deductions. Some of the key features of MS Excel are mentioned as under:

- Hyperlink allows you to link one file to another file or page with the use of Excel.
- Clip art helps you to add images. You can also add audio and video clips.
- Charts allow you to make effective presentations of trends or performance variation, etc.
- Tables are created with different fields, for example, name, age, address, roll number, so we add a table to fill these values.
- Mathematical functions include add, subtract, divide and multiply.
- Logical functions include average, sum, mod and product.
- Images and backgrounds for the sheet.
- Macros are used for recording events for further use.
- We can add database from other sources with data feature.
- Sorting and filter is used to sort data and filter so that repetitions will be removed.
- Data validation tools.
- Grouping and ungrouping of data.
- Page layout features include themes, colours, sheets, margins, size, backgrounds, breaks, print, titles, sheets height, width, scaling, grid, headings, views, bring to front of font or back alignment, etc.

Microsoft PowerPoint

Microsoft PowerPoint, more known as MS PowerPoint, is a program that creates presentations and slide shows. This software application has virtually replaced 35 millimetre slide shows of the past. MS PowerPoint enables the user to create dynamic, informational slide, shows through the use of text, graphics and animation. Slide shows created with the software are often displayed on projection screens for business, training or educational presentations, although they can be distributed as stand-alone files. The slides could either be printed on transparencies to be used on overhead projectors or could simply be saved in a file for use on liquid-crystal display (LCD) projectors. Additionally, the slides can be arranged and printed as handouts for reference. Some of the key features of using MS PowerPoint are:

- PowerPoint provides an array of pre-designed templates from which you can choose a particular template to make your slides. You can also start with a blank presentation and set the colours and fonts, etc., according to your own specifications.
- You can use an auto layout or a blank screen to make your slide. You can then choose to add a combination of text and graphics to suit the needs of the presentation and apply animation to either of these elements to create a dynamic effect.
- You can add as many slides and make them as content rich as your system can handle; there are no limits imposed in the software itself.
- Once the slide show is complete or nearing completion, you can preview it and rehearse your presentation to get a feel for the length of time the presentation will run. You can go back and do some editing on the presentation structure and contents to adjust to the time available.
- Once finished, the slide show can be run from within PowerPoint or saved as a PowerPoint viewer file for access on systems that don't have the full version installed.
- Video and audio can also be added into your MS PowerPoint presentation.
- For more advanced uses, Adobe Flash and other applications can be used to add customised special effects and interactivity.

When using PowerPoint, it is important to remember that the 'slide show' is a presentation tool and not the presentation itself. Learning how to use this application well is not synonymous with being a good presenter. The uses of PowerPoint seem to be endless. Almost any presentation can be enhanced through visual and sound effects, and this application has become the standard tool to do so.

Microsoft Outlook

Microsoft Outlook or MS Outlook is the standard task management and communication software found in most business settings. Its integration with the corporate exchange server allows the user to communicate with iterations of Outlook on other computers. In other words, co-workers can share contacts, calendars and personal messages through the software. Whether for personal or business use, Outlook can provide a user with a variety of tools and features such as:

1. **Email:** The most common use of MS Outlook is its email functionality. When Outlook was introduced, it was designed to be a simple email client, not a full-functioning information manager. The email feature includes support for a variety of web-based email accounts (including

Microsoft's own Hotmail and Live mail), Post Office Protocol (POP3) accounts, Internet Message Access Protocol (IMAP) accounts and exchange accounts.

2. **Calendar:** Users can enter appointments, events and meetings and have them displayed on the Outlook calendar. It can also be set-up to remind users of those appointments and events via a pop-up message, email and even through a text message. Outlook is also designed to handle multiple calendars, so a user can have a personal calendar with personal events (birthdays, dinner dates, etc.) and a calendar for business purposes (meetings, business trips, etc.). If your company uses an Exchange server, you will be able to share calendars with co-workers and access any calendars they happen to be sharing. This is perfect for setting up a meeting time or scheduling appointments with clients.

3. **Contacts:** Outlook features an address book function. It offers space to add personal information for a user's contacts including photos, home pages, email addresses, phone numbers, birthdays and more. The contact list is then integrated into Outlook's email function, making it simple to contact clients from one place. If your company has a networked telephone system integrated with Microsoft Outlook, a user can dial contacts simply by clicking the phone number in the contacts list. If using Outlook on an Exchange server, a user can share and access contacts from other users on the network.

4. **To-do list:** Outlook can provide its users a daily to-do list to stay on task. Simply enter the tasks that need to be completed, with a due date and time and Outlook will offer reminders and display the list prominently on its start page. If using an Exchange server, employers can create to-do lists for employees to complete.

5. **Syncing:** Outlook allows a user to synchronise (synced) email, calendars, tasks and contacts with various web-based services, such as MS Office online. It also can be synced with any Windows mobile phone, allowing for the ultimate portability of a user's essential information. Whether on the go or working from home, a user can access any information needed.

INTERNET SKILLS

The Internet is not just your web email. It is everything that goes over those wires from one computer to another: the email itself, websites, messenger (such as Yahoo Messenger or MSN Messenger), phone calls on Skype, messages from an automated teller machine (ATM) to a bank and the list is unending. Because of all these things, the 'Internet' is a gigantic library, as well as a worldwide message board, telephone network and publishing medium. It is open 24 hours a day and you can find anything you want there and say anything you want.

Current events and blogs as well as information about almost any subject are available in depth and are up to date. This is incredibly valuable for every subject you can imagine. Many of the colleges and research organisations are 'on the web'. If you appreciate the richness of the Web and the Internet and get the benefits yourself, then you will be better able to utilise the services on them. You don't have to know how to do those technical things yourself. If you know what is useful, you will be able to manage yourself.

You need to learn new skills to understand how to use the Internet so that you can use it effectively, and to be able to get control of the information and communication. Internet skills would enable you to:

- Obtain more information
- Communicate with others electronically

- Social networking
- Perforating commercial transactions electronically
- E-learning
- Developing your own websites/blogs

Browsing Web

Microsoft Internet Explorer and Google Chrome are currently the most popular Internet browsers. (Many Mac users prefer the Safari browser.) The competition between the two browsers to dominate the market has led to continuous improvements to the software. Google Chrome has recently entered the market of browsing the net and also getting very popular. Once you spend time on the Web, you'll feel that there is no limit to what you can discover.

A website has one or more related web pages, depending on how it's designed. Web pages on a site are linked together through a system of hyperlinks, enabling you to jump between them by clicking on a link. In order to locate online data, the web servers that host the information, each have a unique numerical address.

With hundreds of millions of websites and more coming online daily, you will undoubtedly find ones you want to revisit. Bookmarks and Favourites save those web addresses, so you can return to them quickly, without having to remember and retype them. When you launch your web browser, a predefined web page, known as the home page, appears. The mobile smart phones have the ability to access information on the web. Connecting to the Net from a device that slips into your pocket is really wonderful.

You can do a host of things using Internet such as online job search, shopping, finding cheaper text-books, learning and planning your trips and buying movie tickets.

Cloud computing is a recent development of the Internet. Instead of buying software, installing it on your computer, upgrading it periodically and storing all your data on your hard drive, with cloud computing you use software applications online, as a service. All you need is your computing device and an Internet connection.

Social Networking

Internet has become a place for human interaction in the 21st century. Social networking sites have exploded in the recent years, allowing millions of people around the world to meet and interact together. Some of the most popular networking sites are:

1. **Facebook:** It has become more or less the standard of social networking with over a billion users. I am certain everyone reading this book has a Facebook account. The primary function of the Facebook platform has been to connect users with friends and family. Businesses create Facebook pages and gather followers, helping with their product promotions and gathering customer feedback.

2. **Twitter:** It provides a platform for users to broadcast short messages—called tweets—to their followers. Along with Facebook, twitter has found tremendous adoption from businesses to increase product awareness among their loyal fans and prospective customers. Businesses often

use these platforms to gather insights about their loyal customers—such as what are customers liking, what are they talking most about, etc. The insights gathered from these platforms allow businesses to fine tune their product offerings to better meet customer requirements.

3. **LinkedIn:** It is the most popular professional networking site and can be a tremendous value for the professionals at any stage in their career. Building a rich network is one of the keys to achieving professional success and LinkedIn is the perfect tool to help you build it. You can connect with your professors, managers, colleagues, customers and partners and stay in touch with them even when you move on to a different role. Then, this network can provide you with future business opportunities, jobs and access to advisors, potential customers, vendors and so much more. The first step is to create a professional and completed LinkedIn profile. Then connect with people you know. It is advisable to gain skills, endorsements and recommendations on the work you have done at various stages of your career as these are publicly visible validations of your skills and achievements. Always remember that investing your time in building a network today can make your life a lot easier tomorrow and the same goes for LinkedIn.

4. **YouTube:** It is not exactly a social network in the traditional sense. It is the world's most popular video-sharing platform accessed by millions of people each day. There are hundreds of millions of videos on YouTube right from cooking *pav bhaji* to dogs skating. But as a professional, the true power of YouTube is that it provides you a free platform for showcasing yourself—be it about your amazing skills or about a product your company is trying to promote.

With these being active, you are always connected to the world and it is often easy to get engrossed in conversations on social networking sites forgetting that these are public platforms. It is vital that professionals keep certain etiquettes and proper behaviour in mind when interacting on these platforms. We often hear in the news about an employee tweeting about the companies' confidential product or making improper comments about co-workers and then getting into big trouble for it. Recently, two girls were arrested by police for making some objectionable comments about a leader on Facebook. Treat all social networking platforms as public and do not disclose, share or forward any information that is confidential or unsuitable for a public audience.

There is much debate about the usefulness of social media, yet each year, millions of new people discover it and dive into. Ashok may be merely curious about how to stay in touch with family on Facebook while Mohan may be steadfastly determined to promote a new business on Twitter. Sudhir may want to contribute his knowledge of mobile technology through a blog. Anupam may want to connect with potential customers through LinkedIn. Each has a different need that requires a different approach to social media. We all play different roles during the course of our lives and with each ones comes a different type of social need.

WORKING IN THE DIGITAL AGE

As technology advances, the world has become increasingly mobile. We have moved beyond the age of fixed telephone lines and fax machines. Smart phone has found its ways into the corporate world enabling an always on, always connected movement—making professionals available and accessible no matter where they are physically located. Here are some of the workplace enhancements enabled by technology that new graduates should expect and be ready for.

Mobile Phone Revolution

iPhone and Android devices are increasingly taking over the world once dominated by mobile pages, Blackberrys and other mobile devices. The ability to receive and send corporate email, review urgent documents and attend conference meetings through one's mobile phone has greatly enhanced productivity in the workplace. Tablets are slowly making their way in as well, especially for applications that require content consumption versus content creation. The mobile computing world is constantly evolving and as a young professional it is important to familiarise with various options available out there.

Virtual Meetings

Thanks to services like WebEx and GoToMeeting.com, it is now possible to attend meetings from anywhere in the world. In most cases, all you need is a computer, tablet or a smart phone and a reliable Internet connection. You can view or present slides, take notes and discuss all at the comfort of your own home or office. These tools help companies save time, effort and money by reducing the hassle and expense of travel. Services like Microsoft Office communicator and Google Talk allow colleagues to quickly communicate with each other via voice calls or instant messaging.

Popular Internet Communication Services

Many companies rely on services such as Microsoft Office communicator and Google chat to enable their employees all over the world to better communicate with each other. The prevalence of Internet telephony and web cameras, have enhanced the experience beyond just text messaging. These technologies are also finding ways into homes for personal use.

Newsgroups

Newsgroups or forums and sometimes just groups, have been around almost since the dawn of the Internet. Today, newsgroups resemble bulletin boards, where people discuss subjects of mutual interest by posting comments. You can find some of the more interesting information on the Internet in groups. After you've explored some online groups, you may be ready to post your own messages—either a comment to something you've read or some totally new question or thought. While the procedure differs depending on the program, the general outline is always the same.

You can start your own newsgroup. If you're interested in starting a newsgroup, don't try it alone the first time around. Find someone who has been through the process before. Many arcane customs and rules have sprung up around creating new newsgroups.

WhatsApp Messenger

WhatsApp Messenger is a cross-platform mobile messaging application which allows you to exchange messages without having to pay for short message service (SMS). WhatsApp Messenger is available for iPhone, BlackBerry, Android, Windows Phone and Nokia and yes, those phones can all message each other! Because WhatsApp Messenger uses the same Internet data plan that you use for email and web browsing, there is no cost to message and stay in touch with your friends.

In addition to the basic messaging WhatsApp users can create groups, send each other unlimited images, video and audio media messages.

Telegram

Telegram is a messaging application with a focus on speed and security; it's superfast, simple and free. You can use Telegram on all your devices at the same time your messages sync seamlessly across any of your phones, tablets or computers. With Telegram, you can send messages, photos, videos and files of any type (doc, zip, mp3, etc.) to people who are in your phone contacts and have Telegram. You can also create groups for up to 200 people or send broadcasts to up to 100 contacts. As a result, Telegram is like an SMS and email combined, taking care of all your personal or business messaging needs—you just have to download Telegram on your smart phone.

24 Higher Level Information Technology (IT) Skills

While the basic information technology (IT) skills described in the previous chapter could be learnt by practice, the following higher level skills involve special efforts and external training resources like graduate and post-graduate programmes and coaching classes to learn and practise. While the basic skills are applicable to all jobseekers irrespective of the nature of jobs they get into, the following higher levels skills would enhance their chances of getting IT sector jobs which are very lucrative and high paying. The relevant certification opportunities also are described further for each skill.

BUSINESS PROCESS MODELLING

Business process modelling is becoming a higher priority amongst the employers. Business analyst is generally the starting point of career in business modelling. There is an increasing emphasis in the organisations to document, understand, optimise and improve their business processes. Managers and business owners are realising that operating their businesses without well-documented processes is just like a pilot flying an aircraft without properly functioning instruments and navigation. Well-documented and streamlined processes ensure consistency, traceability and effectiveness.

Business process modelling is a combination of various steps such as process mapping, process discovery, process simulation, process analysis and process improvement. This knowledge is a key area for most IT consulting companies. The skills required for a business modelling professional include:

- Business modelling terminology
- Business Process Modelling Notation (BPMN)
- Service-oriented architecture (SOA)/Business process management life cycle and methodology
- Communication with business users
- Apply analytical and statistical analysis
- Capture business requirements

There are various certifications available to acquire expertise in business process modelling.

- IBM Certified Business Process Analyst—WebSphere Business Modeller Advanced Edition V7.0 certification—candidates must possess the skills outlined above and pass one test. See *www.ibm.com/certify/certs/15002204.shtml* for more information.
- BCS, The Chartered Institute for Information Technology, has a certification programme for business modelling professionals, titled as 'Certificate in Modelling Business Processes Practitioner'. This certificate focuses on the investigation, modelling, analysis and improvement of business processes. The certificate is relevant to anyone requiring an understanding of business processes,

including business analysts, business managers, business change managers and project managers. See *www.certifications.bcs.org* for more information.

There are no formal entry requirements for the course; however, candidates should be suitably prepared and possess the appropriate skills and knowledge to fulfil the objectives.

DATABASE MANAGEMENT

Database expertise is another area where employment prospects are quite high in the IT sector. Companies are looking for professionals with knowledge and/or experience in Microsoft SQL Server and the Oracle Developer Suite. They also value professionals with database certifications.

A database professional manages, organises, stores and accesses the information used by the company. Companies hold a lot of information that needs putting into reports or documents. As a database professional, your main responsibilities will include:

- Improving the effectiveness of the database tools and services
- Ensuring all the data complies with legal regulations
- Making sure the information is protected and backed up
- Regular reporting to the teams you work with
- Monitoring database performance
- Improving the technology used
- Building new databases
- Monitoring data entry procedures
- Troubleshooting

Oracle Database Certifications

Oracle runs its certifications under the auspices of Oracle University hardware and software, including all components of a storage area network, using Brocade management tools and consoles. The Oracle Database certification has separate tracks for database administration, application development and implementation for database versions 11g, 10g and 9i.

Oracle owns the Open Source MySQL database as well and offers associate, developer, administrator and cluster administrator credentials for that platform. Most of the Oracle DBMS credentials require candidates to attend authorised training classes to qualify for the related exam, but MySQL credentials often do not. The Oracle certifications also represent a true ladder, as it is generally necessary to earn the associate-level credentials first, professional-level second, master third and lastly the expert-level credentials. The Oracle Certified Professionals (OCPs) have the following kinds of certifications:

- OCP 11g Credentials
- Oracle Database 11g Administrator Certified Associate
- Oracle Database 11g Administrator Certified Professional
- Oracle Database 11g Administrator Certified Master
- Oracle Database SQL Certified Expert

For further information on the above certifications, you may visit *http://education.oracle.com/pls/web_prod-plq-dad/db_pages.getpage?page_id=143*

ICCP Certified Data Management Professional (CDMP)

The Institute for the Certification of Computing Professionals (ICCP) offers its own Certified Data Management Professional (CDMP) credential at mastery and practitioner levels. These credentials include education, experience and test-based examinations to warrant professional-level skills and knowledge. The difference between practitioner and mastery level depends on the examination scores and professional database-related work experience. The CDMP is an excellent credential for individuals who are interested in establishing as general database professionals, especially those who seek to demonstrate skills and knowledge that aren't tied only to one specific database platform. It is a useful credential for anyone who works in the database arena and wishes to establish or improve upon their professional credibility.

For more information, go to *http://iccp.org/certification/designations/cdmp*

Microsoft SQL Server Database Certifications

This certification is particularly popular in the organisations that use Microsoft's Visual Studio environment for software development and offers a broad range of tools and add-ons for business intelligence, data warehousing and data driven applications of all kinds. Microsoft offers database-related credentials at every level of its certification programme, from the Microsoft Technology Associate (MTA) all the way to the Microsoft Certified Architect (MCA) programme. Certification programmes offered by Microsoft include:

- MTA
- Microsoft Certified Technology Specialist (MCTS)
- Microsoft Certified IT Professional (MCITP)
- Microsoft Certified Master (MCM)
- Microsoft Certified Architect (MCA)

You can visit *http://www.microsoft.com/learning/en/us/certification/cert-overview.aspx* for more information on Microsoft certification programmes.

IBM Certification Programmes

IBM has long-standing and well-populated IT certification programmes encompassing over 500 individual credentials. One of the company's major certification categories is called 'Information Management' which includes 39 different credentials covering platforms such as DB2, Informix, InfoSphere and Websphere. The range of credentials offered includes Database Associate, Database Administrator, Advanced Database Administrator, Solution Developer, Solutions Expert and more.

It is difficult to list all the certifications offered by IBM. To get full list of these certifications and their details, visit *http://www-03.ibm.com/certify/certs/dm_index.shtml*

SAP Sybase ASE Database Certifications

Sybase is another well-known DBMS platform that has been around for a long time and is now a part of software giant SAP. This certification programme is well developed and recognised in IT circles. The company offers associate and professional-level credentials for administrators and developers, with two other specialist credentials on Sybase IQ and SQL anywhere as well. The names of the SAP certifications are as follows:

- ASE Administrator Associate
- ASE Administrator Professional
- ASE Developer Associate
- ASE Developer Professional

Visit *http://www.sybase.com/support/education/certification* for more information on SAP certifications.

MESSAGING/COMMUNICATIONS

Messaging and communications is another skill set that promises better remuneration. Companies are particularly interested in hiring employees with experience in unified communications and messaging systems, which was one of the highest paying IT skills. A related skill that also ranked among the highest paying was VoIP and IP telephony.

Smart phones are becoming more and more integrated into IT systems for emails and other applications. With the smart phone use increasing and the capabilities evolving, it can also be useful to utilise this today and in the future.

IT ARCHITECTURE

The term 'IT Architect' or 'IT Architecture' is used a lot in the IT industry. The IT architect is involved in the design phase of a system or a set of systems. They will need to know what a system is required to do, what is involved in providing that system, what business process or problem is involved and how it links to other systems. In many cases, the IT architect or system architect will need to have a broad view of a company's IT infrastructure or requirements. They will need to know the most effective way of providing an IT solution that meets the company's requirements, budget and other constraints.

The use of standard tools for designing systems is recommended, due to widely accepted best practices and efficiency benefits. The IT architect or system architect has standards for diagram symbols, methods and types. A common standard is the Unified Modelling Language (UML). The UML is a large language for diagramming and includes a lot of areas of system design, many of which are relevant to the design part of a system architect's role.

The systems or software that the IT architect or system architect defines includes details about various components and how they work together. This could be at a high level involving many systems around the department or company or at a lower level involving a particular system that includes many linked components. The IT architect comes in here:

- To confirm the current and proposed definitions of a set of systems or a single system, between the architects, the technical teams, the users and any management teams involved.
- To describe the details of linked systems or system components for various technical teams. Different teams may be responsible for different areas of a system or different systems altogether. Communication between these components is common and someone needs to define and document them.

Companies are looking to hire enterprise architects as well as system, network, application, data, information and security architects. Among the certifications in this area, EMC-proven Professional Technology Architects, Security Certified Network Architects, Microsoft Certified Architects, SNIA Certified Architects and the Open Group's IT Certified Architects are rising in value. You can visit websites of respective vendors to get more information about these certifications.

IT SECURITY

Security of IT systems is a big issue today. Having a potential candidate for the job with knowledge of security in IT infrastructure is a great help. This helps companies to keep its systems secure and data protected. Large IT security departments employ an Information System Security Manager to supervise and take care of the management and training for the rest of the security team. Typical role of an IT security person includes:

1. To manage the implementation and development of an organisation's IT security
2. To make sure security policies, standards and procedures are established and enforced
3. To coordinate information security inspections, tests and reviews

As an entry-level person, you get involved in the day-to-day operations of IT security management and you will work under the guidance of the Information Systems Security Manager. Your role would be to analyse and evaluate networks and security vulnerabilities as well as managing security systems such as antivirus, firewalls, patch management, intrusion detection and encryption on a daily basis. Sometimes, you may have to interact with and advise the organisation's non-technical employees during the staff meetings, teleconferences or other situations in which, security issues need to be addressed. You need to equip yourself with the knowledge of:

- Security tools that are currently available
- Business security practices and procedures
- Hardware/software security implementation
- Encryption techniques/tools and various communication protocols

CISSP Certified Information Systems Security Professional (CISSP)

The Certified Information Systems Security Professional (CISSP) is known as the 'gold standard' of security certifications. It is governed by the International Information Systems Security Certification Consortium or ISC.

ISACA Certifications

Certified Information Security Manager (CISM) is a globally recognised Information Security Manager designation and is developed specifically for experienced information security managers and those who manage designs, oversee and/or assess an enterprise's Information Security (IS). The CISM certification promotes international practices and provides management with assurance that those earning the designation have the required experience and knowledge to provide effective security management and consulting services.

Certified Information Systems Auditor (CISA) is a globally recognised Information Systems Auditor designation. Possessing the CISA designation demonstrates proficiency and is the basis for measurement in the IS audit profession. With a growing demand for professionals possessing IS audit, control and security skills, CISA has become a preferred certification programme around the world.

For more information see *http://www.isaca.org/CERTIFICATION/Pages/default.aspx*

Microsoft Certified System Administrator (MCSA)

The Microsoft Certified System Administrator (MCSA) is designed to make sure you have the skills to effectively manage and troubleshoot systems running on the Microsoft Windows operating system. There are recommended courses to take if you are just starting out on Microsoft products. Microsoft has recently revamped their certificate programmes to be more target-oriented.

See *www.microsoft.com/learning/en/us/mcse-certification.aspx* for more information.

Unix/Linux Certification

The UNIX and Linux certifications are very popular on the market. There are various vendors who have created several certifications for you to prove your UNIX- and Linux-based knowledge. In the Linux certifications world, the leaders are Red Hat and LPI, but also other companies like Oracle are near behind them. In the UNIX certifications world, we can find three leaders: Oracle with Solaris, HP with HP-UX and IBM with AIX. Also, BSD has its own certifications.

See *certification.about.com/od/linux/* for more information or search on Google for Unix and Linux certifications.

PROJECT MANAGEMENT

Having the ability to plan and integrate projects efficiently can be a great help. A project manager is the person who has the overall responsibility for the successful initiation, planning, design, execution, monitoring, controlling and closure of a project. The job title is used where long cycle project type of products and services are produced and delivered, which includes software design, development and implementation.

The project manager must have, in addition to general management skills, a combination of skills including an ability to ask probing questions, detect unstated assumptions and resolve conflicts. The key is to recognise that risk directly impacts the success and that this risk must be both formally and informally measured throughout the lifetime of the project. Most of the issues that impact a project arise in one way or another from risk. A good project manager can lessen risk significantly, often by adhering to a policy of open communication, ensuring that every significant participant has an opportunity to express opinions and concerns.

Project managers use project management software, such as Microsoft Project, to organise their tasks and resources. These software packages allow project managers to produce progress reports and charts almost on real time basis. Having knowledge of project management software such as MS Project or Timeline is important.

The Project Management Professional certification remains in demand. Even more important is the experience of managing complex IT projects and delivering results on time, and on or under budget. Project management is one of the top 10 skills needed for mid-level employees, which also includes project planning, budgeting, scheduling, project integration and management.

See next chapter for certifications in project management from Project Management Institute (PMI) which has chapters in India.

DATA MINING

Data mining is sorting through data to identify patterns and establish relationships. It is the technique of extracting specific types of information or patterns from large databases, such as data warehouses. Advanced statistical methods sift through large volumes of data, providing answers to questions that were once too time-consuming. Data mining parameters include:

- **Association:** looking for patterns where one event is connected to another event.
- **Sequence or path analysis:** looking for patterns where one event leads to another later event.
- **Classification:** looking for new patterns (may result in a change in the way the data is organised).
- **Clustering:** finding and visually documenting groups of facts not previously known.
- **Forecasting:** discovering patterns in data that can lead to reasonable predictions about the future (this area of data mining is known as predictive analytics).

Today, data mining is primarily used by companies with a strong consumer focus—retail, financial, communication and marketing organisations. It enables these companies to determine relationships among 'internal' factors such as price, product positioning or employee skills and 'external' factors such as economic indicators, competition and customer demographics. It further enables them to determine the impact on sales, customer satisfaction and corporate profits. Finally, it enables them to 'drill down' into summary information to view detail transactional data.

With data mining, a retailer could use point-of-sale records of customer purchases to send targeted promotions based on an individual's purchase history. By mining demographic data from comment or warranty cards, the retailer could develop products and promotions to appeal to specific customer segments. For example, Big Bazaar can mine its sales history database to recommend buying behaviours of individual customers. Visa Credit Card company can suggest products to its cardholders based on analysis of their monthly expenditures.

Wal-Mart uses data mining to transform its supplier relationships. It captures point-of-sale transactions from over 2,900 stores in six countries and continuously transmits this data to its massive 7.5 terabyte data warehouse. Wal-Mart allows more than 3,500 suppliers to access data on their products and perform data analyses. These suppliers use this data to identify customer buying patterns at the store display level. They use this information to manage local store inventory and identify new merchandising opportunities.

There is a huge potential for persons who understand data mining and related fields such as information on demand, content management and unstructured information management. It is a lucrative career choice for the dedicated tech whiz. Not only will you get to look through data on a wide variety of subjects, you will also play a major role in the future policies adopted by the companies that hire you. Progression in this industry makes data mining a popular choice for those with an avid interest in the worlds of statistics and computing.

WEB DESIGN/DEVELOPMENT

Web design is concerned with designing Web pages and sites. While web designers usually need to possess general design skills, such as an understanding of the drawing and a knack for creating aesthetically pleasing combinations of colour and form, they also need to have an understanding of web-specific design factors—screen resolution, image compression, usability, accessibility and website architecture. Web designers are responsible for everything from designing a website's 'look and feel' to incorporating features such as e-commerce, online community, search engine optimisation, animations, interactive applications and advertising hosting into the site—all while ensuring that the site's design is optimised for the specific technologies supporting it.

These careers require a combination of skill in visual design and proficiency with technology. Most web designers work at advertising, marketing, design agencies or at web consulting firms, which build and manage websites for client organisations. Working as a freelance web designer is another option. As the Internet evolves, new technologies come into play and the needs of Internet users change, there will be a need for new skills among web designers.

The work of web designers determines whether people stay on a site or leave and whether they do what the site wants them to do while they are there. If the website's goal is to generate e-commerce, sales results ultimately provide the measure of the success of the web designer's work. If the website depends on advertising or subscriptions for its revenue, then online ad click and new subscribers will be the measure of success.

Web design is a specialised function within IT and a key role in the web development. Web designers create the look, feel and navigation for websites using HTML programming, which is the basic computer language for creating web pages, as well as a number of computer graphics programs. Their work includes defining the user interface, creating catchy graphics or animated images and choosing the style, fonts and other visual elements to make a site appealing. Web designers are also increasingly facing the need to optimise the pages they design for the wireless devices.

Web designers need to be familiar with HTML and JavaScript and understand the way web graphics such as JPEGs and GIFs work. They should also be proficient with industry-standard graphic design softwares such as Adobe Photoshop and Illustrator, and web layout tools such as Microsoft FrontPage and Adobe's (formerly Macromedia's) Dreamweaver. The multimedia design field has many companies that are developing new and better design tools all the time, but the industry is dominated by applications from Adobe, including Director, Shockwave and Flash.

Web design is a high-profile role. The work and job performance are viewed and judged by thousands of people every day. While that can be extremely satisfying and even exhilarating, it is a two-edged sword: If you make a mistake, the entire company can be affected. Still, if you are an artist at heart, have a perfectionist streak and thrill at the thought of having your work viewed around the world, then you may love this profession.

IT OPTIMISATION

The design and implementation of IT infrastructure are crucial to the success of any organisation. Over time, additional services and ever-changing and demanding IT needs require continuous effort to streamline systems and resources to maximise the performance of current assets, technologies, application and services, while remaining flexible to support the future needs.

Simplicity, adaptability and sustainability are the key. A consolidated, seamlessly integrated network can reduce operating expenses and simplify IT management requirements. These strategies must also ensure the environment remains continuously optimised and architected to evolve in-line with long-term business objectives. The IT Optimisation solutions provide a range of strategies that focus on infrastructure simplification, operational efficiency and retention and growth.

The IT optimisation allows businesses to respond rapidly to changing business priorities and align their IT infrastructure with the company strategic goals. As the business grows, volume and complexity of data processing systems and workload on company's server increase, resulting in greater demands on IT infrastructure. Increased demand means increased cost of operations and maintenance. Businesses are faced with the imperative to do more with their IT infrastructure for less. Optimising IT environment can bridge the differences between the inadequate IT infrastructures and the current need for IT to facilitate business growth.

The IT optimisation is the process of modifying your IT infrastructure so that it is more consolidated, flexible and automated. An optimised IT infrastructure facilitates the integration of new business applications. It fuels growth by managing costs with enhanced IT asset utilisation, reduces operating expenses and makes it easier to keep the entire IT infrastructure in-line with the growth objectives of the company. All businesses, regardless of size, can enjoy the benefits of IT optimisation. An effective approach to IT optimisation involves three stages:

- Simplify the IT infrastructure and manage assets for a positive financial impact on the corporate strategy.
- Increase operational efficiency to enhance the flexibility and minimise power consumption.
- Retain and expand IT infrastructure to align with company's business goals, without costly renovations.

Cloud computing, though relatively new at the moment, is destined to be big in the future because it's a great way for businesses to cut costs. Companies already have started realising the value of cloud computing. For example, if the company uses *Salesforce.com*, it would like to hire people who are not only familiar with the cloud, but are familiar with *Salesforce.com*. The IT experts predict a solid future for IT professionals with experience in IT optimisation, including virtualisation and cloud computing. However, these jobs may end up in service providers, rather than IT departments.

NETWORKING

Network engineer is involved in the design and maintenance of the hardware and software necessary for a computer network. They are high-level technical analysts with a specialty in Local Area Networks (LANs) or Wide Area Networks (WANs). Many colleges now offer degrees in network engineering. There are now MBA programmes that specialise in network management.

Network engineers usually have a bachelors degree or higher. They may have had internships or specialty projects within the network design and engineering field. The job prospects for network professionals are quite good from entry level, and with increasing responsibilities and specialisations, they acquire years of experience and specialty certifications. Network engineers are typically promoted to senior-level engineers and may focus extensively on specialty areas such as design, performance optimisation or network security. Several of the certifications within network domain include certifications from Cisco, SNIA, EMC, Brocade and Avaya.

25 Enterprise Resource Planning (ERP) Knowledge

Most information technology (IT) professionals are aware of enterprise resource planning (ERP) and its endless expansion through just about every industry. If any company has not yet gone the ERP route, it probably will soon. That means you are going to deal with ERP eventually right from day one of your employment and that means there are two options today. You start learning ERP now or you wait until someone makes you learn it after you join the company. The best move is to take the initiative to educate yourself on ERP even before you seek employment. We trained our students in SAP R/3 which helped them to demonstrate to the companies that they understand ERP. They were not supposed to be experts; however, they had enough knowledge and skills to understand ERP and particularly SAP/3. SAP training, even though limited, was a good employability enhancement initiative at the institute.

Just imagine a major business with different departments working in tandem with each other to bring profit for the company. Each of the department might be using different software for their day-to-day work. For example, in a car-making industry, spare parts are being managed in a software system; people information uses different software and sales uses something else. Using different software applications brings in the problems of their maintenance and possibility of speedy flow of information across the business functions. This is where ERP plays its role and companies opt for ERP applications which are generally huge packages like SAP, Oracle Apps, etc. These packages once implemented bring the corporate information flow to all the departments and will provide a standard process of workflow in the organisation. It does not matter what type of business it is. The ERPs cover all integral parts of very expansive and comprehensive business processes.

Some central features of ERP that must be understood are as follows:

- **Business process reengineering:** ERP is about leveraging a company's information, as well as the information resources of partner companies, in the pursuit of more efficient ways of doing business. A company's business processes leverage existing resources and information availability optimally in order to achieve the most efficient operation possible. By reconfiguring information resources, combining and extending applications and partnering with other companies in information sharing, new possibilities emerge in terms of how business processes may be implemented. Making business systems better is a central ERP objective.
- **Database integration:** Traditional businesses store information by business function. Financial information in an accounting database, customer data in a customer database and so on. The ERP aims for integration of databases into a super database that enables logical links between records that ERP applications require. The ERP platform software simply creates convenient and easily maintained bridges between existing databases rather than requiring the awkward generation of new databases from old.

- **Enhanced user interfaces:** ERP applications cease to be stand alone and become steps in a process. A user interface initiates down-the-line processes in highly efficient ways like a trigger. The ERP-integrated databases also offer wider reporting options via application interfaces than conventional systems do. It is important to learn what options are useful and how this extended reporting may be enabled.
- *Data* **transport between companies:** With growing Internet applications, sharing of strategic information between partner companies and logistical data between the supply chain partners is increasingly important. The enhanced databases and interfaces of an ERP-based company are made more valuable if the partner companies are involved. This brings in need for a broad and detailed knowledge of the various data communication options.
- **Extended and distributed applications:** A conventional information system is like a farm covered with ponds. You go to a particular pond and take a bucket of water to water your plants. In an ERP environment, the ponds are converted into an irrigation system. The water is routed to the section of the farm where it is needed. This includes sharing water with neighbouring farms. Similarly, even if the users have different needs, they make use of different parts of database records. It is essential to understand how to facilitate this diverse use of common database and how a particular development environment can enable it.

HOW TO GET EDUCATED

This gives you some basic idea about ERP. There are many versions of ERP evolved over the years. It is advisable to get little more information about ERP before you appear for the campus placement process.

First, you can request your institute management to facilitate ERP training for you, may be at some cost. If your institute takes lead, it can negotiate with the ERP training institutions and get good fees structure. Alternatively, you may attend ERP training with a suitable institution at your own cost. There are many training institutions who train in ERP applications. Some of them also provide certifications. The certification is quite expensive. What I would recommend for you is to acquire knowledge of ERP prior to your campus placement season. You can always think about certification later when you have your own resources or you find a company to sponsor you for the certification.

You may also take some of the following initiatives to acquire knowledge about ERP on your own:

- Develop contacts and start dialogue with anyone and everyone who has done ERP implementation. These can be your friends, institute alumni, professors or visiting faculty or a guest faculty who might be in your college. Get ERP selling companies representative to talk to the students of your class. Start asking questions and getting perspectives.
- There are paper journals, online journals and books by the score that all focus on ERP. Do online searches and you will turn up with more reading material than you can cover in five years. Pick some good sources and start reading.
- If you are pursing any IT-related programme, choose one of the ERP-friendly development environments such as 'Java'. For example, learn J2EE. That is a good beginning to get into an ERP career.
- If your institute offers ERP as an elective, do opt for it. Having such courses on your curriculum vitae (CV) can make a big difference when you're pursuing that first ERP implementation.

Career Benefits of ERP

If you are considering making a career in ERP, a self-motivated ERP education is justified. You will simply be more attractive to a large number of potential employers if you are ERP knowledgeable than if you are not. While many available ERP positions seem to want at least one implementation experience, this is not a big hurdle. You can overcome this issue by pursuing certification. Having an ERP knowledge base but no practical experience is certainly a much better skills position than not having any ERP knowledge at all.

If you put in efforts in learning ERP and find that your company would not be getting into it soon, your career and potential advancement still are greatly enhanced and will prove beneficial. Even if your company is not working with a branded ERP system, it still has to effectively integrate its business operations with its customers and suppliers. The tasks involved in this kind of operations include setting up portals, designing shared business-to-business applications and accommodating the partner companies (suppliers and customers) into integrated and distributed processes. You still become valuable if these tasks are on the table and you are the one with some ERP know-how.

What and Why of SAP

The SAP is an enterprise software developed by SAP Corporation, one of the world's largest software companies. SAP stands for **S**ystems **A**pplications and **P**roducts in data processing. As a technology, SAP has been used widely among the industry players. It is the number one ERP company in the world. Most of the fortune 500 companies are using SAP and implementation of the SAP application as per the needs of the companies' policies is quite a challenge. There are many jobs in the market with huge potential in career growth. Potential candidates need to learn real-time technology in SAP and start attending interview and get a career in SAP. The SAP courses are much in demand today.

There are more than 50 modules in SAP and each module is highly integrated with each other. There are some functional modules and some technical modules.

Functional modules are as follows:

- FI/CO (Finance and Controlling)
- HR (Human Resource)
- PP (Production Planning)
- MM (Material Management)
- SD (Sales and Distribution)
- PM (Plant Maintenance)
- PS (Project System)
- QM (Quality Management)
- BIW (Business Information Warehousing)

Technical modules in SAP are as follows:

- Programming (ABAP)
- BASIS

The SAP training covers standard process, referred to as best practices, given by SAP. Therefore, for functional modules, having three to five years of domain/functional experience helps. If you are coming from business management streams, it is likely that you will have the basic process knowledge from your past experience or from the various courses covered. There are certain new dimensions added to the functional modules, which are as below

- CRM (Customer Relationship Management)
- SCM (Supply Chain Management)
- SEM (Strategic Enhanced Management)
- APO (Advanced Planner Optimiser)
- EP (Enterprise Portal)
- SRM (Supplier Relationship Management)
- XI (Exchange Infrastructure)

For technical modules, previous understanding of C, C++ or Java helps to understand the subjects better. Additionally, knowledge of database and operating system helps to understand BASIS easily. No previous experience is mandatory for learning technical modules. If you are from IT or technology stream, you are in a better position to learn these technical module of SAP. Others will need special efforts to learn them.

SAP has also come out with various technical and functional combination modules such as ABAP + HR or ABAP + SD and dual functional modules such as SD + CRM, PP + MM, FICO +SD, HR + SD and HR + CRM.

Which Module Is Good for You?

It can be very confusing to choose a module suitable for you. It depends on your educational background and domain experience. A SAP-based career can be across various roles in an organisation. These can include administration, programming, warehousing, sales, maintenance, manufacturing, finance and distribution. Each area of specialisation requires relevant education, domain expertise and SAP training. Hence, it is important to consider carefully your area of specialisation, so that your career goals can be realised. SAP training and certification are critical on this developmental path.

So get into SAP module which suits your experience and match the domain knowledge. Most of my students opted for Sales and Distribution (S&D) or Materials Management (MM) modules because our institute specialised in Operations Management which delivered course in supply chain and logistics management. Both are very challenging career options today. If you plan to specialise in marketing, S&D module would be most appropriate. If you want to make a career in Finance, FICO module is the best. Same is with HR module. You need to ensure that a particular module suits your career objective and this will finally enable you to be successful in SAP consultancy role.

Thousand of SAP consultants widely work in different parts of the world. SAP has invested millions of dollars in research and development (R&D) and product development. More and more customers are migrating to SAP and there is a perceptible demand for employees with SAP skills worldwide. This is not expected to abate any time soon since more organisations are beginning to optimise and standardise their operations based on SAP's 'best practices'. A sound foundation in SAP in one or more modules is the starting point. Just to give an example, the director of Global SAP service centre of Colgate-Palmolive in Mumbai offered to absorb 25 out of our first batch of 60 students.

SAP Certification Programme

The SAP certification is an expensive affair. Therefore, before going ahead with certification, it is important to know about the different levels of SAP certification. The advantages one obtains by completing them are detailed below.

Associate SAP Certification

This certification covers the basic knowledge one needs for being a SAP consultant. It ensures successful attainment of SAP solution information and implementation skills. With associate certificate one can:

- Achieve the highly valued mark of excellence sought by clients.
- Implement tasks skilfully and confidently.
- Have access to a broad community of SAP peers.

Professional SAP Certification

This is an advanced level of certification and requires proven experience on project handling, knowledge about business processes and a detailed knowledge of SAP solutions. Through professional certification one can:

- Demonstrate experience through a meticulous testing process.
- Lead activities and responsibilities as well as execute them.
- Have access to a broad community of SAP peers.

Masters SAP Certification (in Development)

A certified consultant in this category requires extensive project experience, thorough project knowledge of SAP and also the capability to create a future IT vision inside intricate project environments. It will involve an expert knowledge of specific areas of SAP software and also the ability to drive improvement and solution optimisation with the help of solid understanding and vision. After the master's certification, one can:

- Secure a position in an elite group of visionary experts.
- Thrive in a peer-reviewed, all-inclusive admissions process.
- Have the ability to guide and make long-term strategies.
- Have the right to engage yourself in master-level conferences, colloquiums and industrial events.

These SAP certifications can help you to enhance your skills and knowledge and gain the expertise and credentials you need to help your organisation's efforts to implement SAP software. Once you are in the organisation, your employer may sponsor you for such certification programmes depending on the company needs.

Being SAP certified is like having a direct passport to the business world because there is hardly any other globally recognised credential that carries the same weight. The SAP-certified consultant knows that he/she has enhanced his/her skills by gaining direct experience and have studied rigorously. The SAP certification is an important milestone in a modern and forward-looking career. The SAP-certified consultants also have direct access to the vast resources of the SAP information network, so their clients can rely on them to have the latest, most up-to-date knowledge and skills. So taking all this into account, SAP certification plays a very vital role in today's market.

26 Professional Memberships and Certifications

I always believed that as a graduate or a post-graduate in any discipline, what and how much you acquire out of syllabus is more important for enhancing your employability prospects. The university education structure makes you comply with the syllabus and also tests your accomplishments on the knowledge confined to the syllabus. However, when you think of the job, it is more of what you deliver or what you are capable of delivering and less of what you have learnt in the institute. Employers are looking for persons who have initiative and drive for continuous learning and knowledge acquisition. Any graduate degree can make you eligible for employment but not necessary make you qualified for a job or a position. Acquiring memberships of professional associations and certifications would make you a different prospect for employment.

MEMBERSHIPS

Whichever course you are pursuing for graduation, you will find some associations or institutions which are dedicated to enhancing knowledge and research in your area of specialisation. You need to analyse the different types of professional bodies or institutes, carefully choose few associations or institutions or societies and apply for their memberships. Most institutions have the facility of student members that facilitates your association with the institutions without incurring much cost. I became a student member of the Indian Institution of Industrial Engineering (IIIE) in 1974 when I was pursuing my masters. Then, I became a graduate member, then senior member and currently I am a Fellow of the IIIE.

Some of benefits of joining a professional association, institution or society include:

- **Professional recognition**
  Most institutions have an assessment process that applicants must pass before they are granted membership. This means that, once you have demonstrated that you have the requisite experience, qualifications and skills, you may join the institution and add the appropriate letters to your curriculum vitae (CV) and business card. Membership shows that you have reached a certain level of expertise in your profession and adds to your credibility. It also shows that you are serious about your career and professional development. My fellowship of the IIIE is recognition of my long-standing contribution to the Industrial Engineering profession.

- **Information and advice**
  The websites of most professional associations offer 'members-only' sections that provide access to a variety of databases and message boards, as well as access to industry news, surveys, reports, updates, career information, jobs and details of events. Some institutions offer comprehensive online downloadable documents and publications and a facility for interacting with the experts in the field. You also receive periodic emails about upcoming events and special activities that may

not be open to the general public. Some features of net may be on variety of subjects, such as running a business, advancing your career or boosting your technology expertise.

- **Networking opportunities**

  When you join a professional organisation, you broaden your relationships and make new contacts on a regular basis. Such networking goes beyond the exchange of business cards—as you attend periodic meetings, become active on a committee or take a prominent leadership role, you will forge lasting ties with others who have common professional interests and similar business concerns. These relationships will be rich, ongoing sources of inspiration and ideas. Institutions may have regional networking and professional development events that you can attend, which can be useful for making new contacts and learning more about what is happening in the sector. National expositions, symposiums and conferences also offer excellent networking and research opportunities. If you wish to raise your profile you can volunteer to join committees and help organise events.

- **Magazines**

  Membership in many groups includes a free subscription to the organisation's magazine. Some associations also offer their members free publications and discounts on compact discs (CDs), journals, videos/digital versatile discs (DVDs) and other materials. There are some excellent monthly or quarterly magazines produced by the institutions. In addition to industry news and articles, the journals and magazines often have a vacancies section which is a good source for seeking employment opportunities in your particular industry or professional sector.

- **Career development**

  Many professional associations offer their members the chance to update their knowledge and acquire new job skills through seminars, workshops, breakout sessions at conferences and online courses. Members are often given priority registration for their organisation's convention and may receive discounts on conference fees or special rates on related expenses, such as hotel reservations. The subject matters each time may or may not be directly related to your specific occupation, it could relate to much broader business and professional perspective. For example, theme of a seminar may be 'Achieving Competitive Advantage through Automation' and it could be organised by the Society of Operations Management (SOM). Continuous professional development is essential if you want to forge a successful career. Professional institutions offer career development programmes, training courses and assessments. There may also be the opportunity to upgrade your membership to graduate, associate or fellow level via further assessments and meeting certain pre-requisites like number of years of experience, etc. It gives added professional credibility.

So, whether you are looking to learn about job postings in your field, network in your professional community, gain access to current events in your career area or just have some fun while meeting new people; joining a professional association is a step in the right direction! Most of these associations have discounted memberships specifically for students. You may start with student memberships and subsequently raise your membership class as you gain more experience. Many of the institutions have certifying examinations that also help you to enhance your knowledge and competence. For example, IIIE has a graduate programme in industrial engineering.

Professional association and institutes generally charge for assessment and accreditation, if available, and there is also an annual subscription fee. However, the benefits generally far outweigh the costs incurred. You may even speak to your institute authorities to take a group membership of some of the relevant institutions or even start a student chapter of that institution in your campus. It is important for you to ensure that you gain value from joining a professional association or institutions. Their websites generally have all the information for you to research before applying for membership.

CERTIFICATIONS

Certifications are a great way to break into a new technology, cover gaps in your CV or advance your current position. Certifications are earned from professional societies/associations or from information technology (IT) vendors such as Microsoft, Cisco, Oracle and others. These may be valid for a lifetime or specific period of time and require periodic renewal. As a part of a renewal requirement for certification of an individual, it is common for the individual to show evidence of continued learning or earning continuing education units.

Most certification programmes are created with major focus on raising the professional standards. The growth of certification programmes is also a reaction to the changing employment market. Certifications are portable, since they are not company specific. Certification is an impartial, third-party endorsement of an individual's professional knowledge, skills and experience to apply a methodology or process or software.

A certification is different from a license. What medical professionals or lawyers or architects receive is a license. A license is a demonstration of ability or knowledge required by law, before being allowed to perform a task or job. The certification is not legally bound. However, some certifications do demand a code of conduct while you pursue a particular profession.

Certifications are available in all industry sectors. They may include aviation, construction, technology, environment, health care, finance and others. Certifications are also available in most areas of professions and occupations including business management, consulting, training, human resource, operations, quality, finance, auditing and others. With a number of multinational corporations (MNCs) and software giants establishing their operations in India, many globally recognised certifications are locally obtainable. Certifications give the companies a confidence that the employee understands international standards and practices of that particular area or professions.

Some certifications demand professional experience, whereas some may be obtained while you are in institution with the help of institute management. We promoted various certifications in our institute which had positive impact on the employability of our students. We achieved 100% placement right from the first batch with top-rated companies in all sectors with packages offered far superior to the industry standards.

CERTIFICATIONS IN INFORMATION TECHNOLOGY

The best people in the IT business are those who are passionate about learning and keeping pace with the technology. Technology is evolving at a pace that is difficult to keep up with unless special efforts are taken to move forward with the changing environment. Continuous education and learning is a must. Certifications play an important part of any IT professional's career. The more you put into them, the more you will get out. A certification also indicates to employers that you take your job seriously and that you are knowledgeable on the respective technology.

There are more than 1,700 professional IT certification programmes and examinations; some sponsored by software vendors, some by vendor-neutral organisations and some by educational institutions. A number of them are easy to obtain. You pay your money and you take a multiple-choice test, if you pass, you're in. Others are quite time-consuming and the costs are quite high. Often, the eligibility to even take the examination is dependent on having years of experience, formal education and/or sponsorship from others who already hold the title, and the examinations are gruelling, multi-day affairs that require hands-on performance of relevant tasks. Most are somewhere in between.

Knowing which certifications are the most important for your specialty can seem an insurmountable task. Before you jump into a specific certification, there are some important questions that you need to ask yourself about your career goals and objectives:

- What demography of IT do you fall into? (security, web development, programmer and so on)
- What are your career objectives?
- What IT career are you most interested in?
- What types of resources are needed (that is, money and time)?
- Will this certification have a significant impact on my career?

Clear responses to the above-mentioned questions should narrow your list of potential certifications appropriate to your career goals. You may refer to the job search sites like *Naukri.com* or *TimesJob. com* or some others for positions matching your career goals and see what IT certifications employers are looking for. You may find that on-the-job experience is what employers are searching for in one or more area of your expertise, so it would be logical to invest your time and money into certification in a different area to further your career goals.

The earlier chapter on higher level IT skills listed some of the certifications in specific type of skills. Those descriptions were relevant there. You may review them as well along with reviewing the certifications in this chapter. You may find some repetition from the certifications described in the earlier chapter. But it is okay to refer to both sections.

Let us have a look at 10 of the technical certifications that actually mean something in today's IT job market in India as per *Silicon India* publication in 2012.

- **Microsoft Certified Technology Specialist (MCTS)**
  Microsoft Certified Technology Specialist (MCTS) helps IT staff validate skills in installing, maintaining and troubleshooting a specific Microsoft technology. The MCTS certifications are designed to communicate the skills and expertise a holder possesses on a specific platform. For example, candidates won't earn an MCTS on SQL Server 2008. Instead, they will earn an MCTS covering SQL Server business intelligence, database creation or SQL server. The MCTS credential enables professionals to target specific technologies and is generally the first step towards the professional-level certifications.
- **Cisco Certified Internetwork Expert (CCIE)**
  Cisco Certified Internetwork Expert (CCIE) is a vendor-sponsored certification, focusing on Cisco's products. It requires that the candidate passes both a written exam and a hands-on lab. Candidates have to choose from one of the several tracks: Routing and Switching, Security, Storage Networking, Voice, and Service Provider. The CCIEs must recertify every two years or the certification is suspended. The CCIE accreditation captures most of the networking company's certification glory.
- **Cisco Certified Security Professional (CCSP)**
  Cisco Certified Security Professional (CCSP) focuses on skills related to securing networks that run Cisco routers and other equipment. Candidates are required to pass five written exams and must recertify every three years by passing one current exam. Before a candidate can take

the CCSP exams, he/she must meet the pre-requisites by obtaining one of Cisco's lower level certifications, either the Cisco Certified Network Associate (CCNA) or the Cisco Certified Internetwork Specialist (CCIP).

- **Red Hat Certified Engineer (RHCE)/Red Hat Certified Architect (RHCA)**
  Red Hat Certified Engineer is one of the well-respected Linux certifications in the industry. The exam is performance based. Candidates are required to perform actual network installation, configuration, troubleshooting and administration tasks on a live system. Red Hat Certified Architect is an advanced certification that requires completion of five endorsement exams. Like the RHCE exam, they are hands-on skills tests. Candidates must have the RHCE certification to take the RHCA exams.

- **Technology Infrastructure Library (ITIL)**
  Technology Infrastructure Library (ITIL) certifications provide demonstration of knowledge and skills involved in management positions in the IT services. There are three certification levels: Foundation, Practitioner and Manager. The manager-level certification requires completion of a two-week training programme and candidates must have the foundation certification and five years of IT management experience. Then, they must pass 2–3 hour exams consisting of essay questions. The ITIL is intended to assist organisations in developing a framework for IT service management. Worldwide, ITIL is the most widely recognised qualification in IT service management.

- **International Software Testing Qualifications Board (ISTQB)**
  International Software Testing Qualifications Board (ISTQB) is software testing qualification certification organisation. It is responsible for the international qualification scheme called 'ISTQB Certified Tester'. The qualifications are based on a syllabus, and there is a hierarchy of qualifications and guidelines for accreditation and examination. It is the ISTQB's role to support a single, universally accepted, international qualification scheme, aimed at software and system testing professionals, by providing the core syllabi and by setting guidelines for accreditation and examination for national boards.

- **Certifications for special situations**
  Many specialist exams are available in IT subcategories that can be helpful to those who want to specialise in those areas. Some of these include:

  - Health Insurance Portability and Accountability Act (HIPAA) compliance certification
  - Sarbanes-Oxley (SOX) compliance certification
  - Database administration certification
  - Wireless networking certifications
  - Voice over IP certifications

In addition, for those who have little or no experience in IT, entry-level certifications such as those offered by CompTIA may help you get a foot in the door as you start your IT career.

You may get more information about the above IT certifications from the following websites:

- http://www.microsoft.com/learning/mcp/mcse/default.mspx
- http://www.microsoft.com/learning/mcp/architect/default.mspx
- http://www.cisco.com/web/learning/le3/ccie/index.html
- http://www.cisco.com/web/learning/le3/le37/le54/learning_certification_type_home.html
- http://www.isc2.org/cgi-bin/content.cgi?category=97

- http://www.isc2.org/cgi-bin/content.cgi?category=817
- http://www.giac.org/certifications/gse.php
- http://www.redhat.com/training/rhce/courses/rhexam.html
- http://www.redhat.com/training/architect/courses/rhexam.html
- http://itsm.fwtk.org/certification.htm
- http://www.comptia.com

CERTIFICATIONS IN OTHER SECTORS

Apart from IT, other most popular domains which provide huge employment opportunities are financial and operations management. Similar to IT, there are hundreds of certification programmes available in different areas such as human resources, finance, banking, operations, project management and quality. Certification is offered by particular professional body or society in order to ensure adherence to professional standards, increasing the quality level of practice and competency in the field. Some certifications are intended to be portable across all industry sectors, while some are in more specific areas such as training, inventory control, purchasing and others. It is not possible to cover all the certification programmes in this chapter. Some of the examples of certification in different areas are described below.

Certifications in Financial Sector

The most known certifications in financial sector, which you may be familiar, are as follows:

- CA Chartered Accountant offered by the Institute of Chartered Accountants of India (ICIA)
- CS Chartered Secretary (Company Secretary) offered by the Institute of Company Secretaries of India
- AICWA Cost Accountant offered by the Institute of Cost Accountant of India (formerly, All India Cost and Works Accountants Association)

More than just certifications, these have become qualifications and are like a license, to practise certain financial disciplines like auditing, costing, etc. These are sort of full-time qualifying certifications and provide great careers prospects. Combination with your other basic disciplines is also feasible. During our times when MBA opportunities were very limited, some of us opted for acquiring AICWA after or along with engineering programme.

The financial sector has grown leaps and bounds in the post-liberalisation era and has given rise to many highly specialised fields, with the field-specific certifications emerging internationally. A critical element of the financial sector reforms is the development of a pool of human resources having right skills and expertise in each segment of the industry to provide quality intermediation to market participants. The National Stock Exchange (NSE) came out with different certifications to provide opportunities for the young graduates to make careers in specific fields like investments and capital market, rather than becoming just a generalised financial graduate. These also are aimed at ensuring that financial practitioners:

1. Follow a certain code of conduct usually achieved through regulations.
2. Possess requisite skills and knowledge acquired through a system of testing and certification.

NSE Certified Capital Market Professional (NCCMP)

The NSE, in collaboration with reputed colleges and institutes in India, has been offering a short-term course called NSE Certified Capital Market Professional (NCCMP) since August 2009 in the campuses of the respective colleges/ institutes. The aim of the NCCMP programme is to develop skills and competency in securities markets. It is a 100 hour programme, spanning over three to four months and covering theoretical and practical training in subjects related to capital markets. Successful candidates are awarded joint certification from NSE and the concerned college. The NCCMP covers following subjects such as Equity markets, Debt markets, Derivatives, Macro economics, Technical analysis and Fundamental analysis.

Your college or institute may approach NSE and introduce this course. For more information visit: http://www.nseindia.com/education/content/module_nccmp.htm

NSE's Certification in Financial Markets (NCFM)

As intermediation involves human expertise more than technological support, it is important that a person providing intermediation in the industry has proper understanding of the business and the skills to help it remain competitive. In order to ensure this, it has become an accepted international practice for personnel working for market intermediaries to be adequately certified.

Such testing and certification have assumed significance in India, as there is no formal education or training on financial markets, especially in the area of operations; while at the same time, the market has undergone a complete transformation in the recent years.

A variety of new functions that need different levels and nature of specialisation and orientation have emerged. The industry has a large workforce with varying levels of professional qualifications, skills and experience that do not necessarily match their work responsibilities.

Taking into account international experience and the needs of the Indian financial markets, with a view to protect interests of investors in financial markets and, more importantly, to minimise risks of losses arising out of deficient understanding of markets and instruments, NSE introduced in 1998 a facility for testing and certification by launching NSE's Certification in Financial Markets (NCFM).

The NCFM Programme

The NCFM is an online testing and certification programme. It tests the practical knowledge and skills required to operate in the financial markets. Tests are conducted in a secure and unbiased manner, and certificates are awarded based on merit of the candidate to qualify the online test.

The entire process of testing, assessing and scores reporting in the NCFM is fully automated. The system is operated through an intranet facility by using a central World Wide Web server, with terminals located at each of the designated test centres to be used as an examination front end. Communication between the central server and the test centres is achieved through VSAT/leased line network.

The test is also offered through the Internet to enable candidates outside the designated test centres to take tests at their convenience. This allows flexibility in terms of testing centres, dates and timing and provides easy accessibility and convenience to candidates. The easy accessibility, as well as flexibility involved in the NCFM programme, has resulted in its wider acceptance among market intermediaries, professionals and students.

The NCFM testing modules are divided into three categories, namely foundation, intermediate and advanced. You may obtain more information on the modules and procedure of registration at http://www.nseindia.com/education/content/module_ncfm.htm

Some of the international certifications in finance and accounts that are now available in India include:

- **CFP^{CM} Certification from Financial Planning Corporation of India Limited (FPCIL)**
  The ICICI Direct Centre for Financial Learning is the authorised education partner of FPCIL for CFP^{CM} certification programmes. The estimated demand of financial planners is around 50,000 CFP^{CM} professionals in banking and financial services industry in India. However, till March 2014, India has only 1,849 CFP^{CM} professionals. This makes CFP^{CM} certification to be amongst one of the most sought after certifications. CFP^{CM} certification programme makes you competent to provide strategic advice in investments, insurance, tax, retirement and real estate needs and it enables you to plan and fulfil such needs. Students pursuing/completed graduation or post-graduation including MBA who want to pursue career in finance may consider this certification to enhance their market value. Professionals already working in financial sector may use it as an added qualification to their career advancements. CFP^{CM} certification is currently available in six cities: Bangalore, Delhi, Hyderabad, Kolkata, Mumbai and Pune. For more details, visit ICICI Direct website.

- **CFA Chartered Financial Analyst offered by IFCAI, India**
  The training and certification as Chartered Financial Analyst (CFA) by the Institute of Chartered Financial Analysts is aimed at fulfilling the huge demand for financial analysts. The CFA is not merely an additional qualification, it is a specialisation that gives a person a distinct advantage over others in the field. The CFA certification enjoys wide recognition all over the country as well as abroad. You may also get exemptions from appearing for certain papers in the various examinations for bank employees with CFA certification.

  The areas that cover the CFA skills include financial accounting, management accounting, financial management, investment management, security evaluation, project planning, venture capital management and credit rating among other things. A career with CFA can be extremely challenging and rewarding in monetary terms and in terms of professional satisfaction.

  The CFA is a three-year programme conducted by the Institute of Chartered Financial Analysts of India (ICFAI), which can be completed through correspondence. Students, fresh graduates as well as the employed are eligible. The three-year programme is divided into modules like foundation, preliminary, intermediate and final. People with professional qualifications like MBA, CA, ICWA and M.Com. are exempt from the foundation module of the course.

  As mentioned earlier, this course is conducted through correspondence, with study material sent at regular intervals. This is supplemented with contact programmes at major metros like Bangalore, Chennai, Mumbai, Delhi, Hyderabad and Calcutta. CFA is recognised by the Indira Gandhi National Open University (IGNOU) as an equivalent to a post-graduate degree which makes the students eligible for admission to PhD programmes in management. Many American universities also recognise the programme and accept it as an eligibility criterion for the pursuit of Ph.D. studies. For more details visit: http://www.icfai.org/homepage/Icfai_home_page.html.

- **Chartered Institute of Management Accountants course (CIMA)**
  Originally founded as the Institute of Cost and Works Accountants (ICWA) in 1919 in the UK, the institute was rechristened as the Institute of Cost and Management Accountants (ICMA) in 1972 and again as Chartered Institute of Management Accountants (CIMA) in 1986. In 2008,

CIMA established a centre for the study of management accounting with the Indian Institute of Management Calcutta (IIM-C).

With 170,000 members and students in 168 countries worldwide, CIMA has grown to be one of the most widely accepted and respected professional qualification in the unique cusp of the fields of management and accounting certification. Comparing with more popular options of CA or CFA in the Indian context, the institute claims that CIMA programme is more business focused with more of management accounting, business strategy and financial strategy. The business focus is similar to that of an MBA, but the entry barriers are low in the sense that you can join in with merely having education qualification up to 12th standard. The CIMA gives you career opportunity in sync with the business and management aspects rather than the more routine jobs like audit. You can become a business person with finance orientation, not just an accountant.

The CIMA examinations can be taken at anytime throughout the year and at the location of one's choice. It has nine centres in India with British Council and other colleges which are the study centres conduct the exams on their own campus. For more details visit: www.cimaglobal. com/India.

- **Association of Chartered Certified Accountants (ACCA)**
  The Association of Chartered Certified Accountants (ACCA) is the global body for professional accountants. Its aim is to offer business-relevant, first-choice qualifications to people of application, ability and ambition around the world who seek a rewarding career in accountancy, finance and management. It has 154,000 members and 432,000 students in 170 countries and a record of helping them to develop successful careers in accounting and business, with the skills needed by employers. It has a network of 83 offices and centres and more than 8,500 approved employers worldwide.

  The ACCA is again available for those who are under-graduates and offers a range of certificates at the foundation, intermediate and advanced or professional levels. Your experience prior or during the course also is counted. For more details, visit www.accaglobal.com/india.

PROFESSIONAL EXAMINATIONS IN INSURANCE SECTOR

Insurance Institute of India is the only professional institution in India devoted to insurance-related education and training (life/non-life/health). It conducts different level of examinations leading to award of certificates, diplomas and fellowships that are recognised by the Government of India, Insurance Regulatory and Development Authority (IRDA) and insurance industry in India and abroad for recruitment/promotions and licensing of agents/brokers/surveyors and loss assessors. These professional examinations lead to two types of qualifications:

- **Professional qualifications:** Licentiate, Associateship and Fellowship. These are core qualifications for insurance sector that signify the level of domain knowledge of the holder. These are well recognised and respected in the insurance industry in India and abroad.
- **Specialised diplomas:** These certificates/diplomas provide specialisation/expertise in a particular subject/area such as marine insurance, fire insurance, health insurance, casualty actuarial science and advanced insurance marketing.

Associate and fellowship qualifications of the institute are recognised by similar institutes outside India, for example, Chartered Insurance Institute (CII) in UK, Life Office Management Association (LOMA), American Institute of Chartered Property and Casualty Underwriters (CPCU) and the Insurance Institutes of America (The institutes) in USA and Insurance Institute of Canada. There is mutual recognition of III qualifications and associate/fellowship diploma holders are entitled to exemptions in the qualifications of these international institutes. The IRDA has recognised the institute as the examining body to conduct pre-recruitment qualifying examinations for insurance agents, both for life and non-life business, as well as for surveyors and loss assessors. For more details visit: https://www.insuranceinstituteofindia.com

CERTIFICATIONS IN OPERATIONS MANAGEMENT

In the following sections are described a few of the certification programmes we promoted to our students in Symbiosis Institute of Operations Management (SIOM). Ours was a MBA programme; however, I believe other institutes offering graduate and post-graduate programmes in other disciplines may also be able to offer these certifications to the advantage of the students. This also gives opportunity for the institute to differentiate itself from other run of the mill institutes who stick to the syllabi of the universities.

Six Sigma—Green Belt Certification

It is a known fact that Six Sigma is in uptrend with the organisations, those who want to survive and grow in this highly competitive business environment. The reliability of products and services, which is the most vital parameter or criteria, needs to be met consistently each time (99.9999%) and then only customer will accept the organisation as brand leader. Read information about Mumbai *Dabawala*s online who collect and deliver over 350,000 lunch boxes to office goers in Mumbai each day between 11.00 am and 01.00 pm; and without making a single mistake. They have been doing it for nearly past 100 years. They have been certified for SIX SIGMA by KPMG, one of the world leading consulting firms.

Six Sigma is a fact-driven, structured defect elimination roadmap for all types of businesses. It assures quality to the customers and profit to the businesses. There is no industry or business or function where Six Sigma cannot be applied. Some of the businesses that significantly use Six Sigma in India are:

Sector	Companies
ITES	ICICI OneSource, Accenture, Mahindra Satyam BPO, IBM Daksh
Hospitality	ITC hotels, GRT hotels
Health	Apollo hospitals
Retail	Reliance retail
Telecom	Bharti Cellular, Vodafone, Siemens
IT	Wipro, Mahindra Satyam, Accenture, Infosys
Finance	Bank of America, American Express, HDFC, HSBC, GE Capital

The list is getting bigger and bigger day by day. Six Sigma is also applicable across all business functions such as operations, engineering, HR, finance, marketing, procurement and IT.

Six Sigma knowledge and certification would be of great help to you if you are aspiring to get employment with reputed organisations that prefer Six Sigma competence. We introduced Six Sigma Green belt certification in SIOM and it had tremendous impact on employability of our students in international organisations. It involved both classroom inputs as well as an industry project to ensure application capability of Six Sigma. Additionally, the individual's ability to generate results increases many fold if he knows Six Sigma methodology. This means even if the organisation is not utilising Six Sigma, the person is likely to generate better results leading to better career path.

To understand and apply Six Sigma, the real need is for basic aptitude. Understanding of basic Math and Statistics is a must as the whole methodology is based on heavy analytical work. Six Sigma practitioners recommend the use of MINITAB software in its application which facilitates easy statistical analysis of the data collected. However, you can also use other statistical software as well or even EXCEL. Generally, two types of certifications are involved in Six Sigma capability. These are:

- Black belts apply Six Sigma methodology to specific projects. They devote 100% of their time to Six Sigma. They primarily focus on Six Sigma project execution.
- Green belts are the employees who take up Six Sigma implementation along with their other job responsibilities, operating under the guidance of black belts.

Six Sigma Green belt certification is adequate for entry-level graduates. You may find various organisations offering training to get certified as Six Sigma Green belt. This certification is also available online. Some certify with project and some certify without doing a project. Doing a Six Sigma project in an industry or business is always advisable. It could be a big or small business. It can even be a hospital, a restaurant, a small scale company and so on. You may even approach your friends and relatives who are running a business and propose to take up a project in that business.

You have better chance to learn Six Sigma when you work with the professionals. You would gain experience and they would get the benefit. Moreover, you may have more flexibility and freedom to operate. The idea is to get a practical understanding of the tools by taking up an improvement project and this project can be taken up anywhere. There are many e-groups with whom you can network and share knowledge and experiences; and get your doubts clarified about Six Sigma.

CERTIFICATION IN PROJECT MANAGEMENT

Project Management Institute's Certified Associate in Project Management (CAPM) is a valuable entry-level certification for project practitioners. Designed for those with little or no project experience, the CAPM demonstrates your understanding of the fundamental knowledge, terminology and processes of effective project management.

Whether you are a student, new to project management, changing career or already serving as a subject matter expert on project teams, the CAPM can get your career on the right path or take it to the next level. If you are a less experienced project practitioner looking to demonstrate your commitment to project management, improve your ability to manage larger projects and earn additional responsibility and stand out to potential employers, then CAPM certification is right for you. To apply for the CAPM:

- You need to have a secondary degree (high school diploma or global equivalent) and at least 1,500 hours of project experience or
- Twenty three hours of project management education by the time you sit for the exam.

Once you have more experience in the project management area, you may go for the next-level PMI certification, which is Project Management Professional (PMP). The PMP credential is the most important industry-recognised certification for project managers. Globally recognised and demanded, the PMP demonstrates that you have the experience, education and competency to lead and direct projects. This recognition is seen through increased marketability to employers and higher salary.

The PMP recognises demonstrated competence in leading and directing project teams. It is meant for an experienced project manager looking to solidify his skills, stand out to employers and maximise his earning potential. To apply for the PMP, you need to have:

- A secondary degree (high school diploma, associate's degree or the global equivalent) with at least five years of project management experience, with 7,500 hours leading and directing projects and 35 hours of project management education.
  or
- A four-year degree (bachelor's degree or the global equivalent) and at least three years of project management experience, with 4,500 hours leading and directing projects and 35 hours of project management education.

Once you have the PMP credential, you need to maintain it. As part of PMI's continuing certification requirements programme, a PMP credential holder will need to earn 60 PDUs (a point system to measure your involvement and contribution to the field of project management) per three-year cycle.

This is an overview of the requirements. For complete details regarding the CAPM and PMP eligibility requirements, please view Project Management Institute India website at http://www.pmi.org.in/

AMERICAN SOCIETY OF TRANSPORTATION AND LOGISTICS (AST&L) CERTIFICATIONS

The American Society of Transportation and Logistics, Inc. (AST&L), www.astl.org, is a not-for-profit premier professional organisation for transportation and logistics professionals. Founded in 1946 in the United States of America by a group of industry leaders, AST&L strives to promote and ensure the highest level of global standards through professional certification in the field of transportation and logistics.

The AST&L's mission is to promote and facilitate education and certification in the fields of transportation, logistics and supply chain management. The AST&L's membership of shippers, carriers, educators, students, consultants and third-party logistics individuals are dedicated to continuing education and are committed to raising the professional standards in the transportation and logistics industry.

KnoWerX Education (India) Private Limited (KnoWerX), www.knowerx.com, represents AST&L in India and provides assistance to candidates in pursuit of their certifications—you can get in touch with them.

Professional Designation in Logistics and Supply Chain Management (PLS)

Due to an overwhelming request for an entry-level industry certification, the AST&L now offers the Professional Designation in Logistics and Supply Chain Management (PLS) to professionals seeking an understanding of the key strategies for improving customer service and increasing the efficiency of their logistics and supply chain operations. The purpose of the PLS is to recognise individuals that have completed a course of study, examining the strategies for improving logistics and supply chain operations, and are seeking to apply this knowledge within their profession.

You must have a bachelor's degree or three years of professional experience. Even final year degree or PG students could take these examinations. The PLS designation is granted to those who have successfully passed the comprehensive examination. Either the full expression or the initials may be used after the individual's name on business cards, stationery, etc.

The PLS designation requires recertification every five years. Requirements for recertification include attending an industry-related conference, industry-related education programme or completing a module in the AST&L CTL certification programme.

Exam Requirements

PLS consists of only one examination. Exam questions are in multiple-choice format. There is a four-hour time limit to complete the exam, although it may be completed in a shorter time period. A score of 70% or higher is required to pass the exam; a candidate who scores below 70% may take the exam again. The AST&L provides the study materials for taking the certification examinations.

You can refer to the PLS study guide. The PLS study guide is available on request from KnoWerX on no charge basis once you register for the PLS exam.

THE ASSOCIATION FOR OPERATIONS MANAGEMENT (APICS) CERTIFICATIONS

Established in 1957 as not-for-profit, The Association for Operations Management (APICS), www. apics.org, is the global leader and premier source of the body of knowledge in operations management. The APICS education and certification programmes are recognised worldwide as the standard of professional competence in production and inventory management, operations management and supply chain management.

Certified in Production and Inventory Management (CPIM)

The objective of this certification is to expand knowledge of production and inventory management concepts, tools, terminology and integration of topics within the operations management function. Anybody who is working in any of the following areas could benefit from this certification:

- Production and inventory management
- Operations
- Supply chain management
- Procurement

- Materials management
- Purchasing
- Finance and cost accounting
- Manufacturing information systems
- Consultancy
- Business process outsourcing

The APICS Certified in Production and Inventory Management (CPIM) programme has been organised into five modules, each focusing on key areas of study that are integral to understanding and mastery of production and inventory management principles. Candidates must pass an examination for each of the following modules to successfully complete the APICS CPIM programme:

- **Basics of Supply Chain Management Entry Module**
  The basic concepts in managing the complete flow of materials in a supply chain from suppliers to customers are covered in the basics module. Supply chain concepts are introduced and basic terminology emphasised, as are relationships among activities in the supply chain. The knowledge of the material in this module is assumed as a prerequisite for the other APICS CPIM modules, which cover similar topics in much greater depth.
- **Master Planning of Resources Core Competency Module**
  The topics of demand management, sales and operations planning, and master scheduling are examined in-depth in this module. Both supply and demand planning for mid-term to long-term independent demand are discussed. Priority planning and capacity planning issues also are addressed.
- **Detailed Scheduling and Planning Core Competency Module**
  This course focuses on inventory management, material and capacity scheduling and planning, supplier relationships and the influence of lean and Just-in-Time philosophies in these areas. The course explains capacity planning in detail, introduces other capacity planning techniques such as processor-dominated scheduling in continuous flow processes and reviews project management techniques.
- **Execution and Control of Operations Core Competency Module**
  The principles, approaches and techniques needed to schedule, control, measure and evaluate the effectiveness of production operations are covered in this module. A broad range of production operations are reviewed including project, batch, line, continuous and remanufacturing environments.
- **Strategic Management of Resources Capstone Module**
  In this course, participants explore the relationship between strategic planning and the management and the execution of operations. The course fosters higher level thinking about how market requirements and social and economic sustainability concerns drive the operations, processes and resource requirements of the firm.

There are no specific eligibility requirements for this certification. Anyone including final year students can pursue CPIM. The benefits of CPIM certification include:

- American management certification available in India
- Amplify functional knowledge of production and inventory management
- Achieve greater confidence and industry recognition

- Accelerated career development and better employment opportunities
- Better capability to understand vocabulary, processes and frameworks of clients
- Better capability to understand supply chain management modules of ERP systems

CERTIFIED SUPPLY CHAIN PROFESSIONAL (CSCP)

The APICS Certified Supply Chain Professional (CSCP) programme is very useful in designing, introducing and implementing cost-reduction programmes by looking beyond just the costs related to procurement and reviewing all real costs within the total supply chain. It increases your professional value and secures your future. By earning the APICS CSCP designation, you will demonstrate significant commitment to the supply chain profession and your career, distinguish yourself as an industry expert and excel with your newly acquired specialised knowledge. As a CSCP you will have:

- The proven knowledge and organisational skills to strategically streamline operations.
- The tools to effectively manage global supply chain activities that involve suppliers, plants, distributors and customers located around the world.
- The skills to create consistency and foster collaboration through best practices, common terminology and corporate-wide communication.
- An understanding of the valuable technologies that drive planning and management of successful operations.

Organisations worldwide increasingly list 'APICS CSCP required' in their job postings. Even in India, many of the MNC industries and consulting firms give priority to candidates with APICS certifications. For all your requirements of APICS certifications you may contact KnoWerX Education (India) Private Limited (KnoWerX), www.knowerx.com.

The purpose of providing names of organisations and their website references is just to make the students aware of what is available. It may not be construed that we are here to market their businesses or promote their services. It is advised that the students discuss with their respective faculty or career guidance officers before choosing to go for any of the above certifications.

Excelling through Placement Process

5

Writing a Perfect Resume or CV 27

Your resume or Curriculum Vitae (CV *or bio-data* [which is an outdated term]) is the first document the employer receives either directly from you or through the placement cell of your institute. People use these words interchangeably for the document, highlighting skills, education and experience, a candidate submits when applying for a job. Though broadly all three mean the same and used for the same purpose, there are very intricate differences between them.

Resume is a French word meaning 'summary' and signifies a summary of one's employment, education and other skills, used in applying for a new position. A resume is, therefore, a document that summarises education, experiences and competencies. It is designed to introduce you to an employer, and highlights your qualifications for a specific job or type of work. They do not list out all the education and qualifications, but only highlight specific skills customised to target the job profile in question. A resume is ideally suited when applying for middle and senior level positions, where experience and specific skills rather than education are important.

Curriculum Vitae is a Latin word meaning 'course of life'. A CV is a more comprehensive document that details all past education, experiences and competencies, including extra-curricular activities and professional contributions. It is designed to introduce you to employers in total. A CV is more detailed than a resume, usually two to three pages, but can run even longer as per the requirement. A CV is the preferred option for fresh graduates, people looking for a career change and those applying for academic and consulting positions.

Bio-data, the short form for biographical data, is the old-fashioned terminology for resume or CV The emphasis in a bio-data is on all personal particulars like date of birth, religion, sex, race, nationality, residence, marital status and a chronological listing of education and experience. The term bio-data is mostly used in India while applying for government jobs or when applying for research grants/ scholarships and in other situations where one has to submit descriptive essays. Generally, the company employment application forms also follow the bio-data format.

We will use the word CV in this chapter for brevity. As mentioned earlier, a CV is the condensed version of your professional life onto a sheet of paper covering experience, education, accomplishments, skills and other background information. Some recommend a single page CV but that is OK for a fresher and may not be appropriate for an experienced applicant. Accommodating my 35+ years of national and international experience in four or five pages is a great challenge for me. The rule is simple; *minimum words and maximum message*.

The employer starts evaluating and making initial impressions about you at this point. It is generally very hard to know what to include and what not to include in the CV. Numerous formats available online further confuse the students. This chapter provides a systematic and structured approach and process for constructing a perfect CV.

First take few sheets of paper and use one sheet each for the following heads of your CV:

- CV focus and objective
- Education
- Experience
- Accomplishments/Achievements
- Other specialised certifications and trainings
- References

Just take one sheet of paper for each of the above and go on scribbling whatever comes to your mind. Do not worry about relevance, appropriateness, English grammar, sentence construction, sequencing of information or anything at this point. First accumulate all the information you have about you, against each of the above factors and which you can present in your CV. Having done that read the following section to refine your document into a proper CV. CVs are tailored to match competency needs of different job profiles. You may, therefore, end up with multiple CVs which could be used for different job profiles.

CV FOCUS AND OBJECTIVE

This summarises the kind of job you are looking for. It can become an objective statement if you decide to use one or can form the beginning of the profile section of your CV to give the reader a general idea of your expertise. I prefer a cover letter to personalise the objective for each job opening. Mentioning the objective on CV limits your job choices and you need to create multiple CVs specific to objectives that reflect the actual job for which you are applying.

Your objective statement should be very precise so that even a clerk should be able to pick up your CV without even thinking about it.

For example,

Do not say
Looking for a position which utilises my education and experience to mutual benefit.
Say
Looking for a marketing management position with an aggressive international consumer goods manufacturer.

Precision of objective statement becomes more relevant and important for electronic sorting of e-applications.

EDUCATION

If you are a fresher or with little relevant experience, place your education section at the top of your CV. As you gain more experience, your education section gravitates to the bottom. Use reverse chronological order for listing of educational qualifications.

If you participated in college activities, received any honours or completed any notable projects that relate directly to your target job, this is the place to list them. Continuing education shows your interest in lifelong learning and self-development. Therefore, mention about any training or certifications received that are relevant to the target position, along with or since the completion of your formal education. Do not list any training that is not related to your target job.

EMPLOYMENT EXPERIENCE

Use reverse chronological order for listing employments starting with the present position. List the title, company name, city/state/country and the years you worked for every job. Addresses and zip codes are not required, although you need them for filling out a company employment application later. You have a choice of listing years only (like 2005–present) or months and years (like May 2005–present). If you have more job changes, year format is better. For example, if you worked from September 2005 to May 2006, just say 2005–6. Most HR persons don't care which format you use. However, be consistent with one style.

Duties and Responsibilities

These are the statements which describe the expectations from the positions you held in the past. Study carefully the written description of the job you wish to apply for. These job descriptions explicitly or implicitly state the employer's expectations with regards to qualifications, experiences and skills. Compare your list of duties and responsibilities under each job with the copy of the applicable job descriptions and highlight the sentences that describe relevant things you have done in your past or present jobs. If you have not done certain things mentioned in the job description, you need to think about your potential capability to manage those or related tasks.

Accomplishments

What you accomplished is more important to the employer than the number of years worked or the responsibilities you were mandated to deliver. That gives them an idea of what you can do for them. Look at your jobs and think about your contribution in each of them in a SMART manner. It means:

1. **(S) Specific:** Being specific and concise with regards to your contributions makes a world of difference. List things you have done that made a difference to your company. This may include skills obtained or used, special efforts and tasks that were appreciated and well received. Some examples:

   - Did you **exceed** sales quotas X% each month?
   - Did you **save** the company ₹ X crore by developing a new process?
   - Did you **control** expenses or make work easier?
   - Did you **expand** business or attract/retain customers?
   - Did you **improve** the company's image or build new relationships?
   - Did you **improve** the quality of a product?
   - Did you **solve** a problem and made a huge impact?
   - Did you do something that made the company more competitive?

Note the verbs in bold. These are known as power verbs which we would discuss later.

2. **(M) Measurable:** Numbers, percentages, currency value and symbols catch immediate visual attention of the reader on the accomplishment being presented. Employers seek people who can provide measured, tangible and verifiable results. What value did you add? Don't be vague. For example;

> *Improved the company's efficiency,* does not say much; but if you say, *you cut overhead costs by 20% and saved the company ₹2.00 crore during the last financial year,* it says a lot.

3. **(A) Achievements/Accomplishments:** If you are at entry level, your achievements thus far may relate more to your training, education and skills. Think of actions you have taken to prepare yourself to be ready for employment. How will your training be of value to the employer? Things like part-time working or volunteering for social cause may be useful. Ask yourself with reference to your college or institution

   - Did I accept any added responsibilities, assignments or special projects?
   - In what way did I improve things? How did I grow?
   - What was I most effective at? Did I exceed goals or expectations?
   - Were there any especially challenging problems that I solved?
   - Did I contribute to team activities? Was I a sole contributor who works independently?
   - What were the challenges? What actions did I take? What result did I get?

   If you have prior experience, you may have a lot to write, but be precise.

4. **(R) Relevant:** The job of an HR department is to match people with positions and it is often that special combination of activities, qualities or skills they are looking for that make the difference. Focusing accomplishment statements on the most relevant knowledge, skills, abilities and work activities of the position being sought is very important. Also, read through many job advertisements and make an inventory of skills requested. Prioritise and highlight your most recent and most relevant accomplishments.

5. **(T) Time frame:** One of the most critical performance indicators is time frame. If your accomplishments are recent and completed on or ahead of schedule, your CV will make a huge difference. Getting projects or tasks done on time is a highly prized quality and when you convey this, it indicates a sense of energy and result-orientation. The recentness of your accomplishments also helps.

Your past accomplishments show employers what you might be able to do for them. Remember, you are trying to convince the potential employer that you will generate a significant return on their investment in you.

Using Keywords

Emailed CVs are e-sorted based on keyword search specific to industry or job descriptions. Without the right keywords, your CV will float in cyberspace forever waiting for an HR person to find it. If your CV contains all the right keywords, you will be among the first candidates to be considered for the further process. Even if you lack one of the keywords, your CV may go to the next sorting cycle.

Job descriptions are an important source of keywords. Pay particular attention to nouns and phrases that you can incorporate into your own CV. Make a list of the keywords that you have determined are important, and then also list synonyms for those words.

Avoid using abbreviations as far as possible as they cause confusion due to multiple meanings. It is better to spell out the abbreviation in full form at least once. However, well known and popular initials such as IIM, NITIE, SAP, etc., are recognised by all. Try to use synonyms wherever possible to broaden your chances of being selected through e-sorting.

Soft skills are often not included in search criteria although many companies use them for initial screening for management positions. For instance, 'communicate effectively', 'self-motivated', 'team player' and others are great abilities and are fine to include in the profile, but concentrate more on job-related hard skills.

RELATED QUALIFICATIONS

Is there anything else that might help you qualify for consideration for the job you are applying for? This includes licenses, professional memberships, certifications, affiliations and sometimes even interests, if they truly relate. For instance, for a job in ERP, SAP training or certification would be an asset or for a job in process improvement, Six Sigma training would be very relevant. Section 4 dealt with a number of such certifications which may be quite useful depending upon the sector which you are looking at.

PROFILE

Last but not the least, after completing the entire CV, write four or five sentences giving an overview of your competence and capability. This profile or qualifications summary, is placed at the beginning of your CV. You can include some of your personal traits or special skills that might have been difficult to get across in job descriptions. Here is a sample profile for a Senior Sales Executive position (Figure 27.1).

Busy HR people spend as little as 10 seconds deciding whether to read the entire CV. Therefore, make sure the profile summary at the top entices the reader to read it all. Write this profile and ask yourself, 'Will it convince the employer to call me instead of someone else?'

Figure 27.1   Sample Profile Statement for Senior Sales Executive Position

Dynamic sales executive with a 10-year track record of surpassing multi-crore rupee sales within highly competitive markets. Exceptional communicator with a consultative sales style, Fortune 500 account management skills, excellent problem-solving abilities and a keen client relationship builder. Aggressively identify opportunities, develop focus and provide tactical business solutions. Enjoy extensive travelling. Core professional competencies include

- *Strategic Sales and Marketing Campaigns.*
- *Key Account Acquisition and Retention.*
- *Executive Presentation and Negotiations.*
- *Prospecting and Lead Generation.*
- *Budgeting, Forecasting and Planning.*
- *Cross-functional Leadership and Staff Development.*
- *Customer Relationship Management.*

Source: http://aresumewizard.com/

REFERENCES

It is not necessary to include references on the CV unless specifically requested. In fact do not give references unless and until they are asked for. If you include a reference, make sure that the referenced person knows you very well. Never add an unknown person as a reference. It is also advisable to add such persons as references whom the employer can contact easily. If possible add the phone number and email ID of the reference.

EDIT/DELETE

Now put yourself in the reader's shoes and read your entire CV from top to bottom, word to word and also between words. Keep your job objective and the job description alongside and check for relevance and appropriateness. Make the thoughts flow smoothly. Cross out things that don't relate. Be careful not to delete sentences that contain the keywords you identified earlier. Rearrange sentences based on their importance to the target job description. Keep related items together so the reader doesn't jump from one point to another.

QUALITY OF CV

Your CV is now ready for finalisation and quality check. An aesthetically attractive and grammatically correct CV reflects your own image and personality.

Honesty Is the Best Policy

Employers feel more comfortable hiring you if they can verify your accomplishments. You may glorify your achievements but do not exaggerate or falsify them. Any exaggeration or untruth will be apparent during the interview and it can cost you the job. If you do not meet a particular criterion, mention it in the cover letter by pointing out something more positive that could be justified. Anything more manipulative can be hazardous. For example, say

> I don't have five years of experience in marketing which you need but can add two years of university training in the subject to three years of in-depth experience as a marketing assistant with HP.

Contents and Structure

- Keep your CV limited to one or two page whenever possible.
- Make your CV easy on the eye and digestible. Don't overcrowd. Avoid large paragraphs (five or six lines maximum) and provide space between different sections.
- Use normal margins (1 inch top/bottom and 1.25 inch on sides). Avoid unusual or exotic fonts. I prefer Times New Roman. Keep number of fonts to a maximum of two at the most. Do not overuse capitalisation, italics, underlines, bold or other emphasising features.

- Do not align 'justify' your CV.
- Make sure your name, address and contact numbers appear on the CV and cover letter, preferably at the top of the page.

Sentences

Make sentences structured, positive, brief and accurate. Never use personal pronouns (I, my or me). Writing in third person makes sentences more powerful and attention grabbing. For example,

> *Do not say*
> *I planned, organised and directed timely and accurate production of core products with estimated annual revenues of ₹10.0 crore.*
> *Just say*
> *Planned, organised and directed.*

Use the list of power verbs provided in Annexure 1 to this section. Make sure that each word means something and contributes to the quality of the sentence.

Paper and Printing

- Print your CV on a good-quality printer and on one side of the paper only.
- Sunlit white bond is the most popular paper. Other option could be slightly off-white or light gray. Make sure that the colour of paper doesn't detract the reader from your message.
- Avoid using papers with dark background and patterns as they create dark masses while scanning or photocopying and make your CV difficult to read. It applies when the company sends your CV to multiple locations by fax.
- Mail your CV flat instead of folded. It makes great impression and eases the scanning of your CV.

Avoid Mistakes

Carefully check your CV for correct grammar and spelling. Nothing can ruin your chances of getting a job faster than submitting a CV full of preventable mistakes.

Spelling Mistakes

- Don't use words with which you are not familiar; use dictionary as you write, and understand all the words which you use.
- Perform a spellcheck on your finished CV.
- Have a friend or two proofread your CV for you.

Punctuation Mistakes

- Be consistent in your use of punctuation and hyphenation.
- Periods at the end of all full sentences; always put periods and commas within quotation marks, where applicable.
- Avoid using exclamation marks.

Grammatical Mistakes

- Do not switch tenses. Use present tense for duties you currently perform (for example, *write reports*) and past tense for duties you performed at past jobs (for example, *wrote reports*).
- Write all numbers between one and nine in letters (such as *one, five and seven*) and use numerals for all 2-digit numbers and above (such as *10, 25 and 108*). If you begin a sentence with a number, spell that number (for example, *Six service awards won while employed*).
- Make sure your date formats are consistent.
- Choose your words carefully. Be on the lookout for the following easily confused words.

    - accept (to receive), except (to exclude).
    - all right (correct), alright (this is not a word).
    - affect (to bring about change), effect (result).
    - personal (private), personnel (staff members).
    - role (a character assigned or a function), roll (to revolve).

- Use action verbs using the power verbs list in Annexure 1 (for example, *increased revenues, directed staff, etc.*).

WRITING A COVER LETTER

Every CV sent by post or fax needs a personalised cover letter even if the advertisement didn't request a cover letter. A good cover letter helps capture the reader's attention and motivates him to go further into reading your CV. Emailed CVs don't need a formal cover letter. Just a quick paragraph in the body of the email, telling where you heard about the position and why your qualifications are a perfect fit for the position's requirements, is adequate.

Let us cover some general rules that apply to most cover letters:

- Never use a generic cover letter like, *To Whom It May Concern*. The HR would be more likely to read a letter that is addressed to them or the company. Drop names if you are being referred by someone in the company. CVs referred by company employees or customers receive serious attention.
- Try to get the name of a person and personalise the greeting such as 'Dear Mr Joshi'. In absence of names use 'Dear HR Manager' or just 'Dear Sir/Madam'. I have even used 'Dear Advertiser' in case of box number advertisement.

- Start with the mention of where you heard about the position. The first paragraph is a great place to state (or restate) your objective. Since you know the specific job being offered, you can tailor your objective to suit the position.
- The second paragraph (or two) is the place to mention your experience specific to the job opening. You really sell yourself here by summarising why you are a perfect match for the position. Pick and choose some of your experience and education that closely relate to the company's requirement.

   Mentioning the company and its needs also shows your understanding of the position and its expectations. Don't make this section too long as the reader might quickly lose interest.
- In closing, let the reader know what you expect from this communication. If you plan to call the person on a certain day, you could close by saying, *I will contact you next Tuesday to set up a mutually convenient time to meet.* If you do not wish to make a call, just close your letter by saying, *I look forward to hearing from you soon.* Remember to say, *Thanking in anticipation of a favourable response* or *Thanking you for your kind attention* or something similar as appropriate.

Remember, your CV is an enticer and a way to get your foot in the door of an employer.

ANNEXURE 1: LIST OF POWER VERBS

A	Analyzed	Benefited	Championed	Composed	Counselled
Abolished	Answered	Bid	Changed	Compounded	Created
Accelerated	Anticipated	Billed	Charged	Computed	Critiqued
Accommodated	Applied	Blended	Charted	Conceived	Cultivated
Accomplished	Appointed	Blocked	Checked	Conceptualised	Customised
Accounted For	Appraised	Bolstered	Circulated	Condensed	Cut
Accrued	Appropriated	Boosted	Cited	Conducted	
Accumulated	Approved	Bought	Clarified	Configured	D
Achieved	Arranged	Branded	Classified	Confirmed	Dealt
Acquired	Assembled	Bridged	Cleaned	Confronted	Debugged
Acted	Assessed	Broadened	Cleared	Conserved	Decoded
Adapted	Assigned	Brought	Closed	Considered	Decreased
Adopted	Assisted	Budgeted	Coached	Consolidated	Dedicated
Added	Assured	Built	Coded	Constructed	Defined
Addressed	Attained		Collaborated	Consulted	Delegated
Adjusted	Attended	C	Collated	Contacted	Delivered
Administered	Audited	Calculated	Collected	Continued	Demonstrated
Advanced	Authored	Calibrated	Combined	Contracted	Deployed
Advertised	Authorised	Capitalised	Commanded	Contributed	Derived
Advised	Automated	Captured	Commended	Controlled	Described
Aligned	Avoided	Carried	Commenced	Converted	Designed
Alleviated	Awarded	Categorised	Commissioned	Conveyed	Detailed
Allocated		Catalogued	Communicated	Convinced	Detected
Allotted	B	Cautioned	Compared	Cooperated	Determined
Altered	Balanced	Cemented	Compiled	Coordinated	Developed
Amassed	Began	Certified	Completed	Corrected	Devised
Amended	Benchmarked	Chaired	Complied	Corresponded	Diagnosed

Differentiated
Directed
Disbursed
Discovered
Discussed
Dispatched
Dispensed
Displayed
Disposed
Disseminated
Distinguished
Distributed
Diversified
Diverted
Divested
Divided
Documented
Drafted
Drew Up

E

Earned
Eased
Economised
Edited
Educated
Effected
Elaborated
Elected
Elevated
Elicited
Eliminated
Embraced
Emphasised
Empowered
Enabled
Encouraged
Ended
Enforced
Engaged
Engineered
Enhanced
Enlisted
Enriched
Enrolled
Ensured
Entered
Entertained

Enticed
Equipped
Established
Estimated
Evaluated
Examined
Exceeded
Executed
Exercised
Exhibited
Expanded
Expedited
Experimented
Explained
Explored
Expressed
Extended
Extracted

F

Fabricated
Facilitated
Familiarised
Fielded
Filed
Filled
Finalised
Financed
Fine Tuned
Finished
Fixed
Followed
Forecasted
Forged
Formalised
Formed
Formulated
Forwarded
Fostered
Fought
Found
Founded
Framed
Fulfilled
Functioned As
Funded
Furnished
Furthered

G

Gained
Gathered
Gauged
Gave
Generated
Governed
Graduated
Grasped
Greeted
Grew
Grouped
Guaranteed
Guided

H

Halted
Handled
Headed
Heightened
Held
Helped
Hired
Honed
Hosted
Hypothesised

I

Identified
Ignited
Illustrated
Implemented
Imported
Improved
Improvised
Included
Incorporated
Increased
Indicated
Induced
Influenced
Informed
Infused
Initiated
Innovated
Inspected
Inspired
Installed

Instilled
Instituted
Instructed
Insured
Integrated
Intensified
Interacted
Interpreted
Intervened
Interviewed
Invented
Inventoried
Invested
Investigated
Invited
Involved
Issued

J

Joined
Judged
Justified

L

Launched
Learned
Lectured
Led
Lessened
Leveraged
Licensed
Lifted
Limited
Linked
Liquidated
Listened
Litigated
Loaded
Located
Logged

M

Made
Maintained
Managed
Mandated
Manoeuvred
Manipulated

Manufactured
Mapped
Marked
Marketed
Mastered
Maximised
Measured
Mediated
Memorised
Mentored
Merged
Met
Minimised
Mobilised
Modelled
Moderated
Modified
Moulded
Monitored
Monopolised
Motivated
Moved
Multiplied

N

Named
Narrated
Navigated
Negotiated
Neutralised
Nominated
Normalised
Notified
Nurtured

O

Observed
Obtained
Offered
Officiated
Offset
Opened
Operated
Optimised
Ordered
Organised
Oriented
Originated

Outlined
Overcame
Overhauled
Owned

P

Paced
Packaged
Packed
Pared
Participated
Partnered
Passed
Penetrated
Perceived
Perfected
Performed
Persuaded
Piloted
Pioneered
Placed
Planned
Played
Predicted
Prepared
Prescribed
Presented
Preserved
Presided
Prevailed
Prevented
Printed
Prioritised
Processed
Procured
Produced
Profiled
Programmed
Progressed
Projected
Promoted
Proofread
Proposed
Protected
Proved
Provided
Pruned
Publicised

Purchased	Rewarded	Repaired	Sharpened	Summarised	Troubleshot
Pursued	Retained	Replaced	Shipped	Supervised	
	Recognised	Replicated	Signed	Supplied	**U**
Q	Recommended	Represented	Simplified	Supported	Uncovered
Qualified	Reconciled	Reproduced	Simulated	Surpassed	Undertook
Quantified	Reconstructed	Requested	Slashed	Surveyed	United
Questioned	Recorded	Researched	Solicited	Synthesised	Updated
Quoted	Recovered	Resolved	Sold	Systemised	Upgraded
	Recruited	Restored	Solved		Used
R	Rectified	Restructured	Sorted	**T**	Utilised
Raised	Redesigned		Sourced	Tabulated	
Ranked	Redirected	**S**	Spearheaded	Tackled	**V**
Rated	Reduced	Salvaged	Specialised	Tallied	Validated
Reached	Re-Engineered	Saved	Specified	Targeted	Valued
Read	Referred	Scanned	Sponsored	Taught	Verified
Realigned	Refocused	Scheduled	Standardised	Teamed	Viewed
Realised	Registered	Screened	Started	Terminated	Visualised
Rearranged	Regulated	Searched	Steered	Tested	Volunteered
Rebuilt	Rehabilitated	Secured	Stimulated	Took	
Received	Reinforced	Selected	Streamlined	Topped	**W**
Retrieved	Reiterated	Sent	Strengthened	Traced	Widened
Returned	Released	Separated	Stretched	Tracked	Won
Revamped	Relieved	Sequenced	Structured	Trained	Worked
Reversed	Remodelled	Served	Studied	Transformed	Wrote
Reviewed	Rendered	Serviced	Submitted	Translated	
Revised	Renegotiated	Set Up	Succeeded	Treated	**Y**
Revitalized	Renewed	Settled	Suggested	Trimmed	Yielded
Revolutionised	Reorganised	Shared			

Source: Adapted from contents provided by resume_edge.com on http://www.jobskills.info. Words edited for redundancy.

28 Success at Written Aptitude Test

Aptitude tests ascertain the professional and personal skills of a person in the context of a particular job in a company. Some aptitude tests also test your technical and technological foundation. Most companies such as Infosys, TCS and Tech Mahindra have aptitude tests in their recruiting process.

WHY APTITUDE TESTS?

Aptitude tests are generally a mix of different tests to determine the technical, logical, analytical and verbal ability of the candidates. Some psychological tests also help the companies to determine the personality, leadership and emotional attributes. These show whether an individual is ready to be a part of a particular company or not. Companies use these tests to filter and shortlist candidates for the further recruitment process. Some companies prefer to use the total score of aptitude tests, group discussions and interview for the final selection.

For you as a candidate, this test is a chance to show your skills and attitude as a professional. Since this test is normally conducted in preliminary stages of the selection process, a good score is extremely important. It is mostly conducted in the multiple-choice format and many companies even choose to have this test online to save time and money.

HOW TO PREPARE FOR APTITUDE TESTS?

These tests are to check what you already know, and if you have the right skills, there is nothing to be scared of. Therefore, relax and do not worry about the tests too much. Just concentrate on reviewing your studies or professional skills to ensure that you don't forget or miss anything while answering the questions. You don't have to do an intense study of whatever you have studied. Just a simple revision is good enough.

1. Take some aptitude testing books and solve the already solved problems in each chapter. The best suggested books for aptitude test are R. S. Agrawal's verbal and non-verbal reasoning books or quantitative aptitude text book. Try as many as possible and daily work out something about aptitude. You may also find plenty of practise aptitude tests online which also provide quick scoring. This would give you an idea about the techniques/formulae that are used to solve such problems. Here, you should also think of alternative ways to solve the same problem.
2. When you get familiarised with methods used in these resources then try unsolved questions, solve them and check for answers. You can also try out the puzzles in Shakuntaladevi's books.
3. Download some aptitude test papers of companies from jobsites and try solving them.

4. Group up with your friend and take up some test. Set your own time limit and start solving a question paper. At the end of the test, compare the method that you used to solve with your friend's method. This will give you the best (fastest) way to solve the problem.

5. Practise makes a man perfect. So, it is all about how far you practise with all the resources (books, question papers, Internet) that are available.

HOW TO HANDLE DIFFERENT TYPES OF APTITUDE TESTS?

Different industries have different standards of skill requirements and, therefore, the aptitude tests are also different. These tests not only demand accuracy but also speed. They do not give you a lot of time to think about your answers. It is not only about whether you are able to correctly answer the questions but also about how fast you are able to answer them. So, quick thinking and answering is the key to success. Leave the difficult questions behind and move ahead. There is no point in losing opportunity to answer questions that you know over the ones that you don't.

These tests also challenge your creativity in approaching to solve the questions. For example,

> How much is 15×99?
> One way is doing normal multiplication that we learnt in school and the other is:
> Look at 15×99 as $15 \times (100-1)$. This takes less time to calculate when compared to former.

So such creative techniques are very important to crack these tests with speed.

Also remember, there is a chance of guessing between alternatives in case you are not sure about the answer. Probability of your answer being correct would depend on the number of choices or alternative answers. Also note if there are any negative markings for wrong answers before majorly depending upon guessing.

Aptitude test is just one step towards a successful job interview. Thus, don't get nervous and give it your best.

29 Success at Group Discussions

A group discussion (GD) is a tool used by companies to assess certain desired personality traits and/or skills of the candidates in a group setting. A group of 8–10 candidates is given a topic or a situation, given a few minutes to think about the same and then asked to discuss it among themselves for 15–20 minutes. Some of the traits and attributes the companies try to assess from a GD include:

- **Leadership skills:** Ability to lead, inspire and carry the team along to help them achieve the group's objectives. Ability to create a consensus, openness and flexibility towards new ideas.
- **Communication skills:** Clarity of thought, expression and aptness of language; willingness to accommodate others' views; ability to make your point in a group and listening and probing skills.
- **Inter-personal skills:** Ability to interact with others, emotional maturity and balance, extent of one being people centric or self-centred, group working skills and conflict handling.
- **Persuasive skills:** Ability to analyse and persuade others to view the problem from multiple perspectives.
- **Analytical capabilities:** Data-based approach to reach to conclusions and to make decisions.

While, it is not possible to reflect all these qualities in a short time, you would do well if you are able to demonstrate a couple or more qualities and avoid giving negative evidences on the existence of others.

A GD can be either topic based or case based. Topic-based GD can be of three types:

1. Factual topics
2. Controversial topics
3. Abstract topics

- **Factual topics**
  Factual topics are about things in day-to-day life, which a person is or should be aware of. Typically these are about socio-economic issues and could be current issues or issues unbound by time. A factual topic for discussion gives a candidate a chance to prove that he/she is aware of and sensitive to his/her environment.
  Examples: *Education policy of India, tourism in India, state of the senior citizens, Indian team's performance in World Cup, etc.*
- **Controversial topics**
  Controversial topics are argumentative in nature and are meant to generate controversy. With such topics, the noise level in the GD is usually high and there may be tempers flying. The idea

behind giving such a topic is to see the maturity level of the candidate in rationally and logically arguing his/her point of view without getting personal or emotional and without losing temper. Examples: *Reservations should be removed, women make better managers, is our society still male dominated, etc.*

- **Abstract topics**

  Abstract topics are about intangible things. These topics are not given often for discussion, but their possibility cannot be ruled out. These topics test your lateral thinking and creativity to make sense out of nothing and make a meaningful discussion.

  Examples: *Jai Ho..., the number '0', Satyamev Jayate, MOM or Make In India.*

CASE-BASED GDS

A case study is a simulation of a real-life situation. Information about the situation is given and candidates are asked as a group to resolve the situation. There are no right or wrong answers or perfect solutions in a case study. The objective is to make you think and analyse the situation from various angles, create options and possibly achieve consensus on one of the option.

Your success at GD depends upon your

1. General knowledge and reading about a given subject or subjects
2. Communication skills
3. Capability to coordinate and lead
4. Exchange of thoughts, views and ideas
5. Addressing the group as a whole
6. Thorough preparations

KNOWLEDGE AND IDEAS REGARDING A GIVEN SUBJECT

- **Knowledge is power.** Knowledge comes from consistent reading, watching knowledgeable TV channels, referring to websites and attending conferences and seminars and discussions with people on various topics ranging from science and technology to politics. In-depth knowledge makes one confident and enthusiastic and, in turn, sound convincing in a GD.
- **Be voracious readers.** The more you read, the better you are in your thoughts. You need to be in good touch with current affairs, the debates and hot topics of discussion and also with the latest in the sector and industry. Chances are that the topics would be around these. Read both for thoughts as well as for information and also to get multiple view points on the same topic. Create your point of view with rationale and responses to likely counter arguments from others. The electronic media will be of good use here. Just put your thought statement on Google and you will be amazed to see arguments in favour as well as against your thought.

If you are not sure whether you could make a contribution to the given topic of GD, adopt a wait and watch attitude. It is better not to speak until you get some understanding of the topic. Listen attentively to others, may be you would be able to come up with a point later. Lack of knowledge, if exposed, creates a bad impression.

COMMUNICATION SKILLS

The power of expression is critical in GD. You need to talk effectively and forcefully so that you are able to convince others on your viewpoint. One who is successful in holding attention of the audience creates a positive impact. Evaluators do not look at your vocabulary. It is the knowledge of the given topic, precision and clarity of thought that are evaluated. Be specific, avoid irrelevant talks and speak just what is necessary. Do not keep repeating a point, do not be superfluous and do not exaggerate.

Active listening brings you points and provides you with data to discuss. If you have an average of 2–3 minutes to speak, the rest of the 20 odd minutes is to be spent in active listening. You may listen to others and then react or proceed to add some more points based on clues you get from listening. This would also make you the centre of attraction as you would appear non-threatening to other speakers.

Non-verbal gestures, such as nodding while appreciating someone's viewpoint speak of you positively. Evaluators watch your reactions and body language. Group behaviour is also put to test to judge whether you are a loner or can work in a group.

Use formal language and not the one used in normal conversations. This does not mean use only a high sounding language. Just avoid words and phrases such as *yar*, *chalta hai*, 'cool' and 'I dunno'.

LEADERSHIP AND CO-ORDINATING CAPABILITIES

The examiner becomes a silent spectator once the discussion starts. You have an opportunity to display understanding and knowledge on topic, tactfulness, skill, assertiveness and other leadership qualities to lead and influence others in the group. Grabbing an opportunity to initiate and lead the discussion is a good way to demonstrate your leadership skills.

- Introduce yourself to the group.
- Introduce the topic and state the purpose of the discussion.
- Make sure no one dominates the discussion and consumes too much time.
- Invite quiet group members to speak.
- Be objective in summarising the discussion and conclusions.
- Thank group members for their contribution.

EXCHANGE OF THOUGHTS

A GD is an exchange of thoughts, viewpoints and ideas among the group members. Your contributions to the discussion, comprehension of the main idea, the rapport you strike, patience, assertion, accommodation, amenability, etc. become the factors for evaluation. You may take a stand on a given subject, which during the course of a GD can be changed, giving the impression that you are open to accommodate others' viewpoints.

Your success in a GD does not depend on how much and how loudly you speak. It is also not a question of what is right or wrong and who is right or wrong. It is about how you receive and present your ideas and view point on the topic. This will prove that your thought and viewpoints have strong foundation of knowledge.

ADDRESSING THE GROUP AS A WHOLE

It is not necessary to address anyone individually by name in a GD. In fact you may not know or remember the names of each and every participant in a GD. Even if you are responding to the view point of one candidate, you don't have to keep looking at him/her for all the time. You may begin your response looking at him/her but you communicate with each and every candidate present. Address the entire group as a whole in such a way that everyone feels you are speaking to them. Address the person farthest from you first. If he/she can hear you, everyone else can.

THOROUGH PREPARATION

While a GD reflects the inherent qualities of an individual, appearing for it unprepared is not a good option. Create an informal GD group and meet regularly to discuss and exchange feedback. This is the best way to prepare. This would give you a good idea about the quality of your thoughts and your ability to convince others. Remember, it is important that you are able to express your thoughts well. The better you perform in these mocks, the better would be your chances of performing on the final day. Also try to interact and participate in other GD groups. This will also provide you with skills to interact and discuss with unknown people.

GROUP DISCUSSION PHASES AND SKILLS REQUIRED

You need to understand precisely the GD process because you are evaluated according to your contribution in various phases of a GD. A GD activity has three distinct phases:

1. Initiation
2. Body of the GD
3. Summarisation/conclusion

Your contribution in initiation and summarising phases will give you higher points. This does not mean that your contribution in the body phase of a GD is less important. The initiation and summarising phases demand different skills as compared to the body of a GD.

Initiation Phase

Initiating a GD is a high profit–high loss strategy. You not only grab the first opportunity to speak when you initiate a GD, you also grab the attention of the observer and fellow candidates. If you can make a favourable first impression during initiating a GD with your content and communication skills, it will help you sail through the discussion. But if you initiate a GD and stammer/stutter or quote wrong facts and figures, the damage might be irreparable. If you initiate a GD impeccably but don't speak much after that, it also gives the impression that you initiated the GD for the sake of starting it or getting that initial kitty of points for initiation. When you start a GD, you are expected to create an environment for a meaningful subsequent discussion. Therefore, initiate only if you have in-depth knowledge and understanding of the GD topic. Some techniques you may use to initiate the GD and make a good first impression are:

- **Quotes:** Quotes are an effective way of initiating a GD. For example,
  GD topic: 'Customer is King'
  Quote: Sam Walton (Wallmart), *There is only one boss: the customer; and he can fire everybody in the company—from the chairman on down, simply by spending his money somewhere else.*
- **Definition:** Start a GD with a definition of the topic. For example,
  GD topic: 'Advertising is a diplomatic way of telling a lie'.
  Define advertising: *Any paid form of non-personal presentation and promotion of ideas, goods or services through mass media such as newspapers, magazines, television or radio by an identified sponsor.*
  Similarly for a topic like 'Is Murphy's Law really applicable to our life', start with the Murphy's Law statement.
- **Shock statement:** Shock statement helps grab immediate attention to your view point. For example,
  GD topic: 'The Impact of Population on the Indian Economy'.
  Shock statement: *Imagine at the centre of the Indian capital stands a population clock that ticks relentlessly. It tracks 33 births a minute, 2,000 an hour, 48,000 a day and about 12 million a year. That is roughly the size of Australia.* Or *Nothing is impossible when one billion Indians work together.*
- **Facts, figures and statistics:** Ensure that your facts, figures and statistics are accurate. Stating wrong facts works to your disadvantage. Approximation is allowed at macro level, but micro level figures need to be correct and accurate. For example,
  Approximately 70% of the Indian population stays in rural areas. But you cannot say *approximately 30 states* of India instead of *'28'.*
- **Short story:** Short story giving the right message is a good way to begin. For example,
  GD topic: 'Attitude is everything.'
  Story: *A child once asked a balloon vendor, selling gas-filled balloons, whether a blue balloon will go as high in the sky as a green balloon. The balloon vendor told the child, it is not the colour of the balloon but what is inside it that makes it go high.*
- **General statement:** Use it to put the GD in proper perspective. For example,
  GD topic: 'Should Sonia Gandhi be the prime minister of India?'
  Statement: *Before jumping to conclusions on such a sensitive issue, let's first understand the qualities a good prime minister of India needs to have. Then we can look at the qualities which Mrs Gandhi possesses. This will help us reach the conclusion in a more objective and effective manner.*
- **Question:** Starting GD with a question makes a different impact. Such question is not really meant for any candidate to reply but to start a general discussion. You obviously get the first opportunity to put forward your viewpoint. Questions should promote flow of ideas. For example,
  GD topic: 'Should India go to war with Pakistan?'
  Question: *What does war bring to the people of a nation? We have had four wars with Pakistan. The question is: what have we achieved?*

Summarisation/Conclusion

Most GDs do not have conclusions, but every GD needs to be summarised by putting forth what the group discussed and a point of consensus, if any, in a nutshell. If the observer asks you to summarise a GD, it means the GD has come to an end. It may also mean that you did very well in GD and he/she wants to see your performance further or you were very quiet during the GD and wants to give you any opportunity to score. If you have not been able to initiate the discussion, try to take the opportunity to summarise on your own and close it. Good summarising would get you good points. Keep the following points in mind while summarising a discussion:

1. Avoid raising new points.
2. Avoid stating only your viewpoint.
3. Incorporate all the important points that came out during the GD.
4. Keep it brief and concise.
5. Do not add anything once the GD has been summarised.

GROUP DISCUSSION ETIQUETTE AND MANNERS

Dos	Don'ts
• Be patient. Stay objective.	• Participate until you have understood the topic.
• Be open-minded but stick to your point as best as you can.	• Don't get upset if anyone objects to your view point or lose your cool if you object to anyone.
• Be active and interested throughout.	• Take the discussion personally.
• Be yourself and natural. Do not try to be someone you are not.	• Use too many gestures when you speak. No aggressive gestures like finger pointing and table thumping
• Seek clarification if you have doubts about the subject.	• Dominate the discussion yourself. Give others a chance to contribute.
• Speak pleasantly and politely in the group.	
• Work out strategies to make an entry. Agree with someone else's point and then move onto express your views.	• Avoid drawing on too much personal experience and generalisation.
• Be assertive, not dominating with a balanced tone.	• Interrupt. Wait for a speaker to finish.
• Respect others' contribution and ideas; agree and acknowledge interesting points; disagree politely.	• Bring out the irrelevant information.
• Think before you speak—'Does it make sense?'	
• Stick to the discussion topic.	
• Be aware of your body language when you speak.	
• Motivate other members to speak.	

SOME PRACTICAL HINTS ON QUESTIONS COMMONLY ASKED.

- **How do I take my chance to speak?** Maintain eye contact with the speaker. You would be able to gauge from his eye movement and pitch of voice that he/she is about to close his/her inputs. You can quickly take it from there. Also, try and link your inputs with inputs from earlier speaker, whether you want to add to or oppose his/her arguments. This would reflect that you are actually being participative rather than just doing a collective monologue.
- **How do I communicate in a GD?** The average duration of the GD provides an average of about 2–3 minutes per participant to speak. Be crisp, to the point and fact based. Avoid making opinions without factual base. Avoid looking at the observers while speaking. Try to speak about three to four times. You, therefore, need to make the most of those 30–40 second slots.

- **How do I convince others and make them agree to my view point?** Do not forget that some topics have been eternal debates, and there is no way you can get an agreement in 20–25 minutes on them. The objective is not to force your line of thinking but to provide fact-based, convincing and logical arguments which create an impact. Stick to this approach.
- **Do leadership skills include moderating the group discussion?** No. Do not try to impose your authority by ordering people when to speak and when not to. This only reflects poor leadership. Leadership in a GD only means your clarity of thought, ability to explore the topic in different perspectives, providing an opportunity to a silent participant to speak, listening to others and probing them to extract more information. Work on these areas.
- **How do I disagree in the best possible manner?** Do not use extreme phrases such as 'I strongly object' or 'I disagree'. Instead use 'I would like to share my views on...' or 'One difference between your point and mine is ...' or 'I beg to differ...'.

GROUP DISCUSSION MISTAKES TO AVOID

Some examples of mistakes made by the GD participants, based on my experience as an observer, include the following:

- **Emotional outburst:** A female participant was offended at a statement by a male participant while explaining his point of view, which implied that women are 'generally being submissive'. When she got an opportunity to speak, instead of focussing on the topic, she resorted to accusing the other candidate for being a male chauvinist and went on to defend women in general. Her behaviour was perceived as immature and demotivating to the rest of the team.
- **Interruptions:** One participant believed that the more he talked, the more likely he was to get through the GD. So, he interrupted other people at every opportunity. He did this so often that the other candidates got together to prevent him from participating in the rest of the GD.
- **Egotism or showing off:** One participant got a GD topic for which he had prepared. He, therefore, started boasting of his vast knowledge of the topic. Every other sentence of his contained statistical data like '20% of companies', '24.27% of population felt ...' and so on. Soon, the rest of the team either laughed at him or ignored him as they perceived that he was cooking up the data. Such behaviour highlights your inability to work in an atmosphere where different opinions are expressed.
- **Get noticed—but only for the right reasons:** One participant knew that everyone would compete to initiate the discussion. So, as soon as the topic ('Negative impact on India by joining the WTO') was read out, in his anxiety to be the first to speak, he did not hear the word 'Negative' and began discussing the positive impact of WTO on India. The evaluator had to stop him and then he corrected his mistake.
- **Managing one's insecurities:** A female participant was very nervous thinking that some of the other candidates were exceptionally good. Her insecurity resulted in her contributing little to the discussion. Even when she was asked to comment on a particular point, she preferred to remain silent. Focus on your strengths and do not worry about whether others are superior to you. It is easy to pick up these cues from your body language. You just need practise!!

Going through an Interview Process

30

Interview is a two-way exchange of information and an opportunity for both parties to market themselves. The employer is selling the organisation to you and you are marketing your skills, knowledge and personality to the employer. The employer wants to know if you have the skills, knowledge, self-confidence and motivation necessary for the job. Note that the employer saw something of interest in your CV, and now wants to determine whether you will fit in with the organisation's culture and philosophy. Your performance in GD also had contribution in your being considered for the interview process. Similarly, even if you have come all the way through aptitude test and GD, you might still want to evaluate the position and the organisation, and determine if they fit into your career plans. It is a simple meeting of minds and hearts where an employee's future gets sealed. It is an exercise which fetches you dividends only if your homework is done right.

TYPES OF INTERVIEWS

Primarily there are two types of interview. One is a telephone interview and other is an in-person interview. The telephone interview normally precedes the in-person interview. Once you are in the process, you may experience one or more of the situations described later. It is rare to have only one interview and only one type of interview prior to a job offer. Most employers will bring back a candidate number of times to be sure that a potential employee will fit into the company culture and the competency framework.

Telephone Interview

A telephone interview is used primarily for initial screening to reduce the expenses. It is used to obtain more information about a candidate's skills and experience than what is available from the CV. During a telephone interview you sell yourself only through your voice and confidence in conversation. There are three basic ways in which the telephone interviews are set up:

1. You initiate a call to HR who shows interest in your background that leads to an interview.
2. A company calls you based on your application or some reference and your interview begins, even if you are unprepared for the call. This will be an opportunity for company to judge your response to such uncertain situations.
3. Based on your application, reference or your CV registered with jobsites like *naukri.com*, a company representative calls you to fix an interview date and time, and it takes place as agreed.

Most companies use the telephone interview method to eliminate candidates who don't have essential knowledge, skills and experience. Candidates who meet the requirements are likely to attend the next level face-to-face interview.

Preparing for Telephone Interviews

Your goal of a telephone interview is to get an opportunity for a face-to-face interview. You have a major advantage in a phone interview in the sense that the interviewer has no idea of how you respond to his questions. All that the person hears is a well-informed and well-prepared interviewee. Use this to your advantage. The following tips might help you to progress from a telephone interview to the next step—the face-to-face interview. The basic preparation for interviews is described later in this section and all those items do apply to telephone interviews as well. In addition some specific steps need to be taken for telephone interviews:

- Have all of your materials about yourself and the employer open and readily available for reference. This includes your CV, job description, your notes about employer survey, etc.
- Have a notepad handy to take notes.
- Turn off call waiting on your phone.
- Place a 'Do Not Disturb' note on your door.
- Check your voice by taping it. Listen to it very carefully and make necessary changes. Also warm up your voice while waiting for the call.
- Turn off your stereo, TV and any other potential distraction.

Write down your responses to some questions and practise reading them aloud. You can get many such sample interview questions from net. By knowing what to say, you will seem more confident when you interact with the interviewer on phone, when the call actually comes.

When you pick up the phone and know that the phone is from a company, ask the HR person to repeat his or her name. Verify the spelling and write it down. Use this name in all your responses and further communication. It is perfectly OK to suggest a specific alternate time to the HR person if you cannot devote enough time to an unscheduled phone interview. In that case, ask for the telephone number and a convenient time to call back.

During phone interview

- Listen first. Do not interrupt. Let the interviewer complete his question before you respond.
- Ask clarification. Use open-ended questions. The more information you gather, the better you can respond.
- Smile, though not seen, changes the tone of your voice.
- Keep a glass of water handy, in case you need to wet your mouth.
- Ensure that you can hear and are being clearly heard. Speak slowly with clear pronunciations.
- Take your time; it is perfectly acceptable to take a moment to collect your thoughts.
- Use the person's title (Mr or Ms and the last name); use the first name only if they ask you to.
- Make sure you are in a place where you can read notes, take notes and concentrate.
- Give short answers.
- Do not smoke, chew gum, eat or drink.

- Do not cough. If you cannot avoid, say, 'excuse me'.
- Do not feel uneasy if you find the interviewer silent on the other side after your response. Just wait. You can, however, ask a question related to your last response.
- Stay focused on the key points you wrote down about your strengths. Avoid negative points while describing your background.
- Demonstrate your enthusiasm and interest through your voice and verbal mannerisms. Sound positive, self-confident and focused.
- Do create a strong finish to your phone interview with thoughtful questions.
- Take notes about how you answered and what you were asked.

FACE-TO-FACE INTERVIEWS

Face-to-face interviews are also known as in-person interviews, where you are invited to present yourself for the interview. The most traditional is a one-on-one conversation. Your goal is to establish rapport with the interviewer and show them that your qualifications will benefit their organisation. Your focus should be on the person asking questions. Maintain eye contact, listen and respond once a question has been asked. The face-to-face interviews could take one or more of the following forms:

Panel/Committee Interview

The interview panel or committee generally comprises three to six members. These members come from different backgrounds and occupations. The panel interviews generally don't have a fix pattern. It could be structured or unstructured. In the structured version, each of the interviewers has specific criteria to assess in you. One person may ask questions about your computer skills, another may ask about educational background. In the unstructured version, interviewers make a broad evaluation. You need to treat each interviewer with equal importance. You may get similar questions from more than one interviewer. Patiently respond to them.

You could be facing your prospective team members or you could be up against HR vice president, the section head, the operations chief, etc. You could also be sent to a recruitment assessment centre for multi-parametric evaluation through various psychological tests for pressure-handling abilities, team-player skills and so on.

Behavioural Interview

Behavioural interviews are aimed at learning how the interviewee acts in specific employment-related situations. These types of questions may be asked in any interview format—telephone, panel or one-on-one. The basic premise is that past behaviour is the best predictor of future actions and performance. The behaviour-oriented questions are not hypothetical and are expected to be answered with some facts. The interviewer is looking for results, not just an activity list. They are looking for names, dates, places, the outcome and especially what your specific role was in achieving that outcome. This type of question generally starts with, 'Give me an example when ...' or 'Tell me about a time when ...'.

Group Interview

This is not very common in India. However, its use cannot be ruled out with modern HR practises emerging. Interviewing simultaneously with other candidates provides the company with a sense of your leadership potential and style. Group interview helps the company to know how you interact with peers, and your persuasion capability in a team setting. Particularly,

---

Are you timid or bossy?
Are you attentive or do you seek attention?
Do others turn to you instinctively?
Do you compete for authority?
Do you use argumentation and careful reasoning to gain support or do you divide and conquer?

It may be considered as an interviewer directed and controlled GD. The interviewer might call on you to discuss an issue with the other candidates, solve a problem collectively or discuss your peculiar qualifications in front of the other candidates. Treat others with respect while exerting influence over others. Avoid overt power conflicts, which will make you look uncooperative and immature. Keeping constant eye on the interviewer helps you with some important cues. If you are unsure of what is expected from you, ask for clarification from the interviewer.

Case-interview

In case-interviews, you may be asked to demonstrate your problem-solving or decision-making skills. The interviewer will outline a situation or provide you with a written case and ask you to formulate a plan that deals with the problem. You do not have to come up with the final solution. The interviewer is looking for how you apply your knowledge and skills to a real-life situation. Speak and reason aloud so interviewers have a full understanding of your thought process.

Stress Interview

Stress interview creates discomfort in you through a stressful and difficult situation. The aim is to test the candidate's ability in stress situations. The interviewers may try to introduce stress by asking continuous questions without giving time to think, by asking you to wait in the waiting room for an hour before the interview, or by openly challenging and confronting your believes or judgement. You might be called upon to perform an impossible task of convincing the interviewer on some issue. Answer each question in calm as it comes.

THINGS THAT AN INTERVIEWER LOOKS IN YOU!

Entire campus looks forward to the interview with enthusiasm, fear and excitement towards the beginning of the final year. The constant thought in one's mind is—what shall make this click! What is it that the interviewer is looking in me!

Here's what the recruiters look for when they hire their future employee.

- Family background
- Education
- Experience
- Stability
- Initiative

- General ability
- Inter-personal skills
- Confidence
- Aptitude
- Pleasant looks

The interview is not just limited to testing your knowledge base, but also your application ability. Often questions are asked which need to be answered then and there. The right answer is not the only thing important. It is also the way in which you understand the question, your attitude and approach to the problem and how you logically arrive at the answer. So, put your thinking caps on!

BASIC PREPARATION FOR INTERVIEWS

As mentioned earlier, the interview process is a two-way process. The company needs good candidates and you need a good company to launch or pursue your career. Interview is an opportunity to present yourself and your skills to your best advantage. Remember that you are actually selling an entire package of yourself and its packaging is just like a product. Make sure you make the most out of it. And YOU are the best one to do it!!

Never take an interview lightly. The interview could be on phone, in your campus, the company's site or even at a third venue like a hotel. Whatever is the type of interview you face and where you face it, there are certain basic preparatory steps necessary. Preparation increases confidence. Research and homework are critical part of preparing for an interview. If you haven't done your homework, it is going to be obvious. Spend time researching the occupation, the organisation and questions you might ask at the end of the interview. Keeping in mind basic attitudes and presentation techniques will help you sail through the interview with success. Some additional preparatory steps may be involved in specific types of interviews, such as panel or telephone interview. Some areas which you need to look at are:

Know Yourself

Do a thorough self-assessment to know what you have to offer an employer. Do a Strength, Weakness, Opportunity and Threats (SWOT) analysis on your CV in relation to the job under consideration covering the skills, experience and personal attributes that you can use to market yourself. Also consider your past jobs, extra-curricular involvements, volunteer work, college projects, etc. Key issues are:

- What is required?
- What you can offer and what makes you offer that?

The skills required fall into two categories—technical and generic. Technical skills are the skills required to do a specific job and generic skills are those which are transferable to many work settings. Communication skills are generic. Negotiation skills could be specific to a procurement job. MS office could be a generic skill while knowledge of AutoCAD could be a specific skill needed for a specific company. Also find good answers for questions such as:

- How have I demonstrated the required skills elsewhere?
- Do I have clear short-term and long-term goals?
- What kind of work environment do I like? (Close supervision? Fast pace?)
- Apart from my skills and experience, what else I bring to this job?
- How do I compensate for the skills which I do not possess?

Not everyone is good in each and every field. Every individual has strengths and weaknesses. Companies look for people who know their strengths and expertise and are able to demonstrate those with evidence from the past background. Companies also appreciate if you have put in efforts in the past to overcome your weaknesses. Many make the most common mistake of claiming to know everything. Know your limits and polish your strengths.

Know the Occupation

Researching the occupation and position helps to tailor your responses to demonstrate your understanding of the position and its competency requirements. If you know all the job requirements, you are in a better position to match your skills with them. The resulting 'shortlist' matched with the requirements will be the one that you need to emphasise during the interview. It is also in your best interest to review other job profiles and compensation surveys for similar occupations. There are several ways to find information about an occupation:

- Acquire a copy of the job profile from the employer or the placement cell of your institute. If you are responding to an advertisement, it provides some details.
- Interact with people working in the field. Read articles about the field from newspapers, magazines and the Internet. Find out future trends in the area including technology.

Know the Organisation

The knowledge of the organisation, prepares you to discuss how you can meet its needs, technically, professionally, socially and culturally. Some of the characteristics that you should know about the organisation are:

- How big is it?
- What are its products and market?
- How is the organisation structured?
- What is its history?

- How are they performing?
- Have there been any recent changes, new developments?
- Where is it located?

Placement division of your institute should have a database of prospective companies who are likely to be interested in your institute. It should maintain a library of company literature and business directories. It also should maintain all the press releases, press reports and visit reports of all such companies. Most medium to large-sized organisations have published information and annual reports. Use Internet and search by industry and company name.

You may even visit or phone the organisation and request information on their products, services or areas of research. Your company visits, study tours, summer internships and final project periods also give you opportunities for interacting with many organisations. Make best use of that interaction in creating placement opportunities for yourself and other students.

Prepare Questions to Ask

Prepare a list of questions to ask the interviewer based on your knowledge and research about the company. Intelligent, well thought-out questions create a good impression and show your genuine interest in the position. Think of the questions for which the answers were not readily available in the company literature. Pick your questions carefully, because this is your chance to show your inquisitiveness and to gather more information about the company. Avoid mentioning negative information discovered by you if any. This information also helps you to compare different employers, so you should ask the same questions to each employer. Some sample questions are:

> • What are the most significant factors affecting your business today? How has been the impact of recession on your business/industry?
> • How have changes in technology affected your business today?
> • How has your company grown or changed in the last couple of years?
> • What future direction do you see the company taking?
> • Where is the greatest demand for your services or product?
> • How do you differ from your competitors?
> • How much responsibility and autonomy will I be given in this position?
> • Can you tell me more about the training policy and programmes?
> • Have any new product lines been introduced recently?
> • How much travel is normally expected?
> • What criteria will be used to evaluate my performance?
> • Will I work independently or as part of a team?
> • What are the career paths available in this organisation?
> • When can I expect to hear from you regarding this position?

The last question is very important because employers want to hire those who are interested in the position and this question demonstrates your interest.

Exercise caution while asking questions to an employer.

• You might get some information about the company during your interaction with the interviewer during the interview. Please ensure not to seek the same information again unless you want to have more clarification about that information.

• For a very large high profile company asking; *What is the history of your company?* Or *How your company was started?*; is ridiculous. You should already have the answer from your research. This question might be OK for medium-sized companies who do not always publish annual reports.

• If you think you have a bright idea about any ongoing activity, you may ask: 'Did the company consider this option ...'

PRESENTING YOURSELF AT THE INTERVIEW

Physical Appearance—Dressing and Grooming

Your disposition for the interview makes the first impression on the interviewer. Right dressing shows seriousness that you place on the position. Though proper dressing on its own will not get you the job, a poor dress sense may exclude you from further consideration. Besides, between two equally good applicants, the company may choose to hire the one dressed more professionally. Here are some guidelines to give you a head start:

Men

- **Shirts.** Long-sleeved. White is the safest and most preferred colour for shirts. Light shades of grey and blue are also acceptable. Tuck in the shirt and do not roll up the sleeves. Short sleeved shirt is not considered appropriate for interviews.
- **Slacks.** Dark colour
- **Jackets.** Optional but preferred in campus interviews. Most accepted colour is navy blue. Generally B-school provided jackets are used. Suits might be a better option for final interview and it gives you more colour options.
- **Ties.** Optional, but preferred. Choose a pattern such as solids, small dots, diagonal stripes, etc.
- **Belts.** Matching with shoes. Small buckles with squared lines look professional.
- **Socks.** Black preferred followed by blue or gray, depending on your attire. No white socks. Socks length should hide the skin when you sit down or cross your legs.
- **Shoes.** Black or brown leather is the best; no sneakers for interview.
- **Hair.** Keep neat, short and preferably parted on the side. Shave off all those facial hair.
- **Jewellery.** The watch and wedding ring are the only acceptable jewellery to go with male attire. Digital watches look cheap. Avoid political/religious necklaces or bracelets.
- **Accessories.** Leather briefcase or folder to hold copies of your CV and other documents. Bring extra copies of your CV, a writing pad and pen. Avoid plastic folders and plastic ball pens as they look cheap.

Women

In India, women have the options of western format or Indian format. Generally institutes have their own dress codes for campus interviews, and students are expected to comply. Nothing too revealing please, in either case!

Western Format

- **Suit.** Three-piece business suit, blouse and skirt or slack and cardigan twinsets. No sleeveless shirts. Short-sleeved blouses are okay when they are tailor-cut or have double breast design to create a business-like look. Long skirt but not with a Cinderella look, or short, where it falls at least two inches below the knee.

Indian Format

The elegance of an Indian sari can get you the much-needed advantage. You can also have fusion by putting a blazer over the sari. White and pastel shade saris are the best for interviews. Dark colours such as navy blue or maroon also look good. Just make sure that the sari is plain and doesn't carry much design. Avoid wearing a sari with heavy embroidery or *zari*. Blouse should not be sleeveless. You can as well opt for a salwar kameez with similar colour standards as above.

- **Panty-hose or stockings.** A must for professional grooming, but nothing with overly fussy patterns.
- **Shoes.** Closed shoes or pumps with 1½ inch heels suggest a professional look. Dark colours are best.
- **Hair.** If longer than shoulder length, should be pulled back. Don't let it fall in front of your face and don't keep fixing it during the interview. Avoid large ornaments and trendy hairstyles.
- **Make-up.** Be subtle; natural is the keyword. Light shades of lipstick and nail polish are recommended.
- **Jewellery.** Be conservative. A simple gold, silver or pearl necklace is best. Avoid gaudy fashion jewellery and those which make noise when one moves.
- **Accessories.** Folders and bags should blend well with the total professional look. Match your purse with shoe colour. Bring extra copies of your CV, a writing pad and a pen.

Timely Arrival at the Interview Site

If the interview is on campus, timely arrival is no big deal. However, if it is off-campus, some special efforts become necessary. Seek help from your placement office. Get clear address and location of the venue, with a direction map if possible. If using public transport, you need to know the nearest train station or bus stop, etc.

- Arrive 5 to 10 minutes early. Arriving early will give you opportunity to interact with other candidates and also read some information on the company in the reception area.
- On arrival, politely tell the receptionist the purpose of your visit and who you are meeting. You may be asked to sit and wait in the reception area.
- Enter into a state of relaxed concentration. Calm your negative self, chatter through meditation or visualisation prior to the meeting. Just relax while waiting, focus on the present moment and take slow and deep breaths to remain calm and confident.

Entering the Interview Room—First Impression

Interviewers make up their mind within the first five minutes of an interview. Therefore, keep in mind the important first impression indicators:

- Knock the door before you enter and ask for permission—*May I come in?*
- Wait for a response from the interviewing team before you actually enter.
- Walk in the door with a confident smiling face and wait for the interviewing team to request you to take seat. Be totally comfortable with the situation.

- When introduced, have a firm, but not painful, handshake. Have good posture when sitting or standing. Introduce yourself in a relaxed and confident manner.
- Keep the bag of your documents and certificates at a place which can be accessed easily if required.
- Do not show your certificates to the interview panel till you are asked to do so.
- Your CV is with the panel. Therefore, do not offload all your achievements and skills onto the panel till requested by the panel.

UNDERSTANDING THE INTERVIEW PROCESS

Regardless of the type of interview, most will incorporate the following stages: establishing rapport, exchanging information and closing the interview. Pay attention to the job titles of the interviewer(s). This can help you decide how much technical detail to provide in your responses.

ESTABLISHING RAPPORT

This is very important because while establishing rapport, first impressions are made and the tone of the interview is set. A good interviewer will introduce himself and take the lead. Follow his lead and respond appropriately. If they are chatty, be chatty; if they are formal, be formal. Some employers deliberately use casual conversation to get to know you on a more personal level.

- Smile and maintain eye contact. This communicates confidence, even if you don't feel it.
- If the interviewer offers, give a firm shake hand. If they don't, it is appropriate to offer yours.
- Wait until the interviewer sits or offers you a seat before sitting down.
- If the interviewer is making small talk, participate. Keep your answers short and positive.

EXCHANGE OF INFORMATION

This is the bulk of the interview. It is your opportunity to let the interviewer know what you have to offer and your chance to learn more about the organisation.

- When you answer a question, look the interviewer in the eye.
- Watch the interviewer's reactions. If he looks confused, ask if you can clarify anything.
- Be aware of what is your body language. Avoid closed postures. Sit upright, but not stiffly.
- Feel relaxed. Control your nervous habits like swinging your foot, talking with your hands or fiddling with jewellery, buttons, pens, etc.
- Show that you are interested in the job by asking questions.
- Try not to appear bored or anxious. Don't look at your watch.

CLOSING THE INTERVIEW

When the interviewer is done with his information gathering, he will ask if you have anything to add or if you have any questions. This is your opportunity to review your skill inventory and make sure that you have communicated everything that you wanted to. If any of your questions have not been addressed during the interview, now is the time to ask them.

- Thank the interviewer for his time and consideration.
- Ask when you can expect to hear from him. If it is not known when a decision will be made, ask if you can phone in a week's time to inquire about the progress.
- If the interviewer offers his hand, shake it firmly. Otherwise, it is fine to offer yours.
- If not already discussed, you can offer to leave a sample of your work or portfolio if you have one.

MAKE THE MOST OF YOUR INTERVIEW

Responses

Most interviewers complain that few candidates are able to give original and right answers and most just give answers provided in the coaching classes. Interviewers like to give a lead in the way they ask the question. It is, therefore, up to you to note facial expressions, the tone of words and thrust of questions and get clues as to where this interview is heading.

You can never predict the question you may have to answer. So, approach the interview with an inventory of important points about yourself that you want the interviewer to know. For example, if you apply for a job as a sales executive, a list of products you sold before, types of customers or market segment, languages spoken, knowledge and experience in the industry should be kept handy.

Be Polite

Listen very carefully and don't interrupt the interviewer. Poor listening skills create bad impression. If the interviewers are serious and soft-spoken, then you should act in the same manner as the interviewer. Avoid loud laughter during the interview. Sometimes, you may know something very well and it just slips your mind. Ask for help from the interviewer. Just in case you are stuck, ask for a hint. *Don't try this too often!* Things might just click.

Be Positive

Face the interview with a positive attitude. Proper preparation would provide you that much-needed confidence and positive attitude. Companies look for employees who are goal-oriented, career-driven, enthusiastic and motivated. Be the employee they want. Don't complain about anything—from your former employer to the weather—and don't apologise for experience that you don't have. Just sell what you do have and let the employer decide if you have what is being looked for. Also, avoid negative words. For example, do not say, 'I have a little experience ..., ' say, 'I have experience ...'. Don't be afraid to repeat important points. In fact, it is a good idea to do that.

Showcase the Important Things

List five important things that fit the job profile of the position. Prepare to present skills that fit such traits. It helps to talk to friends familiar with the job profile or your placement officer.

Be Tactical

If you are experienced, the interviewer already knows your current salary and benefits package. For campus interviews the companies come up with a package and generally you have option to take it or leave it. Your placement office, however, should be negotiating the package in the interest of the students. When the topic of salary comes up, avoid spelling out a figure of your expectations as much as possible. State that you know that the company will make a fair offer which would do justice to your qualifications and experience. If you are offered the position during the interviewing process and you want the job, then accept it. If the offer is not acceptable for any reason, ask for time to consider the offer.

Be Calm, Have Clear Verbal and Sound Non-verbal Communication

Calmness shows emotional maturity and is essential during the job interviews. Calmness does not imply being unenthusiastic or apathetic, but recognising that you are nervous and not letting it come in the way. A clear verbal communication implies clarity of thought process, while body language and facial expressions assist in establishing a good rapport with the interviewer. Pauses, silences and gestures may all indicate what you mean, understand or would like to emphasise.

Look Beyond the Obvious

Your interview team wants you to address some core queries about you. Try and look beyond the upfront questions to explore their real intent and expectation. If they ask you about your perception of the company's policy of say flexible timings, they want you to present your expectation from such a policy. Think of alternatives before you criticise anything. If your work involves individual research besides team work, don't go overboard about team-player abilities. Balance your answer and mention how, sometimes, individual work is more productive though teamwork is needed to put into action ideas generated by individual research.

Don't Get Scared

Interviewers are not lions. They are looking for excuses to hire you and not spill your guts. Don't be over defensive and meek. That conveys low self-esteem. If you face your interviewers with fear in your eyes, they won't like what they see. Don't be afraid to 'blow your own horn' as long as you can substantiate what you are saying with examples. Third party observations can also be mentioned. For example, *My last employer told me that I was promoted because of how I handled conflicts with clients.*

Know Next Steps

Remember that your goal is to get opportunity for the subsequent interview. Ask about the next step in the interview process as well as the hiring timetable. If you do not receive a positive response and you are sincerely interested, explain them why this information is important to you and then ask again about the next step and timetable.

DEALING WITH SPECIFIC TYPES OF INTERVIEWS

Panel Interview

1. **Give variety to your answers**
   Different panels might be comparing notes. Don't give a stock answer to all of them. Repackage your skills so that they sound different. If you showcased project 'A' as your major achievement in your job earlier, talk about project 'B' before the next panel.

2. **Fine-tune inter-personal skills**
   Pull out your group management and group presentation skills. Look for the personality type of each interviewer and try to connect with each one of them without getting personal. Take your time in responding to questions. Maintain primary eye contact with the panel member who asked the question, but also seek eye contact with other members of the panel as you give your response.

3. **Prepare for stress**
   You'll be up against a time crunch in a panel interview. In one-on-ones, the interviewer might be taking notes, allowing you little breathers, but no such luck with four people firing questions at you. Use stress control techniques to soothe your nerves.

4. **Rehearse well**
   Your placement office should organise mock panel interviews. Alternatively rehearse with your family members or friends. Ask them to fire non-stop questions at you. Ask for serious feedback. Questions about qualifications and work experience are usually generic; so, what your mock team asks you should be pretty close to the real stuff.

See yourself answering with ease the questions you expect. Then replay your answers and ask yourself these questions:

- How interesting were your observations?
- Did most of your responses begin the same way?
- Did you use 'we' often, suggesting team-player attributes?
- Are there traces of humour in your responses?

THE SUBSEQUENT INTERVIEWS

Some companies have a practise of scheduling multiple interviews with multiple teams. Most companies, however, bring you back for second and sometimes third or fourth interview for various reasons. Sometimes they want to reconfirm their earlier observations and conclusions about you. Sometimes they have difficulty deciding between few short-listed candidates. The interviewer's supervisor or other decision-makers in the company may want to have a 'look' at you before the final selection is made. The second interview could take a variety of directions and you must prepare for each of them.

- If meeting the same person again, you do not need to be as assertive of your skills. You can focus on cementing rapport, understanding the company and its culture and how your skills mesh with them. Probe tactfully to discover more information about the internal dynamics. You might end up negotiating a compensation package; so be prepared.
- If meeting a new person or team, it could be starting all over again from the beginning.

The second and the subsequent interviews are generally held at site. The site, however, could change depending upon who is in the interview panel. It may be the last step in the process before an offer is made or could lead to the next level of the selection process. Both the employer and the interviewee have specific goals to be achieved during the subsequent interviews.

Employer's Goals

1. Identifying and conforming specific qualities: In the first interview, employers have identified many general qualities important to their organisation. In the second interview, employers try to see if you have the specific qualities they are looking for.
2. Identifying organisational fit: Employers also want to see how others in the organisation respond to you and if you fit their corporate culture.

Interviewee's Goals

1. View the facilities; meet employees of the organisation.
2. Determine if the company, the job and the people are a strong fit for you.

INTERVIEW QUESTIONS AND RESPONSES

Interviewers use five different types of questions—directive, non-directive, hypothetical, behaviour descriptive and stress inducing. Being aware of the different types helps you in the preparation stage as you build your skills inventory. It also helps you focus on exactly what is being asked and what the employer is looking for in specific questions.

Directive Questions

The interviewer is looking for very clear and focused information. If you have completed research on yourself, this type of question should be easy to answer.

> **Q:** *What skills do you have that relate to this position?*
> **A:** *I have very good communication and inter-personal skills that I have refined through summer and part-time jobs. In addition, I am fluent in both English and French.*

Non-directive Questions

The interviewer asks a general question and does not seek specific information. You determine the focus of your answer. Be structured and concise in your reply.

> **Q:** Tell me about yourself.
> **A:** I have a bachelor degree in Science and masters in Business Administration with HR specialisation. In addition I have recently completed a certification course in SAP, HR Module. These have given me a strong background in many of the principles of human behaviour and the recruitment, training and development functions. I have done my summer project with XYZ company in reviewing their compensation policy; and my final project is in the area of competency management. Competency management was my elective subject and area of major research. These have enhanced my capability to do justice to the position under consideration. I love and enjoy working with people, have leadership abilities and I am a proven team member in my earlier academic experience and short experience with the company.

While answering such questions, keep in mind that the employer wants to know how your background and personality qualify you for the job. Your answer, therefore, should cover four areas: your education, related experience, skills and abilities and personal attributes. As you talk about these areas, relate them to the profile of the job you are seeking.

Hypothetical or Scenario Questions

The interviewer describes a situation which you may encounter in the position and asks how you would react in a similar situation. This is to test your problem-solving abilities. When answering such a question, try applying a simple problem-solving model to it—gather information, evaluate information, seek solutions, weigh alternatives, make a decision, communicate the decision, monitor the results and modify if necessary.

> **Q:** Suppose you are working in our laboratory on your first day and a fire breaks out at a nearby work station. What would you do?
> **A:** Before I start working in any laboratory, I always locate the emergency equipment, such as eye washes, fire blankets and alarms. I would also review the safety protocols. So in this situation, I would be aware of these. As soon as I notice the fire, I would shut down my experiment and if the fire is significant, I would pull the fire alarm and help to evacuate the laboratory. In the case of very small flame, I would ask the staff member at the station what I could do to help, which would vary with the type of substances involved.

Behavioural Questions

These questions relate to what you did in a particular situation rather than what you would do. These become relevant if you have prior experience. Situations chosen usually follow the job description. The logic is that past performance is a good prediction of future potential in managing similar situations. There is no right or wrong answer to this type of question. When preparing for such questions, review the skills and qualities that the position would require and identify specific examples from your past which demonstrated those traits.

Q: Give me an example of a work situation in which you were proud of your performance.
A: While working as a sales executive for XYZ company, I called on prospective clients and persuaded them of the ecological and economic benefits of recycling. I also followed up on clients to ensure that they were satisfied with the service they received. This involved both telephone and in-person contacts. I increased sales 34% over the same period in the previous year.

Stress Questions

Some questions will surprise you and possibly make you feel uncomfortable during an interview. The interviewers want to see how you react in difficult situations or sometimes to test your sense of humour. Such questions may directly challenge your response or say something negative about you or a reference. Sometimes they ask seemingly irrelevant questions like 'Which is your preference, fruits or vegetables?' or 'If you were an animal, what type of animal would you be?'

The best way to deal with such a question is to recognise what is happening. The interviewer is trying to elicit a reaction from you. Stay calm. If humour comes naturally to you, you might try using it in your response, but it is important to respond to the question. What you say is not nearly as important as maintaining your composure.

Q: Which do you like better, lions or tigers?
A: Oh, lions definitely! They appear so majestic and are very sociable. To be honest, I think that seeing The Lion King four times has probably contributed to this!

Just to round up what has been said earlier, great interviews result from careful groundwork. You can ace your next interview if you:

1. **Set goals for the interview.** It is your job to ensure that the interviewer knows as much as he wants about your skills, abilities, experience and achievements. If you sense there are misconceptions, clear them up before leaving. Don't leave the meeting without getting your own questions answered.

2. **Understand the basic question behind every question.** 'Why should we hire you?' Be sure you answer that completely.

3. **Understand the interviewer's agenda.** He has the responsibility of hiring the right candidate. Your responsibility is to demonstrate that you are the one. 'Are there additional pluses here?' 'Will this person fit the organisation's culture?' These and other questions will be on the interviewer's mind. Find ways to appropriately respond.

4. **Watch those non-verbal clue**s. Generally, words constitute only 30% to 35% of the communication. Facial expressions, body movements and gestures convey the rest. Keep eye contact. Lean slightly towards the interviewer to show interest and enthusiasm. Speak with well-modulated voice that supports appropriate excitement for the opportunity before you.

5. **Be smart about money questions.** Don't fall into the trap of telling the interviewer your financial expectations. You may be asking too little or too much and in each case ruin your chances of getting that job. Instead, ask what salary range the job falls in. Postpone money discussion until you have a better understanding of the scope of job responsibilities.

6. **Don't hang out your dirty laundry.** Be careful not to criticise your earlier employers or the college. State only positive aspects of your previous experience. Even if you disagreed with a former employer, express your enthusiasm for earlier situations as much as you can. Whenever you speak negatively about another person or company, you run the risk of appearing like a troubled person who may have difficulty working with others.

ANNEXURE–I

Typical questions asked in interview and your possible responses

1. **What are your biggest accomplishments?**
   You may begin your reply with: 'Although I feel my biggest achievements are still ahead of me, I am proud of my involvement with... I made my contribution as a part of that team and learnt a lot in the process'. It will be good to close your answer with specifying what attributes and circumstances made you succeed.

2. **Tell me about yourself.**
   This is a pet question of most interviewers. Remember the underlying question: 'Why should I hire you?' You need to have a short statement prepared in your mind including examples of achievements from your academic and work life that closely match the elements of the job before you. It should not sound like a rehearsed puppet talk. Talk about things you have done well at your college and how you wanted to perform in the first job.

3. **Why should I employ you? Why should I choose you over someone else?**
   Your answer should list out strengths that you feel are relevant to the job. Talk clearly about problems that you have solved in the past and highlight the quality required. Below are some suggestions. You need to structure them to suit your requirements and also give appropriate details and examples.

   - I have the experience and knowledge relevant to this job.
   - I have good co-ordination skills.
   - Good analytical skills.
   - I can persuade people to see my point of view and get the work done.
   - My greatest asset is my ability to motivate people even during emergencies; I do not lose my cool.
   - I have good entrepreneurial skills.
   - I have consistently met my deadlines and targets.
   - Can say 'no' to people when required to do so!
   - I am very co-operative with my subordinates and would like to see them grow.
   - I am a good team-player.
   - I am very flexible and have the ability to work hard under difficult work conditions.

4. **Do you have offers from other companies?**
   A difficult question! You are on thin ice here! Since you are in the job market you must have applied to other companies or would have some offers from other companies. Best thing is not to lie. The interviewer could be checking your honesty. He may also be trying to find out how

focused you are. Do you apply randomly or is there a well-planned strategy? Your answer should match your career goals.

5. **What salary are you expecting?**

   Try not to get into salary details early in the interview. If pressed, you could say that it all depends on the job and would like to discuss after the competencies are matched. Say this in a convincing tone.

   In case this question comes up during later interviews, give a direct answer. If you have done homework, you would know how much other people in similar jobs are paid. Quote the range upfront. Work out how much is your worth based on the market value of the job and your skills. If you bring some extra skills to the table, do not hesitate to ask for more than the market value. Do not sound apologetic while quoting the figure you have in mind.

6. **What kind of a culture are you comfortable with?**

   It is better to be frank about your preferences. Your interviewer will get a clear idea about your expectations.

7. **Which is more important to you—salary, perks or growth opportunities?**

   This one will reveal the real you. So be sure what you are going to say. Be true to yourself and diplomatic. If you think this is a negotiation move, say clearly what you are looking for.

8. **What do you know about our company?**

   Never give your opinions about the company. Stick to reported facts that you have gathered from media or net. Talk about the product portfolio, size, income and market perceptions of the company. No negatives please.

9. **Your qualifications are excellent, but you may be overqualified for the position we have to offer?**

   Point out that more experience can never be a drawback. If you are multi-skilled, then highlight that a company on fast track needs multi-skilled people. Also, emphasise that the company's future growth will be an exponential function of your experience.

10. **How has your experience prepared you for your career?**

    Though academic courses provided the foundation of knowledge, I think the design projects, reports and presentations have prepared me more for my career. Internships have given me the confidence and problem-solving skills. I also refined my technical writing and learned to prepare professional documents for clients. By working on multiple projects for my college while keeping up my grades, I have built time management and efficiency skills. Additionally, I've developed leadership, communication and teamwork abilities. In general, life has taught me determination and the importance of maintaining my ethical standards.

11. **Describe the ideal job.**

    Ideally, I would like to work in a warm environment with individuals working independently towards team and/or individual goals. I am not concerned about minor elements, such as dress codes, cubicles and the level of formality. Most important to me is an atmosphere that fosters attention to quality, honesty and integrity.

12. **What type of supervisor have you found to be the best?**

    I have been fortunate enough to work under wonderful supervisors who have provided limited supervision, while answering thoughtful questions and guiding learning. In my experience, the best supervisors give positive feedbacks and constructive criticism with a view to support career growth.

13. **What do you plan to be doing in five years' time?**

    I plan to focus on getting globally recognised certifications in my areas of expertise and serve in leadership roles both at work and in professional/community organisation(s).

14. **What contributions could you make in this organisation that would help you to stand out from other applicants?**

My industriousness and learning ability have been valuable assets to my previous company. My self-learning abilities will minimise overhead costs and my industriousness at targeting needs without prompting will set me apart from others. Additionally, one thing that has always set me apart from others is my broad interests and strong writing abilities. I am not a typical 'left-brained' engineer and with my broad talents, I am likely to provide diverse viewpoints.

15. **What sort of criteria are you using to decide the organisation you will work for?**

Most importantly, I am looking for a company that values quality, ethics and teamwork. I would like to work for a company that hires overachievers.

16. **What made you choose your major?**

My academic interests are broad, so I sought civil engineering to achieve a great balance of mathematics, chemistry, physics and, most importantly, environment.

17. **Have your university and major met your expectations?**

My college has exceeded my expectations by providing group activities, career resources, individual attention and professors with genuine interest in teaching. My major has met my expectations by about 90%. I would have enjoyed more choices in elective courses and would have preferred more industry-based learning.

18. **What made you choose this college?**

I chose this college for the following reasons: My budget was limited. I was keen on the course and this college was the best recognised college for this course within the industry. I saw the website and was impressed with activities of student groups, and the people communicated in a very friendly manner.

19. **List 2–3 of your greatest achievements since you've been in college and why?**

Receiving the Outstanding Student Member Award and College of Engineering Student Service Award! I got involved with student activities to overcome my debilitating shyness. Receiving these awards was a sign of accomplishment in the transition from dragging myself to participate and to feel energised by it.

I also received the best Web Site Design Award for my department of civil engineering.

Without training in web design, I competed against not only the other student sections, but professional sections around the nation. Despite competing with more HTML-experienced people, I brought this award to my section.

Some of the other achievements of mine include earning the highest grade in an organic chemistry class of about 200 people. I worked very hard for this grade and loved the subject, so it was a great feeling to see that the hard work paid off.

20. **Which subjects have you enjoyed studying the most and why?**

I have enjoyed hydrology, fluids, solid and hazardous waste management, water and wastewater treatment and oceanography because I love water and environmental topics. Calculus and linear algebra excite me because I love logic. I enjoyed the writing and analysis in economic history. Business law thrilled me because I have a strong interest in legal matters.

21. **Which subjects did you dislike and why?**

Introductory soil elicited little interest in me, most likely because the professor was inexperienced, the book was ineffective and I had little spare time in that semester to look into other resources.

22. **Do you have plans to continue your education?**

Yes, but not immediately. I plan to continue part-time with either an MBA or an environmental engineering masters, depending on which will be more beneficial to my work.

23. **How would a professor who knows you well describe you? And how would one who does not know you well describe you?**

A professor who knows me well would likely describe my personal qualities: sweet, down-to-earth, smart, hard-working and conscientious. As specific examples of those who did not know me well, my soils professor and soils teaching assistant each considered me smart and respectful and both thought that I must have enjoyed the class a lot, due to my performance.

24. **Given the chance, how would you alter your education?**

Knowing now what I like the most, I would have used my electives for extra math and psychology classes, since I tend to be well-rounded enough that a variety of classes are unnecessary; my personal reading is diverse enough. I have found that mathematics and psychology are helpful to all career and life paths.

25. **Which part-time job did you enjoy the most and why?**

Working for PM Environmental was most enjoyable to me, since I felt like I was significantly contributing to the company, and I enjoyed learning on my own.

26. **Interests**

Some of my interests include dogs, hiking, snow-shoeing, water sports, writing, reading (especially Charles Dickens' novels), skiing, drawing, crafts and computers.

27. **What are your strengths?**

My strongest strength is the ability to teach myself difficult material, regardless of the subject (with the exception of theatre and drawing blood from dogs, which I have no talent for). Additionally, I have always excelled verbally and look forward to writing opportunities.

28. **What are your weaknesses?**

I tend to try to do too many things, leaving little time for myself. I have worked on balancing myself for the last several months. I am also working on improving my public speaking skills.

29. **What sort of serious problems have you experienced and how have you handled them?**

There was a fire in my apartment building at the end of January during one of my semesters at the university. I was able to rescue my pets and the neighbour's dog, as well as my textbooks and backpack. I, however, lost most of my mementos and possessions. While the firemen were preparing their hoses, I drove to school (with the animals in the car) to meet my laboratory partners, who were waiting for me. I explained the situation, emailed my professors and rushed back to the apartment.

Fortunately, I had insurance. I missed about a week of school to deal with insurance matters and find a new place to live. In order to salvage my grades and sanity, I dropped a course and honoured my existing student group and research commitments. Staying active socially and keeping myself well-rounded were the best healing tools for me. Within a few weeks, I was caught up and had recovered reasonably from the loss of sentimental items.

Remember, the above list of questions is just a guide. You need to prepare your own answers to suit your actual situation and your own life experiences.

Pre- and Post-Interview Follow-up 31

PRE-INTERVIEW FOLLOW-UP

Nowadays the executives and HR managers are very busy and may fail to select and notify candidates within one or even two months of posting an employment advertisement. Don't let this deter you. If you have applied for a job, follow up. Make them tell you that they rejected you. Never assume that they did. A short follow-up letter mailed three weeks after submitting a CV will differentiate you from other candidates and suggest to hiring managers that you are unusually interested in the position. A good follow-up letter will:

- Remind the employer of your resume.
- Express your continued interest in the position.
- Help you stand out from other applicants.

POST-INTERVIEW FOLLOW-UP

Beyond thanking your interviewers for their time as you leave, it's vital that you follow up in written form. If the competition for a position is tight, a follow-up thank you note can mean a lot. If the HR is slow to hire, the arrival of a thank you note can serve as a reminder about the candidate who's awaiting the next move.

Just after you've completed the interview, take note of anything specific you discussed and make a point of referencing it in your thank you letter. It may seem like a small detail, but this tactic really makes an impact.

Always write a thank you note immediately after the interview. If there are a number of interviewers, then send a copy of thank you letter to each person. According to a survey, less than 20% of applicants write a thank you note after an interview, and 94% recruiters said that a thank you letter would increase the applicant's chances of getting the job or at least help him/her stay in the running, provided he/she is otherwise qualified.

A thank you letter should be short. The purpose is to simply thank the interviewer for his/her time, and reiterate some of the important things you discussed and learned about the company in the interview. Summarise your qualifications and how they meet the expectations of the position. Add some key qualifications that you forgot to mention in the interview. If the interviewer shared some information about the company and its culture, mention how much you appreciated it. Standing out amongst other candidates will occur if you thoughtfully consider this follow-up letter as an additional interview in which you get to do all the talking. Propose useful ideas that demonstrate your added value to the team.

Don't try for the hard sell. You had your chance in the interview. The thank you letter just reinforces what you have already said.

Fifteen minutes of your time and postage are very inexpensive investments in your career!